beautiful mystery

beautiful mystery

LIVING IN A
WORDLESS WORLD

Danilyn Rutherford

Duke University Press
Durham and London 2025

© 2025 DUKE UNIVERSITY PRESS. All rights reserved
Printed in the United States of America on acid-free paper ∞
Project Editor: Liz Smith
Cover design by Dave Rainey
Typeset in Portrait, Canela, and Proxima Nova
by Westchester Publishing Services

Library of Congress Cataloging-in-Publication Data
Names: Rutherford, Danilyn, author.
Title: Beautiful mystery : living in a wordless world / Danilyn Rutherford.
Description: Durham : Duke University Press, 2025. | Includes bibliographical references and index.
Identifiers: LCCN 2025004843 (print)
LCCN 2025004844 (ebook)
ISBN 9781478029250 (hardcover)
ISBN 9781478061458 (ebook)
Subjects: LCSH: Rutherford, Danilyn. | Rutherford, Danilyn—Family. | Mothers of children with disabilities—United States—Biography. | Communicative disorders—Patients—Family relationships. | Grief. | Disability studies. | Mothers and daughters. | Anthropology.
Classification: LCC HQ759.913 .R884 2025 (print) | LCC HQ759.913 (ebook) | DDC 306.874/3092 [B]—dc23/eng/20250604
LC record available at https://lccn.loc.gov/2025004843
LC ebook record available at https://lccn.loc.gov/2025004844

Cover art: Photograph courtesy of the author.

CONTENTS

Prologue vii
Worlds Without Words 1

I leaving the ground
What to Expect 13
Diagnosis 21
Early Intervention 31
What Millie Remembers 47
No Future 55

II the lessons
Proximity to Disability 71
The Sovereignty of Vulnerability 91
Becoming an Operating System 107
Proprioceptive Sociality 133

III millie's flock
Cross Country 151
What Social Worlds Are Made Of 163
The Rest of a Life 181

Epilogue 191

Acknowledgments 195
Notes 199
Bibliography 209
Index 221

PROLOGUE

If you look at the right time, you can see them: improbable flashes of neon green flitting from tree to tree. Craig discovered them as soon as we moved in, less than a month after our daughter, Millie, was born. Feral parakeets. I was in Millie's room assembling the changing table when Craig called me up to our roof deck to look. "Right there!" I squinted at the patch of sky between two trees. The swarm of dots looked black until the flock wheeled and the green feathers caught the sun. "We have to show Ralph." Later that day, while Millie was napping, the three of us climbed up to look. Perched in his father's arms, Ralph stabbed his chubby finger at the horizon.

Some say they're descended from escaped pets that somehow found each other, these monk parakeets that live in the treetops. Others say a flock was released when a deal in the exotic animal trade went bad. Chicago isn't the most welcoming environment for these tropical exiles, but they've made it their home, breeding in the wild here for nearly forty years. That fall, the birds were bright against the sky; I watched for them with each changing season. In July, when the trees explode with new growth, you're less likely to see them than to hear them. A lone screech pierces the morning birdsong. Trills, cackles, and squawks mark sundown. In the winter, you'll see their dwellings, bundles of brown leaves suspended where the bare branches reach for the sky. Nestled beak to tail feathers—that's how I always pictured them. Warming each other and waiting for spring.

After Craig died, I was the one who took Ralph to the roof deck. Every April, we scanned the treetops and listened for their voices. In January and February, we surveyed the nests for signs of life. At the beginning of the summer, my mother drove down from Wisconsin with flats of marigolds and morning glories, and she squeezed in next to us and searched the sky. Did I ever take Millie to see the parakeets? Probably not. On that first day, she was a newborn, a soft little ball curled up in her crib. By the end of our time in Chicago, she was almost too heavy to carry up the stairs. But even then, she still couldn't follow my gaze. She wouldn't have noticed what I was looking at.

I WAS A WIDOW by the time Millie got her first wheelchair. I was also a newly tenured professor. My daughter, who is now an adult, does not walk on her own, or speak, or communicate with signs or symbols. Millie was three and her brother was six when her father died suddenly of a heart attack. I was two weeks away from learning whether my promotion had gone through.

When the monk parakeets soared among the treetops, I longed for Millie to see them. I wanted her to experience this flash of wonder. Her disability felt tragic. I mourned all the things we might never share. Now I wonder whether I had it backward. Maybe Millie was the flash of wonder, and I was the one who couldn't see. Across the gulf between our species, I watched the monk parakeets and pondered the mystery of their existence. My own daughter has proven as fascinating to me, as much a stranger to the landscapes I used to take for granted. Millie has brought me into a world that stretches much further than the one that I once thought of as my own.

A MONTH AFTER CRAIG died, Ralph joined a support group at his elementary school for bereaved children. At the end of a session, the school psychologist pulled me aside. My son didn't seem to care about homework and grades. She was worried. "Ralph is floating above his life." Her words stung, and I thought of my own life, and Millie's. How far above the life of a typical mother—or professor—was I floating? How far was Millie floating above the lives of most toddlers her age? But was this really such a bad thing? This isn't a story about learning to fit in. It's a story about learning to fly. And, in the end, we had company up there in the air.

Worlds Without Words

In December 2020, National Public Radio ran the first report in a series on the fortunes of disabled people seeking health care during the pandemic.[1] One of these people, a middle-aged woman named Sarah McSweeney, lived in a group home in Oregon. Afraid that she had contracted COVID-19, the staff took her to the hospital. "That afternoon," the reporter said, "[the nurse at the group home] received a phone call from the doctor in the emergency room." The doctor was confused. Sarah McSweeney was multiply disabled. She couldn't speak for herself. And yet her care provider had brought with her a legal document stating that her client wanted all medical interventions. The nurse at the group home explained. "We had her at full code. So all treatment. Because she was young and vibrant and had a great life. And that was her wish, that's what we gathered from her. She wanted to be alive."

"That emergency doctor would be the first at the hospital to raise a question that would shadow decisions about McSweeney's care," the reporter went on. "Why does a woman with significant and complex disabilities have a legal order that requires the hospital to take all measures to save her life?"

One by one, McSweeney's service providers offered an answer to this question by describing the woman they knew. A woman who loved manicures and pedicures. Who loved having her makeup done. Who enjoyed the mall so much that she was learning to use a voice output device so she could get a job greeting customers at the door. McSweeney had her dark hair dyed red so it clashed with her wheelchair. She loved country music. She loved watching people swing dance at country bars. The manager of the group home chimed in: "Her smile would bring a smile to everyone in the room."

But the doctors who cared for McSweeney pictured her differently: as a quadriplegic patient who "couldn't even use her hands." Over the course of the next three weeks, they made decisions on the basis of what they saw as her poor quality of life. During her stay in the hospital, she contracted aspiration pneumonia and grew seriously ill. At a critical moment, the hospital ethicist advised against intubating her. When her care providers protested to the doctor, he scoffed. "Oh, can she walk? And talk?" He used his middle and index finger to mimic two moving legs.

A week later, McSweeney's lungs failed, and she died.

When I heard this story, I was making dinner in my kitchen in Santa Cruz. I wasn't really listening to the radio when it came on. I used to love *All Things Considered*, but the coverage during the pandemic had soured me on the program. If I heard one more show about the suffering of middle-class schoolchildren, I was going to scream. But these words froze me in place. Jeanette, one of Millie's care workers, who stuck with us throughout those difficult months, stepped into the kitchen to prepare Millie's meds. "Hi!" she called out, her dark brown eyes smiling above her mask. The daughter of a farm foreman, with a three-year-old son at home, Jeanette confronted COVID with the unflagging good humor of a Mouseketeer. I shook my head and pointed at the radio. "They're talking about someone like Millie."

The story I was hearing was about more than whether Sarah McSweeney had a life worth living. The report captured our dominant American views of what makes a person a "whole person." Forced to justify their client's existence, McSweeney's care providers spoke of her career goals and consumer preferences; it makes sense that they had so much to say about her trips to the mall. But her care providers also spoke of something more profound. What struck me so hard was not McSweeney's capabilities but her relationships. To focus on the first is to beg the question: Would it have been okay to deny her a ventilator if she had been less vivid, ambitious, and fun? To focus on the second is to give thought to the impression McSweeney made on the people interviewed for the story. Those who worked with her learned how to ask her direct questions and recognize when she answered "yes" or "no." But they had to experiment with a variety of activities and pay close attention to her responses. How many games of twenty questions did it take for her to name her favorite country star—Kenny Chesney—and pick the perfect pink for her nails? Her care providers went to all this trouble because it is their job to help their clients gain access to mainstream society. But they also acted for other, more intimate reasons. Without saying a word, McSweeney pulled others into her orbit. With them, she created a new way of being together. She created a world.

I've lived through a similar process of creation. This book relates the lessons I have learned from my daughter, Melitta Alta Rutherford Best, who is in her early twenties as I write this. Millie, as we call her, doesn't walk or talk, and she communicates exclusively through sounds and gestures. But she's taught me how to fashion what Michele Friedner and Emily Cohen call an "inhabitable world"—a shared space of dwelling, both real and forever in the making, that evades the limits that mainstream society places on what it means to be a person, to relate to others, and to live a meaningful life.[2]

Language isn't an essential ingredient when it comes to making worlds—or at least not in the form people often take for granted. People talk to each other, they reach agreements, and they speak from the heart. But there's more to communicating than what they can express in words. Among the many things language does, utterances describe thoughts and perceptions. But they only do this when a speaker belongs to a community where there's a link between their voice or signing hands saying "this tree" and the bark they're slapping in the forest. The same is true of all the other ways of communicating that scholars describe as sign use.[3] Weathervanes point in the direction they do because they are pushed by the wind. But someone raised in their absence might not know what that little metal rooster is doing on your roof. This book explores my journey with Millie to a different side of our lives together—a side where co-presence matters more than convention, where we struggle to make ourselves felt, instead of insisting on making ourselves understood.

IT'S NOVEMBER 2023, and I catch sight of Millie when I reach the foot of the stairs. She's sitting in a high-backed chair, and she's rocking back and forth, head down, intent on her work. Her work is a salmon-colored, crocheted octopus, a gift from her care provider Julie, who has a sharp sense of Millie's obsessions. The octopus has tentacles—obviously!—and Millie is holding them in her field of vision, moving her head back and forth to shift her angle on these alluring shapes. Every so often, she brings a tentacle to her mouth and brushes it gently across her lips.

Millie is wearing a cotton hoodie and leggings under her orthotics, plastic sheaths that run from her knees to her feet, where they are squeezed into shoes designed to be worn with them. Millie is long-limbed and built like an athlete—a five-foot-tall version of me. I clomp around the house and knock things off counters. When she's gliding in her wheelchair, Millie is ethereal—not an ogre, but a sprite. Her hair, which is a color midway between auburn and dirty blonde, is cut in a pixie. She looks like Julia Roberts playing Tinker Bell when she smiles. Right now, Millie is not smiling. She hasn't registered my arrival. I take a seat close to her and say her name. A beat goes by, and then another, and her face lights up. She lifts the octopus off her lap and gives it a playful shake. I study her profile. Did she recognize my voice? Is that the meaning of this pleasure? Or did a tentacle catch the sun?

Six years ago, I left the local university and started working for a New York–based foundation. I haven't been back to Santa Cruz in over a month. I want to believe Millie is happy I'm home. But I never see more than part of the picture, foothills of a mountain range barely visible above the clouds.

I don't understand my daughter. What she likes to eat, what she likes to touch, what noises she prefers: I think I have a grip on this. But much of what Millie does still seems inexplicable to me even after more than twenty years of living together. Millie hums, and I assume she's happy; she cracks up, and I tell myself she thinks I'm hilarious. But then her humming turns sour, and her laughter spins out of control, and I'm faced with the possibility that she's actually in distress. And, yet, the mystery Millie is to me has pulled me close to her. It has also made me wonder whether I have ever truly understood any of the other people I have loved.

Other parents—and other academics—have had similar experiences. In *A World Without Words*, the sociologist David Goode reported on research he'd done in the 1970s on children exposed to German measles in utero. Here's a description of Bianca, a nine-year-old with cognitive disabilities, cerebral palsy, and sight and hearing impairments, as the staff at her school experienced her: "While in class, she appeared to be generally unaware of her surroundings or the actions of teachers and therapists. She was not 'with it,' as [her teacher] would say. She was considered to be one of the most 'low functioning' children in the school."[4]

But at home Bianca was a different person than "Bianca-as-she-existed-in-the-organization-of-a-special-education-school." To put it more precisely, she was a person: someone with aims and a personality, someone you might even call imperious. When Goode fed her, she let him know when he wasn't doing it correctly. She wanted her milk cold, and if he poured it too long before serving it, she ordered him to get her a fresh glass. She did this through facial expressions, vocalizations, and gestures. Instead of using a formal language, Bianca and her family communicated via "guessing games," which yielded what Goode calls "routine signs" made of conventions that lived and grew. "If, when Bianca stamped her feet at the dinner table, she quieted down after her parents gave her a piece of fruit, then the pounding was interpreted to have meant 'I want fruit.' If she refused fruit but did not mind being picked up and taken to the couch, then the pounding was taken to have meant 'Take me to the couch.'" "As some of my notes indicate," Goode writes, "when one watched Bianca and [her mother] Barbara communicating, it was artful, balletlike in precision, and uncannily accurate."[5] This "lived order of communication" was also highly idiosyncratic and tightly tethered to Bianca's life with her family.

To "get" Bianca, as Goode argues, "you had to be there and for a long time."[6]

I love Goode's book. I also love the wealth of more recent writings by other scholars, like Joshua Reno, whose book *Home Signs* covers similar ground.[7] But I'm fascinated by what comes before the conventions, before the second, third, or umpteenth iteration that tells Bianca's parents that their daughter's stamping foot is demanding fruit. It turns out to be something less explicable than routine or habit—not the solution, but the problem, not the prize, but the desire. At a conference on assistive and augmentative communication, I happened upon a session that I found surprisingly moving. Some Japanese engineers had come all the way from Tokyo to explain a scanning device they'd designed to capture otherwise imperceptible movements in people considered to be in a permanent vegetative state. They looked for patterns in how these individuals reacted to different kinds of music. They wanted to hold open the possibility that they were alive to their surroundings and that they cared about the sounds their world contained.

The engineers' research was built on the same foundation as Goode's research, a foundation consisting not of surety but of faith, that the being before them was a someone. Someone with a take on the world and a stake in how others treated them. Someone whose pleasures they could imagine making their own. Signs, routine and otherwise, rest on this tacit belief: that we are confronted with a person, and there's more to them than is immediately evident. Medical professionals and school systems describe Millie as severely to profoundly cognitively disabled. But the force that has shaped my life with her is not disability, or even difference: It's cognitive mystery, to give a name to the puzzle of a mind and heart that seem impossible to plumb.

In the United States, where Millie was born and raised, one response to cognitive mystery is to impute intentionality: to act as if someone is trying to communicate in situations when it's not clear that they are.[8] You squeeze into a crowded subway car. Someone elbows you in the ribs, and you turn to glare at them. They look away. It rankles. Did someone shove them, or do they not like your looks? Hope, fear, and doubt are common companions when the intentions of others seem opaque. In response, people try to make their behavior make sense.

People do the same thing with their pets, gods, and ancestors.[9] I'm on the wharf with my partner watching the sea lions that congregate on the struts below the walkway. Our poodle cocks her head, and we can tell what she's thinking: "They have fish that bark?" Animals supposedly don't have language. But who doesn't talk to their cat? Evangelical Christians talk to God and are sure He talks back by shaping the course of daily events. Ethnographers working in other parts of the world have described conversations in which the spirits speak in the sound of the wind, the shape of a chicken's entrails, or a rip in a piece of cloth. A French expert on religion, Pascal Boyer, went so far as to suggest that the very idea of spirits reflects the evolutionary value of imputing intentionality in the face of cognitive mystery.[10] That shadow stirring in the bushes might not be a leopard. But it's better to be safe than sorry when your life is at risk.

People apply the same kind of logic with newborn infants, who, when you think about it, are a little like gods. A baby's lips curl into an expression somewhere between a smile and a grimace. "You're happy!" we exclaim. Then comes the burp. We talk to babies and we act like they understand us: This is how children learn to speak. Honed over the course of our species' history, this strategy works by virtue of what developmental psychologists have described as a deeply felt impulse: Communication begins with "basic affiliative need."[11] Babies want to connect with the adults around them—that's why they copy them, look where they're pointing, and gaze into their eyes. For their part, adults want to connect with their babies. That's why adults work so hard to get their attention and make them smile.

Service providers who work with people like my daughter try to provide the same kind of "social scaffolding" that researchers have shown is so important for typically developing babies.[12] School districts hire aides, teachers, and therapists to help Millie and others like her function as normally as possible. Their goal is to prepare them to become productive workers and citizens by teaching them to communicate in ways that the average American can understand. Their efforts can lead in unexpected directions. Sometimes the sheer pleasure of establishing a connection takes precedence over any other purposes an interaction might fulfill. Autistic authors and bloggers have acted as emissaries from worlds without words, using letterboards and laptops to describe the breadth of their experience. "My language," Mel Baggs explains in a video on the topic, "is about being in constant conversation with every aspect of my environment."[13] When Baggs flaps, hums, and stims, they are communing with the things around them, from the branches outside their window to the chain dangling from the shade. Cognitive mystery—that puzzle presented by an inaccessible mind—can spark efforts to normalize those who seem different, to make disabled people fit a typical mold, under pressure from the unequal social orders in which so many of us live. But it also directs us toward ways of living more creatively and humanely with beings very different from ourselves.

At the heart of this book, thus, are questions of ethics. Philosophers have long relegated people like Millie to what Eva Feder Kittay has called the "margins of moral personhood."[14] They supposedly don't deserve equal treatment because they lack the traits that make the rest of us fully human: rationality, autonomy, foresight, and the ability to use language to demonstrate that these exist. Yet moral personhood doesn't exist in isolation. We offer it to one another, and we claim it for ourselves, as we go about our daily routines. Life with Millie has forced me to confront cognitive mystery and, for better or worse, find a way to relate to it. To live with Millie is to find personhood in a space in between what we can know of one another and what we cannot.

"YOU HAD TO BE there, and for a long time."

I'm a rower, a runner, a meditator, and a pretty good cook. I'm descended from four generations of college graduates; my grandmother majored in math at Barnard in the 1910s, and two of my three siblings have PhDs. My great-great-grandfather was a German American minister; my Scottish American father was a deacon in the local Presbyterian church. I have ancestors who were killed in the French and Indian War. I'm pretty sure they deserved it. With America's roots in slavery and the theft of Native land, I'm one of the people my country loves.[15]

Most importantly for my purposes here, I'm an anthropologist. This book belongs to an unusual genre—more personal than an academic study, more analytic than a memoir. I've done my best to write in a way that draws near—near to my daughter, and near to the forces involved in shaping our lives. I have not written a medical mystery novel or a bildungsroman. Millie still doesn't have a diagnosis, even though I have a chapter on the topic. Doctors have misunderstood Millie and failed to define her in biomedical terms. This is significant for a variety of reasons, but it's not why I wrote this book. You'll see me change, but my character development is also not the point.

What follows starts as a travelogue, then opens up like an accordion. I begin on the South Side of Chicago, where Millie was born, and end on the Central Coast of California, where she lives now. Midway through, I stop at some way stations, where I pause to expand on some lessons I've learned. Part I explains how I arrived in Millie's world; part II describes what I found there; part III pays homage to our fellow inhabitants, our local experts and companions, and the stuff from which Millie's world is made. I write from two standpoints: that of a mother, and that of a scholar. As I hope my readers will come to realize, these two viewpoints are intimately connected. Thanks to Millie, the mother and the anthropologist are one and the same.

In *The Body Silent*, his remarkable memoir documenting his gradual loss of feeling from the neck down, the anthropologist Robert F. Murphy portrays the shrinking of a social world. He could still write—he published important work until the end of his life—and he could teach, thanks to some jerry-rigging that made his building accessible. But the threads that once attached him to friends and colleagues slowly dropped away. Other professors stopped asking for his opinion. Waiters talked to his wife instead of him. Murphy's memoir offers a searing critique of the boxes into which our society places disabled people. In what follows, I bear witness to the damage wrought by this violence. But my trajectory has been different. Millie's disability has welcomed me into a world that grows with each passing year.

Most academic books begin with a detailed road map. This one does not. My goal in this chapter is not to tell you where we're going. It's to offer you reasons for coming along.

THE WRITTEN VERSION OF the report on Sarah McSweeney on the NPR website features images. There's a picture of her, followed by portraits of the individuals the reporter interviewed for the story—long-haired, middle-aged women who pose gravely for the camera. Several of these women stand against the gray clapboards of a wooden building, perhaps the one where McSweeney lived, near windows reflecting trees and sky. The piece ends with a photograph of a collection of painted rocks that residents and staff had placed in memoriam outside the group home. There are flowers, rainbows, cartoon faces, and the silhouette of a woman reclining next to a tree. One of the rocks reads, "The world just lost some sparkle." This world is the world that Sarah McSweeney made.

I thought of McSweeney a few years ago when I turned sixty. Among other things, I celebrated by baking myself a cake made with lemons from my garden. My partner carried it into the dining room, and I perched on a chair next to Millie and started singing "Happy Birthday." Startled by the commotion, Millie rocked uncomfortably on her stool. At the climax of the song, she tucked her face into her shoulder and grimaced, clearly frustrated by the noise. We've been through this ritual many times, and it always feels forced. But I can't stand the thought of skipping these little ceremonies. On birthdays and holidays, it feels crucial to affirm to myself and others that we are a family and that Millie belongs. When the cake arrived on the table, Millie lunged for it hungrily. I quickly cut her a slice. She leaned forward eagerly as I guided forkfuls into her mouth. Our dog stood by to catch the crumbs.

Later, when it was time to tuck Millie in, I sat on her bed and spoke softly into her ear. "Thank you for helping me blow out the candles." I often hear Millie at night during the hour or so it takes her to fall asleep. I sometimes mistake her for the owls that nest in the trees around our house. She coos, and I can imagine her fingering the coverlet, swaying softly, entertained by things the rest of us can't see. But now Millie was still. She was leaning slightly forward, her head lifted off the pillow. Her eyes were steady, and her lips were curved into a slight smile. "We *Rutherfords* like cake, but you *Bests* are supposed to like pie," I whispered. She chuckled—right when I pronounced her last name. A jolt went through me. Did Millie know she was a Best? Or was it the warmth of my voice and the closeness of my breath that had stirred her? I searched Millie's face. Her expression had gone blank. I still don't understand Millie. But, for a moment, I could have sworn she understood me.

Millie survived the pandemic—Zoom school, disinfected vegetables, itchy masks, and all. But I lived in fear she would end up in a hospital alone. COVID or not, that day may be coming. When Millie is Sarah McSweeney's age—forty-five—I'll be eighty-four. Neither of my parents lived much longer than that, and my mother's dementia separated her from her children. What happened to McSweeney could happen to my daughter when I'm no longer around. Perhaps writing this book has been a wishful project. I'm trying to reassure myself that Millie will always have a social world, one that can defend her from this fate or, if not, commemorate her once she's gone. You might think someone has to meet certain criteria to participate in social life, or even to deserve to live. It's not just disabled people; our enemies are also beyond the pale. But I can't get away from the fact that on this warming, warlike planet, we are in it together whether we understand each other or not. It's not the job of people like Millie to be the teachers of people like me. Still, there are things we can learn from them. Grappling with cognitive mystery may be key to the survival of all our worlds.

part I
leaving the ground

What to Expect

Leafing through photographs in the storage room of the house I am trying to sell, I come across a series of shots of Millie as a baby. There she is, strawberry blonde and made of circles: round face, round eyes, round nose, round rosebud mouth, round rosy cheeks. She is looking at the camera; her expression is alert, even wise. In another picture, taken a year or so later, she has long hair held back in a barrette, and she is resting in my arms, smiling wryly, as if she were about to tell a joke. Who is this little girl? But then I recognize the blue and purple shirt Millie is wearing, and I remember that day in Ventura, the California beach town where Millie's father grew up. Millie's aunt took that photograph with a high-speed digital camera. More precisely, she took hundreds of pictures of Millie roughly sitting in that pose, then deleted the ones where Millie was cross-eyed, or drooling, or chewing on her tongue. What these photographs capture is false, a falsification of Millie's infancy. But it is also true—true of the person I wanted my daughter to be when she was small and often inconsolable, inexplicably out of reach.

MY PREGNANCY WITH MY first child, Ralph, had taught me what to expect during my pregnancy with Millie: Day by day, the changes would unfold, turning me into a living calendar, marked by personal milestones, from my first four-hour nap to the last time I could see my toes. I was gestating my second baby, along with my first book, in Princeton, New Jersey, where I came for a yearlong residential fellowship. My routine was fixed. At 8 a.m., I dropped Ralph at the preschool, then headed to my office. I worked on the book all morning, then had lunch with my colleagues. After that, I returned to my office until teatime, when I made my way to the drawing room to eat a cookie, smile blandly at the physicists, and stare at the ducks in the nearby pond.

Life was quiet. My evenings were spent with Ralph, who was mostly skipping the terrible twos. On weekends, we were joined by Craig, who commuted back and forth to Chicago, where he worked for a consulting firm. We took walks in the damp forest that bordered the grounds. Craig and Ralph chased squirrels around trees.

I met Craig in college when he was a bearded Marxist in overalls. We were roommates in a co-op at the end of fraternity row. Craig had light red hair, a collection of plastic dinosaurs, and endless enthusiasm. I was absent-mindedly dating a fellow rower when I realized I was happier coming home to Craig than I was going out. I kissed Craig, and we spent the night on the co-op roof. From then on, our lives were cemented together. We held steady through the years I spent in Indonesia as an English teacher, through Craig's transformation into a certified public accountant, through the months we spent living together and the months we lived apart. Craig's life strategy was to get a high-paying job so he could retire early, move to Montana, and spend his time hiking and baking and selling pies. When we announced to our friends that we were getting married, they rolled their eyes. As they saw it, we'd been married from the day we met.

On our first visit to Southern California to meet Craig's family, I woke up next to him on a sofa bed staring into the eyes of a freckled three-year-old, her face only inches from my own. Craig's mother was an immigrant who called people "nincompoops" and cackled when she laughed. For years, she ran a childcare center in her home. She was a fervent supporter of family planning. "Not everyone needs to have kids," she said cheerfully and somewhat pointedly to me once; neither of us was sure I was the type. Craig inherited his love of toddlers from his mother along with his turned-up nose. I resisted the idea of having children, but he gently wore me down.

I was midway through my doctorate when Craig's firm transferred him to the London office. We were there for seven years, and we timed our first pregnancy to coincide with the completion of my dissertation. I gave birth to Ralph a week before the chair of the anthropology department at the University of Chicago called to offer me a job. I took the job, and we moved to Chicago, where Craig's firm had just opened an office. Two years later, Craig mounted a quiet campaign to convince me to have a second baby after we learned I would have a year off to finish my book.

Craig was delighted about the pregnancy. So was I, to a point. When the chair dialed my number on that day in London, Ralph was milk-drunk on my shoulder. Midway through the conversation, he softly mewled into the phone. "Children are great as long as you don't fetishize them," she told me. I was taken aback, but in principle I agreed. My tenure clock would soon be ticking, and I had plans.

When I was seven, I spent hours poring over the family atlas, charting water routes from our home in Wisconsin to distant continents. When I was a teenager, I planned road trips on blue highways through the farmlands to the Pacific, where I would turn right and head to the Yukon or left to the South Pole. I thought of my life as a journey. I'd spent some time deciding on a destination—making and remaking my own life strategies—but I hadn't been standing still. I'd had trouble starting my dissertation—I spent months spinning my wheels, scrawling sentences and anxiously erasing them. Although it had taken almost a decade, I'd gotten my PhD and a job. Over the next nine months, I was going to finish my book. I'd find a publisher, and in three years, I'd come up for tenure.

Craig's pie shop in Montana? That could come later. Craig taught me to catch lizards with little nooses made of grass, so we could admire their blue bellies before setting them free. He pulled the car to the side of the road so we could smell the prairie and look at the clouds. I gazed with him at the heavens and snuck glances at my watch. Mostly we rolled happily along. But at night, the fear of failure sometimes seized me out of nowhere, like a leopard dropping on me from a tree. My husband and son, and the future child inside me—they were my beloved fellow travelers. I was the one with the map.

DURING THE MONTHS I was pregnant with Millie, the idea of having a disabled child briefly crossed my mind. I came across an article in a back issue of *Harpers* around the time I was scheduling my amniocentesis. At thirty-nine, I assumed the procedure was more or less mandatory, never stopping to ask myself why. The author, Michael Bérubé, was a professor and the father of a boy with Down syndrome. His portrait of his son moved me: the warmth and specificity of his love for him, the way he saw adorable quirks where others might have seen flaws. It was adaptive for humanity, he argued, to include individuals who approached life with a sense of wonder and whose thoughts unfolded at a slower, more deliberate pace.[1]

Sitting in my office after returning from the clinic where they did the procedure, I wondered what we would do if the results came back positive. If the anomaly were something serious, we'd schedule an abortion; I told myself I wasn't a martyr. But the thought of Down syndrome gave me pause. Terminating the pregnancy would be the rational thing for us to do—but would it be easy? I pushed the thought away.

As it turned out, Down syndrome wasn't in our future. Throughout our year in Princeton, everything was fine. The millennium came and went without the world ending. Everything was still fine the following summer when we returned to Hyde Park, where we greeted the doorman, unpacked the U-Haul, and resumed residence in our apartment, panting from the humidity and heat. My water broke a few days after my due date while I was sitting at my computer in my office on campus. I walked two blocks to the medical center and checked myself in. The midwife examined me, then sent me home to wait for contractions. There were none, and Craig and I had dinner at a local café. Then we walked back to the hospital where I was induced.

It was gloomy out—far too gloomy for a summer evening. A crow cawed in the distance. Craig and I held hands, but we didn't talk. I wasn't focused on having a baby. I was distracted by thoughts of my upcoming midcareer review and edits to my book. I wasn't worried about the induction; my son had come into the world the same way. I remember idly wondering whether I was capable of going into labor without a jump-start. No matter; I had little ego invested in my uterus, and I didn't want more kids.

At the desk, a bored receptionist checked me in. A nurse guided us into a small delivery room and sat me down in an exam chair, which was covered in gray vinyl, flanked by monitors, and fixed to the floor. It faced a television suspended from the ceiling that broadcast nothing but static. Craig stayed long enough for a briefing from the midwife and to watch me flinch as another nurse inserted the IV. Then he stepped out to make a work call. And so my labor began, with little more fanfare than a trip to the dentist.

WHEN I TAKE MILLIE to a new specialist, the doctor always takes a medical history, and the first questions are invariably about her birth. Were there complications? The simple answer—the one I always give—is no. And yet, in retrospect, there were vague signs, little whispers warning me that something about my daughter's infancy was going to be off-kilter, not quite sunny and bright.

In large part, it was a matter of lighting. The hospital room in London where Ralph had been born was brightly illuminated, and I was in labor long enough for the sun to set, then rise, then sink again, casting the glow of a sunny January afternoon across the walls. The delivery room for Millie's birth in Chicago was dark, kept that way on purpose by the midwives. What I remember is dim and foggy. Sitting in the chair while they injected the oxytocin. Leaning against Craig during a contraction. Someone putting my feet in stirrups. Somehow finding myself with a baby on my lap. I have one vivid memory: A nurse measured the baby's head circumference, checked the growth chart, and then measured it again. There's a certain comfort in knowing that in some part of my brain I sensed from the start that something was off.

BUT THERE WASN'T ANYTHING up, the nurse told me, and the pediatrician concurred, discharging me and my daughter for the short car ride home. I introduced a highly curious Ralph to his new sister, and we embarked on this new phase in our lives. We were aided by Dovita, the Lithuanian nanny Craig had found for me by making friends with one of the doormen in our building. Dovita arrived at 7 a.m. every morning and marched into our bedroom to steal Millie from my arms so we both could get to work. Later, when we began the process of seeking a diagnosis for Millie, Dovita objected. "There's nothing wrong with Millie; she's perfect," she insisted.

Millie was perfect, in her way, but something was missing. A spark, a sparkle, a little flame, hints of the grown-up this newborn would become. Ralph, like his dad, was born with a sense of humor. From the moment he drew his first breath, he was already the person he is now. Millie seemed to be in hiding. It was not something I could talk to a doctor or even to Craig about. But when I looked in my daughter's eyes, I saw a cipher. Even as I threw myself into the happy rounds of the first weeks with my new daughter, I felt a slight queasiness, even dread.

For the most part, I put this dread out of mind. I'm a multitasker. Craig once teased me for bringing books on dates: You never knew when there would be some downtime, I reasoned, and it paid to be prepared. There's a picture of me sitting with Ralph in a rocking chair in London. He's two months old, and he's stretched out on my nursing cushion fast asleep. I have a yellow legal pad perched on his stomach, and I'm furiously writing.

At the same time I attended to Millie, I did a final round of revisions to my book, met with editors, and applied for grants. No one caught me writing on top of Millie, but there are pictures of us together where I look distracted by these tasks. For Millie's first Christmas, we took the kids to Ventura. Millie was five months old. There's a shot of me in Craig's parents' house with Millie on the sofa; I'm holding her upright and wishing she would smile. She is limp—low muscle tone, I later learned to call it—and vacuous; her eyes are unfocused, her tongue protruding from her mouth. I catch my mother-in-law frowning as I pose Millie for the picture, but she quickly rearranges her face. It was easier to focus on the scary if surmountable hurdles I had to leap over on my march toward tenure than to face the fact that Millie was not clearing her own. In her career as baby, she was not on track to succeed.

DURING THAT FIRST YEAR, I became involved in a network of advocates working for the West Papuan cause, and I was invited to Washington, DC, for a board meeting. Craig, Millie, and Ralph came along; it was early January, and we arranged to stay with neighbors from our year in Princeton. In the evening, we lounged in the couple's living room and caught up. We discussed our jobs, but mostly we discussed our children.

I have a vivid memory of sitting on the floor with Millie while we were chatting. We were talking about milestones, and my colleague was remembering which of her children did what at what age. We may even have pulled out a copy of *What to Expect the First Year*. In the latest edition, the entry for six months, Millie's age at the time, reads something like this: "Paging Miss Personality! There she is, smiling, waving, talking, and entertaining anyone in her orbit. She's probably able to bear weight on her legs when you hold her upright and may even be ready to hit the road, albeit at a crawl."[2] Back then, the entry started with a list of everything your baby "should," "will probably," "may possibly," and "might even" be able to do.[3]

While the others continued the conversation, I quietly took a mental inventory. Sometimes Millie seemed to look at very small items, like raisins, I told myself, remembering reading something about that. And if I propped her up on the floor with her legs crossed and her arms holding her weight, she might even be able to sit on her own. After everyone else left the room, I tested this theory. I got Millie into position. She stared impassively. I held my breath and watched her. She was trying, I told myself. Or was she? I suppressed the impression that flashed into my mind: This was kind of like building a house of cards. A moment passed, then Millie tumbled onto her side.

That counted, right?

It felt strange. I wanted to be proud of Millie, the way I'd been proud of Ralph. Nothing had prepared me for the sheer pleasure of his presence. He was a miracle, and that made me a miracle, too. Ralph crawled early and walked early, and his first words were a full sentence—"eat hot dog"—announced at a barbecue when he was eighteen months old. Ralph erupted with joy when I tickled him.

When I tickled Millie, she looked confused.

I HAVE ANOTHER VIVID memory from that trip to Washington. Our flight home was delayed by snow, and the airline gate was crowded with frustrated travelers. Millie was screaming, and Craig and I were desperately trying to get her to stop. We took turns carrying her, bouncing her, pushing her back and forth in her stroller. I blushed and avoided meeting our fellow passengers' eyes. Finally, exasperated, I laid her down on the carpet, flat on her back, in the midst of the rolling luggage and wet boots. She suddenly stopped crying. I stared down at her, and it dawned on me. I had nothing to give her. She wanted to be left alone.

Diagnosis

As Lennard J. Davis taught his readers at the dawn of disability studies, before normal was a character trait, it was a curve, plotted on a piece of graph paper, with a fat middle and skinny tails.[1] In the nineteenth century, the Belgian astronomer and statistician Adolphe Quetelet used the "error curve" to record the distribution of human features. Sir Francis Galton sliced that bell-shaped bump into sections and redrew the diagram so that those with "desired traits" occupied the heights.[2] Some of us, the privileged ones, fight for a place in the top percentile: better than 99 percent of the population in some measurable respect. In the past, to be perfect was to be divine, an ideal state unattainable by fallen mortals. Now the ideal is within reach. *What to Expect* teaches new parents to expect the norm, to love the norm, to long to exceed it. It takes a database of accomplishments—this many weeks for rolling over, this many weeks for pulling up—and cobbles them together into a fantasy: a baby who is miraculously average (or above average) in all respects.

In 2000, the year Millie was born, the transformation that Richard Roy Grinker describes in *Nobody's Normal* was well underway. In the United States, our capitalist society had stigmatized unusual minds; now it was embracing them. There were drugs to sell for sadness and tech jobs for people on the spectrum. What had once been a mark of shame was at worst a common ailment; at best, a source of income and even pride. I should have gotten on that bandwagon early—hell, I had a doctorate in anthropology. But when it came to human brains and bodies, as opposed to human cultures, there was only so much difference I could take.[3] I thought of myself as a rebel, but at heart I was a greyhound, eager to run down any rabbit that materialized on the track. I expected the norm, I loved the norm, I longed to exceed it. And behind this was a desire even more fundamental—for acceptance, for a nice warm place next to the hearth.

During that year in Princeton, I received some wise advice from a historian, who pulled me aside in the hallway one day. "Don't pin your life's dreams on tenure. Job security is a rare thing. If you get it, good for you. If you don't, don't beat yourself up; you'll be just like everyone else." I nodded, but only part of me believed her. I didn't want to be just like everyone else.

Until I did.

"PARENTS WORRY TOO MUCH." I could almost hear our pediatrician's voice as I sat in the clinic waiting room on a cold winter morning, my toe gently rocking Millie's car seat. Craig sat next to me, wearing a suit under his parka. It was the end of January, and we were there for Millie's six-month checkup. A two-year-old stood near the train set in the middle of the room, holding an engine in his fat little hand. I watched as he examined it. Then he looked up gravely and met my gaze. I glanced down at Millie, who was staring at her nose, her left eye slightly off-kilter, not tracking with the right.

When Ralph was a year old, I had called Dr. Monroe in a panic. Seconds earlier, Ralph had scrambled onto his baby jogger, then stood upright, chortling, before plunging face down onto the hardwood floor. Ralph's shrieks were still filling the apartment when Dr. Monroe picked up the phone. She cut me off after a few words. "If he's crying, he'll survive."

Dr. Monroe's style suited me. I wasn't the type of mother to look for trouble. But now I was worried. That summer, I had ignored an ant I found strolling across my kitchen counter. The next morning, my sugar bowl was alive with black specks. These niggling concerns: Would they really add up to nothing? I was beginning to wonder. I needed someone to talk me down.

And it wasn't just me. Craig had been harboring his own doubts. After the trip to DC, he'd spoken them out loud. "Does she look at you? She never looks at me. That doesn't seem right." He'd taken the morning off so Dr. Monroe could reassure us. We were probably overreacting. Maybe Millie was nearsighted. When I was eight, I couldn't find the chalkboard, let alone read it.

The two-year-old had figured out how to get the engine to roll on the wooden track and was making soft train noises as he pushed it back and forth. Again, he sensed I was looking; turning, he locked eyes with me and grinned. Who was I kidding? I wanted Dr. Monroe to find the problem and fix it.

A nurse called the two-year-old and his mother. We were next. First came the weighing and measuring. Millie lay on the scale, pink and placid, and held still as the nurse recorded her length and eased the paper tape measure around her head. Then she repeated what the nurse in the delivery room had done: She jotted down Millie's head circumference, looked at the growth chart, then took a second reading just to be sure. As she led us to an exam room, I caught Craig's eye—what was the deal with Millie's head? Before we had a chance to collect our thoughts, Dr. Monroe burst through the door, a sweet-faced medical student trailing behind her. With her reading glasses and cropped gray hair, she looked like someone hired to play a doctor on TV.

After repeating the head measurement and looking in Millie's ears, Dr. Monroe turned to us. "Do you have any concerns?" she asked brusquely, as if she had something better to do.

Craig and I spoke at once. "Her eyes?" At Millie's three-month checkup, I had mentioned that she hadn't been making eye contact. Dr. Monroe had shrugged. "Kids develop at different rates." Before I had a chance to remind her of this conversation, Dr. Monroe was flashing a light into Millie's pupils. "Alternating esotropia," she pronounced. "It's very common. You can look it up. If it doesn't resolve itself by her next appointment, we can look into using a patch." Craig must have raised an eyebrow because she went on. "If you patch the strong eye, that forces the weaker eye to develop normally." She paused and looked back at her clipboard before fixing us with her cool blue eyes. "Anything else?" Craig and I shared a glance. Without waiting for an answer, Dr. Monroe turned to leave. "Good. Then we'll see you in three months." Good? I needed more talking down than that. I tried to picture Millie in an eye patch.

Neither of us were satisfied, but we swallowed our objections. It was in our nature to trust doctors. I threw myself back into the paper I was trying to write. A month later, Craig, Millie, and I returned to the same waiting room. The eye turn was much worse. From a nearby sofa, a woman with a preschooler glanced at Millie, saw that she was cross-eyed, and looked away. When it was our turn, Dr. Monroe took one look at Millie and immediately got on the phone with one of her colleagues, an optometrist whose office was down the hall.

In a few moments we were in another exam room. I sat with Millie in the exam chair, inspecting the equipment and wondering how an eye test for a baby would work. But the doctor, a young man with spectacles and dull red hair, wasn't interested in Millie's vision. Instead of opening his box of lenses, he looked at her and frowned. "Did you really say she was seven months old?" The question jolted me; was I failing a quiz? Buzz. Wrong answer. That couldn't be Millie's age. Then the optometrist got on the phone with one of his colleagues, a neurologist who worked at the children's hospital down the street. "It's not her eye turn I'm worried about; it's her muscle tone," he told us as he waited to be connected. "You'll want to have her seen right away. Early intervention can make all the difference." All the difference? All the difference in what? Early intervention for what? I had no idea what this man was talking about.

I pulled Millie closer, letting her warmth seep into me, and stared down at the linoleum. Seconds ticked by. An irrational idea took hold of me. I'd brought this on. Whatever this bad thing was, I had worried it into existence. I had thought frightened thoughts, and now they had come true. Finally, I looked at Craig, willing him to speak for both of us. Craig studied the optometrist's face, then cleared his throat. "And the eye patch?" The optometrist shook his head. "No need."

Miraculously, the neurologist had an opening the very next day. Craig pushed Millie's stroller, and as I followed them silently to the exit, the shock and guilt dissolved into fury. Dr. Monroe's face flashed into my mind, and I pictured myself screaming at her. "You promised us nothing was wrong!"

Before leaving the clinic, Craig stopped at the reception desk to ask for a copy of Millie's growth chart so he could take notes at appointments and update it himself. I have a version of it in my files in which the curve for head circumference follows a smooth upward slope but then plunges. The drop comes precisely at ten months, when Millie's new doctors started recording what the measuring tape actually read. Millie was not in the fiftieth percentile, but in the third—a clear sign that her brain was not developing normally. It was also what the eye turn was telling us.

I never took Millie to see Dr. Monroe again.

MY MEMORIES OF THAT last morning in the clinic are bright as a new penny: the smell of alcohol, the shapes on the eye chart, the fluorescent lighting, the red rubber mallet hitting Millie's knee. But after the appointment, I don't remember much, even though that night marked a watershed in our lives.

We were living in a townhouse Craig discovered for us during the year I was on leave in Princeton: a pretty, vertical box of a home. We moved in shortly after Millie's birth. Over the past nine months, I had spent hours doing dishes in the kitchen, watching for cars while Ralph and Craig played ball in the auto court, and nursing Millie near a living room window that looked out over a park and Lake Shore Drive. From our bedroom, the early morning traffic sounded like the ocean; I sometimes dreamed I was sleeping on the beach.

On that evening after our conversation with the optometrist, Craig had to come upstairs to find us. I needed to pack. I was turning forty the next day, and we'd made plans to drive to Wisconsin to spend the weekend with my parents. The bath was running for Ralph, and I was probably chatting with Dovita, who had just offered to change Millie's diaper before heading home. Craig usually burst through the front door in a fit of good cheer. Did he seem a little quieter, a little more subdued? Maybe. I'm not sure. I do remember the words that were racing through my mind: "Something's wrong, something's wrong, something's wrong."

After we ate, after I did the dishes, after Craig read Ralph a story and kissed him goodnight, after I nursed Millie and rocked her to sleep, after all that, we would have talked. There wouldn't have been much to say. We'd been through this kind of thing before. Fifteen years earlier, I had returned to the Bay Area after two years in Indonesia to learn that Craig had a tumor in his chest. He'd been having trouble catching his breath while surfing; the doctor had ordered a chest x-ray. Craig had gone in for a biopsy and was waiting for the results while I was flying home over the Pacific. His eyes grew moist when he described the worst-case scenario. After that, there had been no more tears and not a lot more talk. As it turned out, the cancer had been treatable, and Craig had soldiered on through six rounds of chemotherapy, constant nausea, nerve pain, and the loss of all his hair. There had been no Hallmark moments, no discussions of love and death. There had been nothing redemptive about the experience. It had been brutally quotidian.

I knew that Craig would respond in the same way to Millie's predicament as he had to his own. He would find a medical library, and he would photocopy articles. He had already created a file on esotropia; as soon as he had a new label for Millie's ailment, his research would begin again. At the office that afternoon, he had probably called around to check on the reputation of the specialist we were scheduled to see. Did he report on his findings after joining me in the living room? Did I sit on the couch, looking at him, but not really seeing him? "Something's wrong, something's wrong, something's wrong." Is that all I could hear as he spoke?

More than anything, I remember wanting it to be over—this not-quite-normal, final normal day. Craig was talking about ways to beat the Friday traffic.

I wasn't listening. I wanted to scream, break plates and shatter water glasses, curl up in a fetal position and moan. I wanted to take Millie in my arms and run. That was my idea of a solution. It wasn't Craig's. "Should we head to Wisconsin right after the appointment?" Craig's question woke me. I had been studying the patterns in the carpet; now I looked up. "Sounds like a good idea." Craig was staring out the window. I watched him for a moment and then climbed the stairs to get ready for bed. Craig followed me. We spent the night in each other's arms.

THE NEXT MORNING, WE loaded the car for the drive to Madison, then Craig left to take Ralph to nursery school. He pulled the station wagon back into the garage as I was finishing my coffee. I called up the stairs.

"Dovita, we need to go!"

"Coming!"

I carried the diaper bag, and Dovita carried Millie, a little blonde bundle in footed leggings and a pink shirt. As I slipped into the passenger seat, I thanked Dovita for her help. She gave me a little nod, then stepped aside to wait for the car to back out, so she could wave as we pulled away.

I turned to Craig. "We can't forget to ask about her head circumference."

Craig had one hand on the steering wheel, and I followed his gaze to the street ahead, which led to a stop sign. A toddler in a yellow windbreaker was standing at the corner looking up at her father. Without dropping her hand, he picked up her doll stroller and carried it across the crosswalk, then set it gently on the sidewalk for her to push.

"I talked to Karin," Craig finally said. Karin was Craig's sister, a PhD in developmental psychology who worked at a clinic in Los Angeles. "Apparently, neurologists aren't known for their bedside manner."

"Has she heard of this guy?" I glanced back at Millie, who was sucking her tongue.

"No."

It wasn't a long drive. The neurologist's office was less than two miles from our house, in the medical center close to my office. I sometimes stood in line for coffee at the Starbucks near the entrance. On days when I was struggling with my teaching or writing, I eyed the interns and residents wistfully. Now I thought of them again. I should have gone to medical school instead of wasting my time on anthropology. I could be doing something that actually helped people. I stared at the glove compartment. Everything I knew seemed so useless. For all I knew, the neurologist was going to tell us that Millie was about to die.

Or not. Maybe he was going to tell us that there was nothing to worry about. It was one of those bright spring mornings when the university looked more like a garden than the monastery it was built to resemble. Would my colleagues think I was playing hooky? I felt a pang of guilt. What a thing to worry about at a time like this.

Millie wriggled when I took her from her car seat, then she sat limp, her legs splayed, her hands motionless by her sides. On the fifth floor, we looked for the door marked Pediatric Neurology. Behind it was a small waiting room. I had been bracing for other patients—boys and girls in helmets and thick glasses, metal encasing their legs—but the row of seats was empty. The receptionist handed us a questionnaire. I scanned the questions. What killed my grandfathers? Damned if I knew. I handed the clipboard to Craig. As he checked boxes, I rested my eyes on Millie's glossy mop of hair. I considered getting her out of her stroller. But I'd nursed her less than an hour ago, and Dovita had just changed her diaper. She was silently chewing on her collar. Best leave well enough alone.

Craig put down the clipboard and felt for my hand. There was a clock on the wall, next to a large photograph of a field of tulips. I listened to it tick.

"You can come in now." I jumped. A smiling young woman in a lab coat had materialized in front of us. "I'm Dr. Kelly's intern."

She left us in an exam room. This time, the large photograph was of a field of wheat, but I was more interested in the poster next to it, a chart featuring color illustrations of a dozen pills and capsules, each accompanied by its brand name and a description of what it was for. A knock on the door jolted me back to the present. It was a nurse, here to take Millie's vitals. On her way out the door, she passed the intern, who smiled at Millie and then double-checked the history we'd filled out. "Was she full term?"

I looked at Craig and wondered if he was thinking what I was thinking. What difference would it have made if the answer was no? I pictured the intern putting down her pen. "That explains everything. You can go home. Premature babies usually turn out fine."

The intern interrupted my fantasy. "Dr. Kelly will be in in a moment."

As if on cue, the door swung open and a burly man in his mid-fifties swept through it, a young woman in a lab coat trailing in his wake. He filled the room, less fat than massive, with a black beard and a head full of graying curls.

Craig stood up. The man shook Craig's hand. "Kelly. This is Abigail. She's a first year." The young woman smiled shyly and tucked her hair behind her ear.

Dr. Kelly nodded in my direction, then took the clipboard from the intern. I sucked air through my teeth; I scarcely registered with this guy. Pulling a pair of reading glasses from his breast pocket, he lowered himself onto the stool, like a circus bear performing a trick.

Dr. Kelly scowled at the chart. "No family history of developmental delay?"

Craig's tone was dry. "Just suicide and cancer."

Dr. Kelly didn't smile. He shoved the clipboard back at the intern. Then he looked from Craig to me.

"Why are you here?"

Craig and I glanced at each other, and we made a silent decision. This guy was a sexist. Craig would tell the story. We'd get more traction that way. As he spoke, Dr. Kelly inspected Millie, as if he had read her user's manual and was checking to be sure her specifications were correct. He pulled out a little mallet and I shifted Millie forward so he could test her reflexes. He shone a light in one eye, then the other. He measured the distance from her shoulder to the bottom of her ear. Millie winced as he blew on her forehead, scrunching up her face and blinking her eyes.

Craig's voice trailed off as he brought the narrative to a conclusion. "Then Dr. Monroe gave us a referral to see you."

Dr. Kelly seemed lost in thought, staring at Millie. Finally he turned to the intern. "Let's test her for Down's mosaicism."

She nodded, writing.

I pursed my lips. What the hell is Down's mosaicism? The arrogant jerk. Pulling Millie back into my lap, I caught Craig's eye. My turn to speak. "But the amnio was normal."

Dr. Kelly shook his head. "Doesn't matter. Sometimes the anomaly isn't present in all the cells. Mosaicisms can slip through the cracks." He turned back to the intern. "Let's also order an MRI." Anomaly? MRI? *Cracks*? Millie squirmed in my lap. I pictured a hole in her brain. Dr. Kelly glanced at her, then answered Craig's question before he could ask it. "We'll have to put her under for that."

Dr. Kelly's pen scratched the paper as he signed the orders the intern had filled out. Then he gathered the forms back into the clipboard and turned to leave.

This is it? That was all the information he had to offer us? Dr. Kelly had examined Millie carefully. He had to have noticed something. Was he holding something back? I looked at Craig and then spoke up. "What about her eye turn?"

Dr. Kelly returned to the stool. "Oh, yes. We'll also order a VEP. Visual Elicited Potential. To test the optic nerve."

Craig's voice was steady. "Can you tell us what's wrong with her?"

Dr. Kelly rose again. "No. At this point, we're just ruling things out."

TWENTY MINUTES LATER, WE pulled up in front of Ralph's nursery school. Craig got out to join the other parents waiting on the sidewalk. I stayed in the car with Millie. The tree-lined street stretched out before me, a slight breeze gently shaking the leaves. Birds chirped. I thought of the drive to Madison, and the deep blue of the sky, and the look I'd see on my mother's face when I told her the news. I hadn't been thinking about my birthday, but now my age hit me like a brick. I was no longer a young woman. Millie's future was my future. What were the next forty years going to be like? I could see Millie in the rear-view mirror, slumped in her car seat, her gaze fixed on the end of her nose. I looked away. We'd forgotten to ask about her head circumference.

Early Intervention

Time doesn't always heal, but it can dull the senses. Three weeks later, in early May 2001, we sat in a small waiting room in a medical building that backed onto an inlet of Lake Michigan. From the road, it looked like a yacht club, an impression quickly dispelled by the receptionist dressed in scrubs. Craig, Dovita, and I took up half of the chairs, with Craig's lanky frame spilling into the center of the waiting room. Millie was in her stroller, staring blankly at the edge of a table strewn with old issues of *Special Parenting*, *Highlights*, and *National Geographic for Kids*.

Millie had already had an MRI. The report noted some thinning in the corpus callosum, the bundle of nerve fibers connecting the two hemispheres of Millie's brain, but it seemed to mean little to the neurologist: "Unremarkable" was Dr. Kelly's verdict. Nothing had come of the other tests either; Millie's chromosomes were normal, her optic nerve intact. This sounded like good news. Was it? I wasn't sure.

In the car, Craig had been uncharacteristically quiet: no silly comments for Millie, no questions for Dovita about her life back in Lithuania. He kept his hands on the steering wheel, his face calm and composed. I recognized this silence. He was on the hunt for information, puzzling out his line of attack.

While we were waiting our turn, Craig exchanged pleasantries with a woman in capris and a baseball cap who was seated across from us. His green eyes were bright as he leaned forward to listen to the woman. She seemed to be in her fifties or sixties and had two children with her: a thin little girl in cut-offs, who watched Craig from her shelter between the woman's legs, and a baby no older than Millie, who was asleep in a car carrier at the woman's feet.

"I'm the grandmother," she explained to Craig. "I bring them because their mom has to work. This is the first time you all have been here, isn't it?"

We nodded. Another woman, this one in her thirties, glanced at us quickly and then looked away. She was perched on a chair at the end of the waiting room with a toddler who had dark eyes, a gentle smile, and a head disproportionately small for his frame. I tried not to stare.

It was the first time we'd come to this clinic, but it would not be the last. Millie had joined the ranks of South Side children who needed early intervention. Early intervention is a federally mandated program, a provision of the Individuals with Disabilities Education Act (IDEA), although no one ever breathed the dreaded word "disability" in our presence.[1] Millie, like all the rest of these children, wasn't disabled. She was "delayed." Millie wasn't broken; she was behind. The point of today's activities was to determine how far behind and what we could do about it.

A freckled woman in leggings materialized in the doorway, frowning at her clipboard.

"Me-lit-ta Best?" She held out her hand to Craig as Dovita and I gathered up our belongings. "I'm Carol Hopper."

"I'm Craig. We call her Millie."

I recognized Carol's name from the day I made the appointment, using the number Dr. Kelly had handed me on a post-it. I thought of my mother. She had bounced back quickly from the news about Millie's problems and had internalized the hopefulness that early intervention mobilized. A few days after my birthday visit, when I called to tell her we'd scheduled the evaluation, she had reassured me. "She'll catch up!" I tried to echo her optimism. "I'm sure it's nothing serious," I said.

Like Craig, I'd been quiet in the car on the way over. His silence sheltered a hard kernel of resolve. Mine sheltered a deep reservoir of denial. I was determined not to panic, not even secretly, and I was mostly succeeding. We were getting help, and help would help. Millie would be laughing and playing with the other toddlers in no time. If not, she'd catch up by high school. And if she didn't go to college, she could always work in a bookstore. That would be a happy life.

In *The Protestant Ethic and the Spirit of Capitalism*, Max Weber linked the pursuit of profit with the doctrine of predestination. Believers had no way of telling if they were damned or saved, and that fueled a compulsion: All that relentless striving kept their minds off their plight. I always found this an easy text to teach: Basically, those Puritans were me. I was a big believer in the efficacy of hard work and positive thinking. Craig needed data; I needed an assignment. We'd both been looking forward to this appointment. Craig would find out what was wrong with our daughter, and someone would tell me what to do. The evaluation would go well—just like Craig's cancer treatment had gone well—and we'd drive home from the clinic feeling reassured. But now the day had arrived, and my stomach felt like lead. I took one last look at the toddler with the small head, then down at my daughter, who was chewing on her fist. Nothing serious? I wasn't sure at all.

Carol led us into a spacious room, equipped with brightly colored mats, mirrored walls, and a long rectangular table with molded plastic chairs around it. "Millie," she said. "That's so cute!"

Craig said, "Our son's named Ralph. Lunch-counter names."

Carol laughed. She leaned down so she was at Millie's eye level and grinned broadly. "Hello, Millie!" Millie took no notice of her; she was still busy with her fist.

"Should I get her out?" I came around to the front of the stroller.

"Sure. We won't get started until the rest of the team arrives."

Carol was the physical therapist. The occupational therapist walked in a second later, followed by the speech and language pathologist and the infant development specialist. The women were in their thirties and looked similar enough to be sisters, perky in their ponytails and cheerleader smiles.

I grinned at Craig, who raised an eyebrow when one of them opened the briefcase she'd brought with her and pulled out a square peg and a board with round holes. I knew what he was thinking. That's our girl! A second later, the joke didn't seem so funny. Stacking cups? Were these tests Millie could pass? Or even take?

Carol went first.

"Let's go over to the mat. Can she tolerate lying on her back?"

"She loves it." I tried to smile.

I gently laid Millie down and sat awkwardly by her side. She had her knees in the air, and she was biting her tongue, studying the ceiling. I flushed, imagining how Millie appeared to these strangers: like a newborn the size of a one-year-old. Carol settled onto the floor in front of her, clipboard in hand. Millie suddenly kicked her legs, hard, in a burst of energy that petered out as quickly as it had started, and she brought her fist back in front of her face and looked at it as if she was thinking of giving it a little taste. Carol took a note and then looked back at Millie. I squinted at the words to see if I could read them, then caught myself: I was being uncool. Dovita was having even more trouble containing herself. She craned her head to get a better look.

"Hey, Millie!" Carol took another note as Millie's feet came to rest on the floor. "Hey there!" Now Carol reached for Millie's ankles and straightened both her knees. "Let's see if you can lift your legs, Millie." Nothing happened. I stared, willing Millie to move.

Still seated on the floor, Carol checked a box, then looked up, startled. Millie had been kicking in Carol's direction and her toes had discovered Carol's arm. "You little rascal!" Carol laughed, and the other women joined in. Did they think this was on purpose? Millie's face tightened in a look of concentration and then went slack.

Carol looked up at me. "Can she lie on her stomach?"

I felt my shoulders stiffen. "Not really." Babies were supposed to reach this milestone by the time they were three months old.

"Can she sit?" I was ready for this, and I did some careful arranging. Millie propped herself up for five seconds before crumpling onto her side "Emerging," Carol muttered. I glanced at Craig. He was making a mental note. Emerging. Strange usage. Look it up. Carol lowered her clipboard. "Your turn, Ginny."

The occupational therapist pulled a rattle from her briefcase. She rose from her chair. "You can leave her on the floor."

She shook the rattle in front of Millie. "Good work!" I studied Millie's face, wondering what she'd done. The therapist could tell I was puzzled and turned to me. "She's paying attention to the noise." A second later, when Millie reached for the toy and wrapped her fingers around it, Dovita nudged me, triumphant. See! I told you she's perfect! Millie shook it once, then flung it to the side.

"Great job, Millie!" the occupational therapist beamed. I felt for Craig's hand. He gave mine a squeeze. It wasn't so bad having all these adults act so interested in our beautiful daughter. The therapist wanted to hear about Millie's emotional life. I described the peaceful expression that dawned on her face when she was lying in a warm bath, how she relaxed when I massaged shampoo into her scalp, how she cried when I plucked her from the tub and rubbed her dry. Her horror of solid food. To demonstrate, Craig gently scooped Millie off the mat and tucked her onto his lap. Dovita put some mashed carrots on a small plastic spoon. Millie gagged as the spoon approached her mouth, and she stuck out her tongue to push it away.

The occupational therapist gave the speech and language pathologist a meaningful look. "Sensory aversion." Another term for Craig to look up. As Dovita wiped the carrot off Millie's chin, the speech and language pathologist pulled a glove out of her briefcase. She used her finger to massage Millie's gums. This time, Millie's lips closed over the spoon, and she sucked a morsel of carrot down. "There you go!" The occupational therapist smiled at her colleague. Both women made a note.

On to the puzzles. The infant development specialist opened her briefcase. I eyed the wooden blocks, but she reached for yet another rattle. "Let's keep her here."

After her victory with the spoon, Millie had gone still, cocooned in her father's arms. The specialist moved the rattle slowly back and forth in front of her face. Millie sat impassively, sucking on her tongue. Next, the woman slid this apparently less interesting rattle back and forth on the table. No response.

I caught Craig's eye. He shook his head slightly. Failing the rattle test. That couldn't be good. Dovita shifted in her seat.

The specialist sighed. "Okay. Lay her down on her back." This time, Millie tracked the rattle, her eyes briefly moving together as the specialist moved the toy back and forth above her face. I let out a breath.

"Does she play with toys?" This woman couldn't let well enough alone.

"Yes. She chews on them."

The specialist nodded. "Does she make eye contact?"

I winced. I knew this question was coming. "Not really. No."

The specialist checked a box.

Then, as quickly as it had started, the evaluation was over. "What comes next?" I asked as the women packed up. Craig's brow was furrowed; I could tell he was bursting with questions. Were they really going to leave without saying anything?

Carol glanced up. "We'll work on a report. In the meantime, we should get you guys started. We'll want to see Millie for therapy twice a week."

"Terrific." I tried to sound happy. Craig put his arm around my waist as we waited for the elevator. I drew him close. We'd debrief later. Dovita stroked Millie's head, clearly relieved the ordeal was over. The evaluation wasn't what we expected, but that was okay.

"Emerging." That had to mean something.

AND SO BEGAN REGULAR trips down the shore for sessions with Millie's therapists. I'm terrible at names, but I still remember theirs.

On the Tuesdays when we had occupational and physical therapy with Ginny, the session often involved a big red therapy ball. I plucked my limp little daughter from her stroller and arranged her cross-legged on top of it. Ginny stood behind Millie, gripping her narrow hip bones, and bounced her gently. Millie responded with a look of concentration, her lips pursed, her gaze fixed just beyond her nose. At Ginny's cue, I straightened Millie's legs, and Ginny tipped her onto her side, then rolled the ball under her to turn her over onto her stomach. Millie struggled to lift her face away from the plastic.

Ginny smiled at Millie's efforts. "Hi, Millie! This is a good position for you." Millie didn't seem to agree. I watched concern gather in her eyes. But it was only when Millie started whining that Ginny rolled her back onto her side. Then came the tricky bit. Dovita held the ball, and I held Millie's legs, as Ginny eased her through the transition from lying to sitting. Trunk rotation involves a suite of intricate movements, none of which came easily to my daughter. I still shake my head in wonder whenever I see a baby twist to reach for a toy.

On alternate Tuesdays, we had speech therapy and Charlotte would be waiting with a high chair, where I sat Millie down while Dovita rummaged in her backpack for a jar of baby food. Soon enough, the fact that speech therapy involved eating no longer struck me as strange. Words come from tongues, Charlotte explained, and the tongue is a muscle. Like Millie's other muscles, her tongue was "low tone": floppy and slow on the uptake. It wasn't a natural when it came to keeping a grape, say, out of her windpipe. This made eating terrifying for Millie, and feeding her torture for us, and it would make it difficult for her to learn to speak. Charlotte started with a manual vibrator, which she used to stroke Millie's lips and cheeks. Then she used a finger, encased in a plastic tip covered with bristles, to massage Millie's tongue and gums. Then came the small spoon, laden with a dot of baby food. Millie would eye the dangerous object as Charlotte waved the spoon in front of Millie's nose before reaching in to deposit the dot on her lower lip. On a good day, Millie would gingerly stick out her tongue to taste the morsel. On a bad day, she'd wail.

I practiced what we learned during these sessions at home. I was on dinner duty, and that meant speech therapy. I queued up an album of calming music and hit play, knowing it would be over before the meal was done. I was just as patient—and diligent—when it came to physical and occupational therapy. I ordered a big yellow exercise ball, a bolster, and a powerful baby monitor. Craig carried Millie's crib from her third-floor bedroom to the ground-floor family room, which had thick carpeting and plenty of room to spread out. I put Millie through her paces, gently rolling her onto her stomach and back upright. When she was seated again, I bounced her gently to reward her for the hard work. I was sure it would pay off, and I was willing to do whatever it took.

It's a good thing I had plenty to do, because it took from May to the end of November for Craig and me to receive the results of the evaluation. While we were waiting, 9/11 happened. As my country's bombs fell on Afghan villages, I carried on. It was like riding a roller coaster in total darkness. I clung to anything Millie did that looked like typical behavior. I studied her face when her dad stepped into the kitchen. Was she listening when he greeted her? Was that a smile? Then I would go to a friend's house, and her baby, who was younger than Millie, would do something basic like point at the dog, and my heart would drop through the floor. The report, when we finally received it, put my fears into words without really explaining anything.

> With a chronological age of 9 months, Melitta's cognition appeared to be at 3 months, fine motor skills in the 3- to 5-month range, receptive and expressive language in the 3- to 6-month range, and gross motor skills were in the 3- to 6-month range with a score on the Battelle of 4 months. This would be considered global developmental delay with some visual impairment and inconsistent acceptance of tactile input. Melitta also displays oral hypersensitivity and does not consistently explore items with her hands. She also seems to have some difficulty with self-regulation and displays a somewhat passive temperament.
>
> Melitta's strengths are that she is visually able to track in all planes, that she is interested in visual and auditory stimulae, that she nurses well and exhibits the ability to dissociate her lower extremities.

Standing in the kitchen, I pored over these paragraphs, then passed the report to Craig. Strengths? Didn't these things come naturally for babies?

THROUGHOUT THOSE MONTHS OF waiting, Craig and I worried a lot about Millie's capacity for movement. It never occurred to us to wonder whether she would ever speak. Of course, she would speak. It would just take her a little longer.

In December, our case manager set up a family conference with Millie's developmental pediatrician. At the meeting, we begged Dr. Grove, who seemed wise and kindly, for an honest assessment of Millie's prognosis. Dr. Grove's office looked out on the harbor, and I watched the winter light dance across his desk as he listed what could cause this degree of developmental delay: a genetic or metabolic disorder, cerebral palsy, a regulatory disorder, autism spectrum disorder. But so far, none of the ailments he knew of fit Millie's profile, so there wasn't much he was willing to say.

Dr. Grove was treading gingerly, scanning our faces for a response. As he spoke, I thought of Dr. Kelly. A knot of rage tightened in my gut. None of these guys would give us a straight answer. Did they take us for monsters? Were they afraid we would hate Millie if we knew she was flawed? When Dr. Grove finished, I looked to Craig for guidance. I could tell he wasn't ready to back down. "Say you have a hundred children as delayed as Millie. How many of them ever learn to walk?" Craig's words were measured, but there were tears in his eyes. Dr. Grove answered calmly, meeting Craig's gaze, then mine. There weren't any statistics that could predict Millie's future, he explained. We'd just have to wait and see.

I began having dreams in which Millie crawled out of her stroller on a sunny autumn morning, sunlight dappling her hair and dress. With her chubby hands reaching out, she trundled toward me, squealing in delight. I always woke right before she arrived. If children develop the parachute reflex—if they use their arms to protect themselves when they fall—there's a good chance they'll learn to walk independently. Even though Millie was developing skills that would allow her to eat from a spoon, there was no guarantee she would ever use her tongue to talk. The therapists weren't teaching Millie to communicate. Instead, as I gradually began to realize, they were teaching us to treat her as if she already did.

ONE DAY IN EARLY spring, when Millie was a year and a half, Dovita and I brought her for a session with her infant development specialist. Catherine had a special chair set up for Millie on the opposite side of the room, facing a mirrored wall. There was a big can of shaving cream and a pan of water on the table next to it. My eyes met Dovita's. Shaving cream?

Catherine chuckled. "Millie, have we got a treat in store for you today!"

Dovita unhooked Millie from her stroller and lifted her into the chair. Catherine handed me an apron to cover her clothes.

She sprayed a pile of soapy foam directly onto the table, scooped up a handful, and rubbed it onto the mirror right in front of Millie's face. Then she reached for Millie's hand and guided it forward so Millie could feel it. Millie initially recoiled at the unfamiliar texture, but before long, she was squeezing the shaving cream between her fingers, her mouth agape.

The shaving cream was bait, it turned out—a ploy for turning Millie's attention to the mirror. Still holding Millie's hand, Catherine pointed at Millie's image. "Do you see who that is, Millie?" Millie's gaze was still unfocused, but her lips curled slightly. "Big smile," Catherine said, pointing to the mirror. "You know who that is!" I squinted at the mirror, trying to see what Catherine was seeing. It was kind of like a smile.

Catherine handed me the can. "You try it now. See if she'll look." I hesitated for a second, then sprayed a fistful of shaving cream into my hand. It was cool and soft, and I liked the way it felt in my palm. "Let's put some more on," I said to Millie. I smeared the blob on the mirror, and Millie briefly glanced at it, then looked away. But when I reached for her hand so she could feel what I had done, she didn't resist me. She ended the session with a blob of shaving cream on her nose.

Driving home along the frozen lake, I thought of "The Mirror Stage," an essay I read in graduate school by the French psychoanalyst Jacques Lacan. I found most of Lacan's writings ridiculously hard to grasp, but this one was straightforward. The mirror stage begins when a mother shows her baby its reflection in a mirror. The baby's sense of itself as a bounded individual, instead of a disorganized bundle of wants and needs, is born out of this experience. For Lacan, this is a key moment in language development: It's what allows a baby to learn to think of itself as "me." Even with the shaving cream, Millie had barely looked at her reflection. That smile, if it was one, had less to do with what she saw in the mirror than with what was in her hands.

How would she learn to use words? Did she even have a sense of self?

My thoughts inched toward an abyss.

But then I reflected on what else was happening during that session. Maybe the real point was the banter—the constant barrage of spoken words directed at my impassive daughter. Millie's therapists treated her as a person, not as an array of symptoms. For them, everything Millie did mattered, meant something, sprang from some purpose, however obscure, that couldn't simply be reduced to the impulses of a developmentally delayed brain.

CRAIG AND I WERE hopeful that we would soon gain a better understanding of Millie's brain. A few weeks after our meeting with Dr. Grove, we loaded Millie into the station wagon for the short drive to the children's hospital. In August, Dr. Kelly had concluded his report on Millie with these words: "I can recommend no further diagnostic testing at this time." Craig read the phrase over my shoulder, then shot me a look. It seemed a bit early to throw in the towel. Soon enough, though, we received a call from the medical genetics department. Dr. Kelly wasn't kicking us out; he was kicking us upstairs.

Dr. Wood was a well-groomed, graceful, welcoming sort of man. The genetic counselor who followed him into the exam room seemed cut from the same cloth. It would be years before full gene sequencing was cheap and widely available. This was the early 2000s: No one was spitting into a collection tube and sending it off to 23andMe. Genetic testing was serious business, and Dr. Wood approached it with care.

He greeted Millie as warmly as he greeted us, squatting to come down to her level. He didn't so much inspect her as admire her, and we ate it up. I took the opportunity to point out her sweetest features. "Look how much she looks like her father," I smiled at Craig. "She has the same cute gap between her front teeth." Later, Dr. Wood documented his observations in a paragraph packed with technical terms for simple things: "brachycephaly," "flat posterior occiput," "inner canthal distance," "palpebral fissures." My mother always had a lot to say about the shape of our ears. So did he.

After conversing quietly with the genetic counselor, who had been watching his every move, Dr. Wood filled us in. "I'd like to test her for Rett syndrome." Craig looked at him quizzically, and he went on. "We're able to look for anomalies in a gene called MECP2. It's on the X chromosome. You only see it in girls." Because girls had one good copy, they survived long enough to be born, he explained. "The results will take around six weeks. Do you have any questions?"

We had plenty, and he answered them patiently. Rett syndrome wasn't inherited; it was the result of a spontaneous mutation that occurred at the instant of conception in around one in ten thousand births. Most babies with Rett syndrome developed normally early on, then started losing skills when they were around one. Others didn't regress but developed at a glacial pace. Girls with Rett syndrome didn't make eye contact and had lots of unintentional hand movements. A lot of them had seizures. They all had ataxia, a movement disorder that made it hard to walk and talk. There was no need to jump to conclusions, the genetic counselor added. Outcomes varied. Physical, occupational, and speech therapy usually helped.

In retrospect, our reaction to this information seems strange. We left that appointment happy. A diagnosis is a story, and we needed one. When your child hits a developmental milestone, it's impossible not to feel as if you're to thank for this achievement. When your child doesn't hit any, it's hard not to feel like you're to blame. When you have a diagnosis, you can tell yourself it's not your fault. What could be more accidental than a flash of karma that leads a strip of nucleotides to break left when they should have broken right? Craig and I didn't share these thoughts, but I know we were both thinking them.

We soon came to recognize the pragmatic advantages of having a diagnosis: easier access to insurance coverage, maladies for her doctors to watch for, the possibility of treatments tailored for her and her kind. A diagnosis would have given us a place to look for answers to troubling questions like "What will Millie be like when she is older?" and "How long will she live?" When the test for Rett syndrome came back negative, we grieved for an hour and then called Dr. Wood's office to make a follow-up appointment. New syndromes came to his attention all the time, he told us. None of us were ready to call off the search.

When you have a story, you have a role. In those early years, if Millie had had a diagnosis, for better or worse, I would have had a part to play. Without one, I floated free. "Global developmental delay" was a description, not an explanation. The only thing for me to do in the face of it was to try even harder than I already had. If Millie failed to gain new skills, it wouldn't be my fault. If Millie made progress, I'd be happy—but not as happy as I would have been if her condition had had an actual label. I needed a fate to fight against. You can't beat the odds when there aren't any.

DURING THE FIRST YEAR of early intervention, I was starting my second research project. Later, when I returned to teaching, I found myself unable to talk about social theory without talking about Millie. I told my students about a game Catherine played with Millie. She propped Millie on the floor, then sat down facing her and rolled a ball in her direction. She always acted like Millie was playing catch, even when the ball just bounced off her foot or leg. All of Millie's therapists did this kind of thing, and I'm sure it was part of their training—a way of helping children reach for new skills. But I sensed deeper currents at work. "It's like this for all of us," I explained to my students. "Meaning comes from other people. I never really know what I'm thinking until I try to explain it to someone else." For the moment, I considered what Catherine's strategy meant for my daughter and decided there were grounds for hope. All that was called for was an act of will. By treating Millie like a normal toddler, I could make her one.

I had the will and, somehow, I found the time. Ralph gave me little trouble; he was merrily making his way through preschool on campus at the Lab School, a cheerful child, his teachers told us, easygoing and full of ideas. But then there was my career. Even now, I still have notes from phone interviews and meetings stored on my computer, and I know I took research trips to Washington, Amsterdam, and Jakarta. I'm not sure how I did it. It was as if I were living two lives: one in meeting rooms with activists, another with my daughter on a cushioned floor. My days were emotionally fraught and intellectually rich. Millie didn't learn to crawl, let alone walk, during those two years in early intervention, and it was only toward the end of the period that she was able to sit cross-legged without tumbling over. Much to my relief, she learned to eat solid food and, even better, drink milk from a sippy cup. She never learned to drink from a bottle. For her first two years, my breasts were all she had.

Meanwhile, Craig was learning everything there was to know about special education. I won a grant to support my research that freed me from my responsibilities on campus. At about the same time, Craig had an opportunity to work with a client in the Netherlands, where a community of West Papuans lived in exile; we made plans to move the family to Amsterdam for the year. By the time we realized how far behind Millie was in her development, it was too late for Craig to back out. I stayed in Chicago, where Millie had access to doctors and therapists. Craig worked all week in a Dutch office park, then flew back across the Atlantic to spend the weekend in Hyde Park.

When he wasn't asleep on the couch, he was strategizing. I came downstairs to wake up Millie just as Craig was finishing a phone call with his sister. "That was Karin," he told me. "She says if you don't know your rights, you're screwed." We're going to need another filing cabinet, I thought to myself. Sure enough, Craig set about hoovering up every scrap of information he could find. He mastered the acronyms: ADA (Americans with Disability Act), IDEA, and IEP (Individualized Education Program). He memorized that magic spell, "a free and appropriate education in the least restrictive environment," and learned to wield it.

All this was preparation for enrolling Millie in the Chicago Public Schools. Her placement felt like a matter of life and death. "Millie said 'tickle tickle'!" my mother announced one day when we returned from the grocery store during one of our trips to Wisconsin. She'd been sitting with Millie on the living room carpet. We'd given Millie a plastic Noah's Ark for Christmas, and my mom had been trying to interest her in a pair of giraffes. My mother was reassuring, if not always convincing. Still, I took her words to heart. Millie was gathering momentum. What if she lost it?

There were two choices when it came to Millie's entry into special education. Millie belonged to the "low incidence" population, we were disturbed to learn, which placed her among children who were medically fragile or significantly delayed. The obvious option was Dunn Early Childhood Center, which was four miles away and run by a no-nonsense doctorate in education. She was honest in our meeting. "Our kids need a full day program, but we can't get the school district to pay for it. If you can send Millie someplace better, I would." Twelve miles away, near the runways at Midway Airport, Blair had a full-day program. Its devoutly Catholic principal had attracted enough funding from private donors to provide a full slate of services.

Millie got into Blair. In June 2003, I prepared my file to come up for tenure. In August, Craig held down the fort so I could take a research trip to West

Papua. While I was gone, my parents accompanied Craig when he delivered Millie on her first day of school. They returned in October for the Blair Halloween party, where Millie dressed like a devil, and I dressed like an angel, for a parade of wheelchairs through the cheerful corridors. Some of the children in the parade were heavily medicated, and I took comfort in the fact that Millie seemed much more alert than some of her peers. I liked and trusted Millie's new teachers and therapists. They seemed to want to do right by her and were filled with optimism. The transition went well.

A FEW YEARS AGO, Ralph, now in his twenties, pushed into my home office. "Mom! You wouldn't believe what I found!" I winced, expecting the worst. Ralph was whiling away the pandemic in Santa Cruz, and he had been rooting around in some boxes stored in my studio. The day before, he'd shown up with a journal I kept in high school and read a few choice passages aloud. This time, instead of my juvenilia, Ralph was clutching Craig's old video camera. I took in his raised eyebrows and the excited pitch of his shoulders. Ralph stands, walks, and emotes just like his father did. And, like his father, Ralph loves devices. I sighed, too absorbed in the email I was answering to object. "You can have it if you want. Does it work?"

Ralph plowed on, ignoring my offer. "There are a bunch of tapes!"

I stared up at him, stunned. I'd known there was a cassette in the camera, but I'd never seen any others. "There's more than one?"

"Yes! Look!" Ralph handed me the camera with the viewfinder opened and pushed a button.

My heart melted. "Oh my god, you were so cute."

Ralph ordered the cords he needed to hook up the camera to our television. One evening after dinner, we sat down together in the living room to watch the life we had lived in the six years before Craig died. There was Ralph, prancing naked across the hardwood floors of our apartment in Hyde Park. I lounge on the couch, my nose in a book, looking up to smile at Ralph, then at the camera as he crawls into my lap. There he was again in his bright yellow parka and fuzzy jester hat, pushing a red snow shovel in my parents' driveway. He's being supervised by my father, who is bundled up and looking rather cold.

From behind the camera, Craig's voice provides the narration. "What are you doing, Ralph?" he asks repeatedly. Every so often, Ralph pipes up. "Shoveling snow!" "What's in the pan, Ralph?" Seated on the kitchen counter, Ralph beams. "Bacon," he announces, triumph in his voice. "Where's your stocking?" Ralph is crawling in front of my parents' fireplace, watched by my parents and my sister and her late husband, who are squeezed together with me on the couch. Stocking? Ralph is confused. What's a stocking?

The next cassette opened with some footage taken at a gate at O'Hare. I am holding Ralph up to the window and showing him the airplanes. Ralph points his finger, then turns to me, excited.

Taking this in, I poked grown-up Ralph in the shoulder. "We look at things, then we talk. That still pretty much sums up our relationship."

Ralph laughed. "Some things never change!"

Ralph inserted the third cassette and suddenly Millie appeared on the screen. My heart skipped a beat. There she was in the sunny kitchen of our Chicago townhouse, standing in her stander, wisps of golden hair floating around her head like a halo. Her gaze is fixed on her fingers, but she is reacting to her father's voice. "Mill-ie. Mill-ie," he sing-songs. "What are you doing, Millie? Mill-ie. Brrrrrr." When he makes a buzzing noise with his lips, Millie looks up and focuses squarely on the camera, her lips curved into a small grin. She's alert—in some ways she looks more alert than she does now—and she's radiant, eyes wide, lips pink, cheeks rosy and smooth as a peach.

Dovita told me Millie was perfect, and she was. Was I too worried to notice? Was I too ready to listen to all those voices telling me she was not? I look at myself in this footage, and I see someone who looks a lot like me: bookish, gawky, amused, preoccupied. But there is a gulf between that woman and the person I am today. It's made of sadness and wisdom. Did that woman realize she was blessed? That they were blessed? Would she have thought differently about her life if she'd known it was all about to change?

As these thoughts raced through my mind, I fell silent. "I'd forgotten how beautiful she was," I finally breathed.

The next cassette opened with Millie in her crib. The camera work is shaky, and this time, the narrating voice is mine. It takes a minute, then I suddenly realize why I'm working the camera: It's because Craig is gone. Millie is sitting erect and laughing. Have I snuck into her bedroom to catch her greeting the day? But no—it's late at night and what looks like joy is agitation. "It's past Millie's bedtime, and she's still awake," I observe. The camera holds steady as Millie's movements grow more frantic, and she thrashes and kicks until one of her feet gets caught between the rails of the crib. I'm not comforting my daughter; I'm a fly on the wall.

What was I doing? I leaned forward, frozen. This was so wrong. I had no memory of making this tape. Had I recorded this for Millie's doctors? Ralph looked at me, concerned. "We don't have to watch this now."

I glanced at him, then back at the screen. "It's okay."

In the next scene, Millie is sitting on my mother's lap facing outward, straddling my mother's thighs. My mother's expression is stony as I talk. "Here's Millie with her grandmother. We're looking for unintentional movements. But Millie is acting pretty calm." The language I'm using confirmed my suspicions; this was doctor speak. Ralph shifted on the couch next to me. I wanted to explain, but I had nothing to say. A moment earlier, my mom, my dad, my sister's husband, and Craig had sprung back to life before us, along with toddler Ralph, quaking with happiness, and baby Millie, touched with grace. Fast-forward, and I am trapped at the bottom of a well. It's the summer of 2004, and Millie's specialists are still looking for a diagnosis. They're considering a spinal tap to test her for a degenerative syndrome that attacks the motor neurons. I'm filming Millie's "symptoms" so they can tell whether it's worth it. The procedure they're proposing is painful and dangerous. I don't know what to do.

The last cassette begins with the only footage showing Craig. It's the summer before Millie was born and he's reading *Henny Penny* to Ralph. Craig's eyes are gentle as he points out the pictures. "Look, Ralph. Who's that?" Hearing me step into the room, Craig looks up, mildly concerned to see me playing his role as family documentarian. "Are you sure it's turned on?" The camera angle goes haywire as I turn the device to check.

Who would have thought back then that we could survive without my husband? Certainly not me.

What Millie Remembers

The sky was steel gray on the morning when my friend's husband led Ralph and me away from the hospital to his car. It was November 23, 2003. A flock of ravens gathered in the distance, their harsh voices carried by the wind. A scattering of leaves swirled at our feet. These were not the leaves that crunched underfoot in October. These were the holdouts, too small to catch in a rake, free but aimless, like tiny plastic bags caught in the wind. Ralph walked silently beside me, clutching my hand. We both were shivering. Craig had just been pronounced dead. We had stepped off a cliff, and we would fall forever through this frigid day.

I'd called my friend from the windowless conference room where the doctor had come to deliver the news. Rachel answered after four rings, and I blurted out my request. I needed someone to bring Ralph to the ER so he could say goodbye. Her husband had waited in the foyer when the nurse led Ralph and me to the exam room. It hadn't taken long. Ralph had looked at Craig's body, then up at me. "Poor Daddy. Can we go home?"

Shortly afterward, Ralph developed a keen interest in zombies. This perplexed me until the child psychologist I found for him explained the obvious.

Of course, Ralph was interested in situations in which someone's father came back to life.

THE NIGHT BEFORE HE died, Craig hadn't planned to be home. He had been on a business trip, and he was supposed to leave directly from the airport to spend the weekend hunting. But the American Anthropological Association was holding its annual meeting in Chicago, and I was throwing a party for friends from out of town. Craig had caught an early flight just so he could help me. He slipped into the kitchen while I was showing some graduate students the roof deck. From the doorway, I caught sight of him holding a glass of wine and giggling uncontrollably at something one of my senior colleagues had just said. I moved within earshot, and the conversation turned to a movie Craig was trying to get me to see. Full of mischief, I crept up behind him. "*Master and Commander?*" I cut in. "A management consultant's wet dream!"

Eight hours later, Craig died in our bed. He was killed by a blockage in the coronary artery that doctors call "the widow maker" because a brief pause in its blood flow can stop a life in its tracks. The first thing I noticed was the shaking, which rattled the metal bed frame. Ralph was curled up behind me. I reached past him and fished for my glasses on the nightstand. Craig lay face up, his back sharply arched, eyes fixed on the ceiling. He was gasping, but the sound he was making was guttural, senseless. I watched, unable to move.

Finally, the shaking ended, and Craig's body gave a final jerk.

The stillness broke the spell, and I pulled my eyes away from my husband. Ralph, jolted awake, had risen to his feet and was standing next to the bed, his small face pale and confused. Light from a streetlamp landed on the travel alarm Craig had given me for my research trip. 5:09 a.m. Beyond the travel alarm was the phone. What do they do in the movies? Call 911. My hand quivered. I'd been wasting time. I sent the clock crashing to the floor as I struggled to free the handset. Yet when it came time to punch in the number, my finger hovered for a second. Should I really be bothering them? Was this an emergency?

"911. What's your location?" The voice was matter of fact.

"The bedroom." I repeated what I'd just told Ralph. "Something bad is happening. To my husband."

"I need your address."

Somehow the right numbers and words made it out of my mouth. "5330. South Shore Drive."

"Is he breathing?"

I shut my eyes. "I don't know. My son is with me. He's only six."

"The paramedics are on their way. Take your son and wait by the front door so you can let them in."

Three of the guests from the night before had stayed over: an anthropologist friend, a Papuan journalist I was close to, and a Papuan scholar I'd just met. I woke my anthropologist friend before heading down to unlock the door; he woke the others. They watched as the emergency vehicles arrived, then retreated to their rooms.

I sat with Ralph on the living room couch while the paramedics worked. Red lights flashed in the darkness; the fire truck had been first to arrive. Ralph's eyes had widened as the burly men rushed up the stairs with their equipment; there was rustling overhead.

Ralph looked up. "What's that sound?"

"They're helping Daddy. It's okay."

It? What was it? It was as if Craig were an alien spaceship that had fallen from the sky, and we earthlings were trying to resuscitate the crew. This had to be a dream. I tried to picture what the paramedics were doing. CPR? Whatever I knew about that seemed beside the point. I wondered what wheels were turning in Ralph's brain. School started in two hours. Would this be an excused absence? Was I still supposed to send him to school?

There was commotion on the stairs. The paramedics were bringing Craig down on a stretcher. My anthropologist friend offered to sit with Ralph. On my way out the door, I called Dovita and asked her how quickly she could make it in. Then I slipped into the front seat next to the driver. In the back, the men were still working on Craig. Now, I know he was probably already dead.

Where was Millie in all of this? Was I grateful she was sleeping? Was I worried she'd wake up? Did I want to spare her from what was happening? Would having her on my radar screen in these critical moments have been too painful to bear? I do remember thinking, as the horror sunk in, of something Craig had said to me as we made our way to the car after the meeting in which the school district agreed to enroll Millie in Blair.

"Let's never get divorced." Craig's tone had been mock grave.

I had squeezed his hand and completed his thought. "Nope. No divorce. That would be a bad idea. Neither of us can do this on our own."

ON THAT COLD MORNING, we returned to the house to find Rachel and my guests making phone calls and coffee. Rachel hugged me, her eyes brimming with tears, and then took Ralph's hand. "No school today, sweetie. You can do whatever you want." What Ralph wanted to do was watch television, which he did for the next twelve hours, drinking root beer in bottles from the corner store. Dovita played with Millie in her bedroom downstairs. I don't remember holding her.

I walked to the closet to hang up my coat. I could feel my friends watching me. This was the moment when I was supposed to break down. But the last thing I wanted to do was shut myself up in the bedroom where Craig had just died. Instead, I went to the kitchen. I wasn't going to cry, not with an audience. I had things to do. Craig had bought me a counter-height table for the kitchen so I could drink my morning coffee and look out the window. I sat at this perch and made lists. Call the coroner. Order death certificates. Call the hospital. Ask them to do an autopsy. Call the funeral home. Find an estate lawyer. Call the bank.

Behind me, the townhouse filled with people. That afternoon, my brother and his family drove down from Ann Arbor, and Ralph's older cousins joined him on the couch. Craig's sister arrived with her husband and daughters on a red eye the next morning.

By then, my sister had taken charge of Craig's closet. As Craig's possessions left the house, other things took their place. The kitchen filled with plants, flowers, baked goods, and visitors. The parents of Ralph's classmates brought us meals until our refrigerator ran out of space. The phone was constantly ringing. Craig's classmates called from as far away as Nairobi. Famous academics whom I'd only met once or twice asked whether there was anything they could do. I was moved and deeply grateful. But mostly I was amazed. A year earlier, one of my colleagues had had a brain aneurysm. I had pitched in for flowers, but it had felt too intrusive to call his wife. How had these people gotten up the nerve to call me?

Craig's death cracked open my household and exposed Ralph, Millie, and me to the astonishing kindness of strangers. It was not an easy adjustment. I longed to have the house to myself. I slept very little. At 2 a.m., I would make my way to the kitchen. Sometimes I put away dishes and organized the stuff on the counters. Sometimes I sat on the floor and wondered why I wasn't dead, too. A friend in England, who somehow knew what I needed, sent me lavender bath oil. I sat in the tub, breathing in the scent, my eyes fixed on the faucet. While my relatives slept, I got up at 4 a.m. to jog through empty streets.

I heard back from the coroner: Other than the one blocked artery, the vessels in Craig's heart were entirely clear. When I called Craig's father, he described some research he'd just discovered. A group of Norwegian men had been treated with the same chemotherapy combination that Craig had in his early twenties. A startling number of them had heart attacks in their forties, Craig's father told me. Could the treatment that saved Craig also have killed him? Neither of us knew what to do with this thought.

As one week turned to two, I spent hours at my table in the kitchen. I opened condolence cards and planned Craig's memorial service. The venue, the speakers, the music, the caterers, the hotel rooms for out-of-town guests. I immersed myself in our wedding's evil twin. Thankfully, Craig had taken out life insurance and, to my surprise, he'd also amassed some savings. That Montana business hadn't just been a dream. Craig's career had embarrassed me—what had happened to my Marxist?—but now I felt only relief. We were set financially for the foreseeable future. I would have to figure out the rest.

One day, I found a message Craig had accidentally recorded in my voicemail. It was a cloudy morning in December, and I was sitting in the kitchen with my flip phone listening to old messages and deleting them. The social security office, the insurance company, my mom, my cousin, hospital billing—and then there was Craig. "No worries," he was saying. "You'll make it." He'd been talking to a driver who was rushing him to the airport. But I felt like he was talking to me, and I hoped he was right.

I SAVED THAT MESSAGE, and then my carrier erased it. Not long after that, I dreamed that Craig's memory had come to say goodbye and I was about to forget he ever existed. I ran into him curbside at O'Hare. He was wearing a soft dark-blue sweater—one I'd gotten him for Christmas—and carrying his travel bag. I was ecstatic to see him, and we chatted happily until he turned to go. "Wait," I called after him. "You already left. How can you be leaving again?" I woke up in tears and immediately thought of Millie. Would Millie remember her father? Would she miss him? Would there be anything that reminded her of the smell of Craig's skin, his gait when he carried her, his hairy arms, his deep voice, his laugh?

Millie seemed to know something was wrong. On the day Craig died, she stopped sleeping through the night. We went to Seattle for Christmas that year, and my eldest brother let me sleep while he wheeled her around his living room. It wasn't until 3 a.m. that her eyes finally fluttered closed. During the day, Millie seemed distracted; I'm sure I did, too. My parents and my sister joined us, and my brother rented a house on Puget Sound that was big enough to hold us all. We took long walks together on the country road that ran along the shoreline. Gulls wheeled in the cold, cloudy skies overhead. Quiet conversations went on around me. They sounded like traffic on a distant highway. Bundled in a scarf and hood, Millie lay motionless in her stroller, exhausted from her struggles. It was as if we were both sealed in a jar.

Those moments in the bedroom, when Craig's life was draining away, were seared into my mind. For Ralph as well, the past could never be a blank. The names of the dead live on in databases. Mail addressed to Craig piled up on the kitchen counter where Ralph could find it. Creditors kept calling looking for the wrong Craig Best—someone who wasn't paying their bills. For years to come, Ralph would be surrounded by evidence of his father's existence. But envelopes and phone calls meant nothing to Millie. I didn't know if they ever would.

During those first few months, I did what I could to keep Craig alive for both my children. On Saturdays, I loaded the kids into the car, and we followed Craig's routine: a quick stop for donuts, then a drive to the North Side to shop for a week's worth of food. Craig had nicknames for his favorite businesses, and I always used them. He had loved Costco's free samples. "Should we go to the snack store first?" My new existence took on a certain clarity. Who was going to get Millie out of the car seat? That would be me. At the memorial service, Craig's best friend described him as an "artist of everyday life." I tried to become one myself.

On those days when Craig seemed so present, I didn't dwell on what Millie would remember. I was too busy enjoying her weight in my arms and the warm smell of her hair. But on darker days, I was scared. I looked at Millie and felt a bottomless sadness. When Craig sat next to her on the sofa, bouncing her and singing in her ear, he always left a dent in the cushion. You could tell he had been there. But not for long. I needed Millie to remember him. I needed everyone to remember him. I needed to freeze our life as it had been before Craig died. I always drove down the same streets that Craig had used when we ran errands. Now, I see why. I was afraid of losing my bearings in a landscape I thought I had no choice but to cross. I was like that cartoon coyote who sprints off a precipice and keeps on running. I could feel the drop coming. But I couldn't bear to look down. What I didn't know then was that I was falling upward—into the open sky, where I could see beyond the horizon I'd been racing toward. I was leaving the path behind.

More than twenty years have passed. Does Millie remember Craig? I want to believe she does, but I may never know for sure. I'm not sure that it matters. When I'm with Millie, I can feel the imprint of his love for her. An imprint that can't fade because it made her who she is. This kind of memory has no need for words.

But back then, I yearned for the day when Millie and I would talk about her father. I couldn't bear the thought that this day would never come. Toward the end of the school year, I was thrilled when the principal at Blair told me how much my daughter reminded her of a former student: same cheerful personality, same dimples, same strawberry blonde hair. They might have the same syndrome, she thought.

Not long after this, I met the girl's mother at a fundraising event at the school. I asked how her daughter was doing. I knew from the principal that the girl had just turned sixteen, and I hoped to hear that she had learned to speak. But the mother shook her head. "Things are not good. Our life's a living hell."

I clutched my empty juice cup and stared at her. I had no idea what to say.

CRAIG'S DEATH TRANSFORMED ME. The worst thing that could happen had happened, and I was still standing, like in those dreams where you can't be killed because you're already dead. I had learned about being the mother of a disabled child from early intervention and the search for a diagnosis. Now, I was ready to learn what Millie herself had to teach me.

No Future

These lessons from Millie were hard-won. The anthropologist Sophie Chao did research in a part of West Papua where oil palm cultivation was poisoning the rivers and scarring the land.[1] Time had ended, Chao's Marind friends told her. The people who made their homes in the dying forest rejected the government's promise that the plantations would spell progress. Instead, they experienced an extreme form of grief with the loss of the songbirds, cassowaries, sago groves, and spirits, the loss of their way of life. I have never had to experience this kind of apocalypse. But I'm moved by the grace with which the Marind responded, keeping faith with a world that was slipping away.

This kind of grace didn't come to me naturally. By the time Craig died, I'd spent decades rushing past other travelers on life's moving walkway, my gaze fixed firmly ahead. I thought I was charting my own route—that atlas, those maps—but plenty of others were on their way to the same gate. In high school, I couldn't wait to get to college; in college, I couldn't wait to get to graduate school; in graduate school, all I could think about was getting a job. When I was five, I fell into a depression when I realized that my friend Lisa would always be a year older than I was; I had been trying so hard to catch up.

Craig and I spent the first years of Millie's life inventing futures, to borrow Sophie Chao's words, from whose vantage point Millie's present would find meaning—someday, we would look back and all this would make sense.[2] Even as the extent of her disabilities became clear, we still saw our daughter through a prism. It was the prism of the person we dreamed she could be: a slender young woman who shelved books, read to toddlers, sang in a choir. With Craig's death, all that ended. Not only did I need to keep Craig alive for Millie, I needed Millie to keep Craig alive for me. Children are the future, the cliché goes; they can't help but call to mind what's to come. My children, by contrast, called to mind what had been—a past when their father was still alive. Craig had known them as they were now. Whatever they became, they would become without him. And that future, in those early months, was unfathomable.

AND YET, TIME WENT BY. Shortly after Craig died, the dean called to tell me I would be tenured. A friend and his wife joined me at a fancy restaurant where Craig had made a reservation six months earlier so we could celebrate. (He had more faith in me than I did.) Craig had booked the kitchen table, which was available for special occasions, and I watched the chefs scurrying, chopping, and searing. The appetizer was a tiny soft-shell crab, delicately breaded and resting on a dime-sized dollop of remoulade. "It's too beautiful to eat," I whispered as much to Craig as to anyone else.

I was given the option of returning to work whenever I felt like it; I scheduled a class for spring quarter, then promptly canceled it. When I wasn't with Ralph and Millie, I was in our guest room sorting photos and gluing them into a stack of albums Craig had bought and never used. Or I was on the StairMaster next to Craig's desk, exercising and reading. Craig had been bugging me to read Patrick O'Brian's ship novels, and I'd resisted. Now I devoured all twenty of them, pumping and sweating. When I finished the last in the series, I wept.

On Friday mornings, while Ralph and Millie were at school, I took watercolor lessons on the north side, speeding up Lake Shore Drive to class with music blasting. We were supposed to work from photographs, but I worked from memory. I was on a pack trip in the Sierras, painting while Craig fished, trying to match the green of the meadow before the light faded from the sky. In August, Craig's parents held a memorial service in the outdoor chapel where we'd been married. Afterward, Millie stayed with my in-laws, and I drove to the mountains with Ralph and a group of Craig's friends. Near the camp where our pack trips usually began, I poured Craig's ashes into a crack in a rock beside a pine tree. I watched as the sparkling dust vanished into the sand and gravel. Afterward, I sat by myself on the granite, warmed by the sun. "We miss you," I told Craig. "But I know where to find you. We'll be back."

Craig's former headmaster, Bill, who led the pack trips and had become a family friend, invited me to spend the anniversary of Craig's death at his house in La Honda. My parents drove down to stay with Ralph and Millie, and I flew west alone. Bill fixed us some sandwiches, and I stood on the patio, looking west across the hills to the ocean, which was growing dark in the distance. After her husband died, Joan Didion found herself unable to give away his shoes because he would need them. She handled the loss calmly because she didn't believe it had occurred. Bill stepped out to hand me a beer. "Craig would be proud of you," he told me. But the spell was broken. On the way back to the airport, the truth dawned on me. My husband was gone for good. I'd done everything his death demanded of me. I'd managed in his absence. But no amount of list-making would bring him back. The next week I found a therapist in Chicago. "You're not going to get over this," she told me. "The sooner you accept this, the better."

EVERYONE TOLD ME I should be worried about Ralph, and I was. He hadn't just lost his father; he'd lost his partner in crime. Craig had three sisters, and he'd grown up with a father who embraced him as his natural ally and companion. They went on adventures together—duck hunting, skiing, flying in a helicopter—and Craig had talked to him almost daily as an adult. Craig treated Ralph the same way his father had treated him. He took him pheasant hunting, allowing him to carry the warm bodies of dead birds in his vest; they rode bikes together over the border into Indiana, stopping at bodegas along the way to buy Mexican cokes; he took him to Colorado and taught him to ski. They took pleasure in doing things I did not quite approve of, and I took pleasure in holding down the fort. I'd take my time feeding Millie breakfast and cleaning up the kitchen. After that, Millie would stand in her stander, and I'd sing to her; if she was contented, I'd grade a few papers or review some of the admissions folders that piled up in my inbox every year. Then I'd carry Millie down to her stroller, and we'd go for a walk around the point, where families held cookouts and waves gently lapped against the rocks.

In the afternoon, the garage door would rumble, and Craig and Ralph would thunder up the stairs. "Don't tell Mommy," I heard Craig whispering in the stairwell after one of their outings. But Ralph couldn't help himself. He ran to me, beaming. "I got to watch them gut a deer!"

"Say hi to your sister," I ordered him, pointing at the stander.

"Hi, Millie," he said, shoving his little face in front of hers, wiggling his fingers and trying to get her to respond.

After Craig died, my family did their best during vacations to fill the gap left by his absence. Ralph and Millie had seven cousins—with one exception, all girls—and their fathers couldn't wait to get their hands on Ralph. They sent me frequent bulletins from the field. My brother who lived in Ann Arbor invited Ralph on a canoe trip, and my nieces, who were slightly older than Ralph, welcomed him into the noisy household, where my sister-in-law nagged him as if he were one of her own. I put him on an airplane to Los Angeles for Easter—the first of his many flights as an unaccompanied minor. While Craig's sister baked, my brother-in-law took Ralph and his daughters to Legoland. Later, the cousins climbed trees in the backyard, before tucking into ham, creamed potatoes, and three kinds of pie. That summer, my other brother invited Ralph to Seattle, where he went sailing and ate chocolate with yet another girl cousin, who was also around his age.

But these trips only went so far, and with Craig out of the picture and Millie in it, there were things Ralph couldn't do. On a sunny Sunday afternoon, eighteen months after Craig's death, Ralph ran up to his room and came downstairs with his father's Frisbee. He stood by the front door. "I want to play catch." Millie was in her high chair, and I had a half a bowl of chili left to spoon into her mouth. After that, I would have to wash her face, clean up the dishes, change her shirt and diaper, and unfold the stroller. It could take us an hour to get to the park across the street; by then, Ralph would have given up and turned on the TV. I hired a graduate student to spend time with Ralph on the weekends. One of his friends was already watching Millie a couple of afternoons a week so I could play with Ralph. When I was bathing Millie or changing her, my attention was entirely occupied. But when she was peacefully staring at her lap or fingering her rattle, I was all his. "Millie, Millie, Millie," Ralph trilled at his sister, then turned to chat with me.

Bound to me by what we had witnessed together, Ralph came to see himself as my deputy in difficult situations. During those first months, he learned to show up when I needed help with Millie and was quick to fetch a clean diaper or a package of wipes. Millie was a fixture in Ralph's childhood: a constraint but also a comfortable presence. Ralph either had all of me or none of me, and he learned to make do.

Ralph was with me when I wheeled Millie into our favorite restaurant on one of our many trips to see my parents. When I took a break from tucking bits of hamburger into Millie's mouth, the woman in the next booth caught my eye. "She's adorable." I flushed with pleasure; Ralph looked up. "You know, a surgeon could fix that eye turn." My smile froze. Around this time, Ralph stopped inviting friends over to the house. "I was very protective of Millie," Ralph told me recently when I asked him what he remembered about those times. "When people stared, I stared right back." His answer surprised me—I had been too wrapped up in my own reactions to notice this. I pictured little Ralph confronting nosy strangers, a pint-sized tough guy drilling holes in them with his eyes. Still, there were limits to his solicitude. "I didn't want to take care of Millie. I was afraid she'd want or need something, and I wouldn't be able to figure out what it was."

BY THE END OF the second year after Craig's death, it was no longer possible to reproduce a facsimile of the family life we'd once had. Ralph was well into third grade in a different building at the Lab School, and I was back to teaching full time. I no longer had just one care provider for Millie; I had four, including doctoral students from our program who needed the cash. If it wasn't care providers, it was friends whose voices echoed up the stairwell. I was afraid of the gas grill; that had been Craig's domain. I used it as an excuse to throw a dinner party. My guests said hi to Millie, then I carried her to bed while they decided who would teach me how to light the burners without blowing up the house. Ralph joined us at the table.

"So what do you work on?" I once caught him asking a student. Ralph was eight.

I offered to teach the first quarter of the required theory course for incoming doctoral students. It was a grueling assignment involving nine hours of class per week. I spent the summer of 2005 reading St. Augustine, Vico, Machiavelli, Hobbes, Locke, Smith, and Hume instead of finishing my second book. I knew nothing about this literature. But thoughts of my own career left me empty. Doing something new and scary made me feel alive. I had a study in the university library, where I spent hours poring over strange old texts. I burst into tears one day, suddenly recognizing where all this energy was coming from. It was Craig. The theme I chose for the course was the limits of human understanding. It was also the theme of my life.

My life on campus was filled with words. For the theory class, I assigned four hundred pages of reading each week. I did it all, and more, and wrote detailed lectures on each of the authors we covered. When I wasn't reading with my students, I was talking to them or grading their papers: A barrage of language, written and spoken, pummeled me every day. At home, Ralph ruled the airwaves.

The History Channel blasted in the background while I cooked. Over dinner, Ralph would explain what he'd learned. Ralph and I talked on the way to campus and on Saturdays when we ran errands. Where did religion come from? he asked me once at a stoplight. We spent the next hour on the topic without exhausting it.

Ralph, with all his language, both delighted and disturbed me. He was slow to read; Craig and I had noticed this during the summer before Craig died. When Ralph was in second grade, I had him evaluated. He had dyslexia and dysgraphia, the psychologist told me, but he was a strong auditory learner. In third grade, Ralph scored in the eighty-fifth percentile in reading comprehension, even though he couldn't read a sentence aloud. When I wasn't talking to Ralph, I was talking about him—with his tutor, his teacher, my sister-in-law, my mom. Ralph was so obviously no longer the young child he had been when his father was still living. It was becoming harder to avoid thinking ahead.

In the midst of all these words, Millie was my refuge. "She's such a soothing presence," a student told me after spending the afternoon with her. Having Ralph out adventuring gave me time alone with my daughter; I found her soothing, too. Millie was developing better trunk control; we could sit together cross-legged, and she'd just started to roll. One day, I left her playing with Mardi Gras beads on the living room carpet while I grabbed a cup of tea. I sat down on the sofa, and suddenly she was lying at my feet, humming gently while she fingered my shoes. Letting Millie play with my shoelaces was strangely calming. Who cared if she tied my feet together? I had nowhere to go. In Millie's world, there were no words, and the future vanished. There was only now.

BUT MILLIE'S WORLD EXISTED within other, more vocal worlds, and these worlds were in motion. I pulled into a parking lot in front of the low-slung building where Millie was completing her first year in the Chicago Public Schools. I sat in the station wagon and took a deep breath before opening the door. I was early. It was May 2004, and I'd come to Millie's early childhood center for her second Individualized Education Program (IEP) meeting. I was channeling Craig. He'd gotten her into Blair; it was my job to keep her there.

The social worker had given me a form to fill out describing Millie's strengths, my concerns, and any ideas I had "for adding to/enhancing your child's education." I'd responded with an essay. It listed all the reasons why Millie should qualify for enough therapy time to merit a full-day placement, which meant qualifying for Blair. "Millie is very cheerful and good-natured; she tolerates therapy well," I started out. "She seems happy at school; she is always smiling in the morning when she gets on the bus." She was strong enough to transition from lying to sitting, I went on. They should work on that; it would give her more options for playing and learning. "I also feel she is on the cusp of a real improvement in communication," I concluded. "It seems very important not to reduce any of the activities included in her last IEP."

Clutching this document to my chest, I made my way past the friendly receptionist to Millie's classroom, where her teacher, therapists, and a school district representative relaxed around the art table.

"So glad you're here!" Millie's teacher welcomed me.

"We love Millie!" her physical therapist chimed in.

The school district representative gave her papers a jolly little shuffle, then called the meeting to order. "Let's be sure to introduce ourselves. Who wants to go first?"

Her teacher started us off. "Millie is such a sweet girl."

The rest took their turn, reporting on Millie's IEP goals and her progress in meeting them before closing with some recommendations for next year. I was loaded for bear, but my prey were bunnies; it took a second to adjust. Somewhat sheepishly, I read my statement aloud, pausing to see how the women would react; several of them nodded as I spoke. The school district representative agreed with me: Millie should have as many minutes of therapy time as she did now, and possibly more. She wasn't going to get booted from Blair.

Everyone at the meeting knew that Millie had lost her father less than six months earlier. Maybe they were being extra nice to us; if so, they didn't seem to find it hard. I looked around the room gratefully. These women were clearly enjoying my daughter. They wanted to understand her. I did, too.

Not that any of us thought understanding Millie was going to be easy. The "Determination of Adverse Effects Worksheet," which described the impact of Millie's "communication disorder," had some unnerving boxes checked. Under "Social Impact," they'd selected "difficulty being understood by peers and/or adults" and "difficulty initiating, maintaining, and terminating verbal interactions." But, in person, Millie's teachers and therapists spoke in the language of potential, not impairment: about what she might do, not what she couldn't.

The psychologist who'd evaluated Millie during her first year at Blair had been encouraging. She'd seen glimmers of comprehension. When she asked Millie to clap her hands, a few seconds went by and then Millie seemed to try to comply. I thought of her comments every time I scooped up some applesauce and pretended that the spoon was an airplane. Sometimes Millie opened her mouth. Sometimes she giggled. Other times, she did nothing at all. Then there were the times when I did nothing at all, and Millie laughed as if I had just told her a joke.

Did I really believe that Millie was "on the cusp of a real improvement in communication"? Or was I just saying these words to be true to Craig's memory, the memory of how he worked so hard to give Millie every advantage, when I knew not to pin my hopes on a behavior that didn't already exist? Either way, I wanted my words to be true.

Millie stayed at Blair for the next four years. Each fall, her speech therapist set the same goal. Spring would come, and everyone would praise her on her efforts even though she always fell short. And the next year, we'd start all over again. Millie did make some strides in physical therapy. One day in her bedroom, she was lying flat on her back on the floor and suddenly heaved herself upright with a jolt. This move allowed her to roll around the living room searching for shoelaces, then sit up to untie them, which made it easier for her to get the job done. In class, Millie smiled when she was happy and cried when she was uncomfortable. She babbled, sometimes in syllables. She swept her arm across the table, possibly to get something she wanted. Did she understand us? It wasn't clear. Did we understand her? Not a lot more than we did when she started school.

NEVERTHELESS, CHANGE WAS IN the air. In the paperwork she completed each year, the school district representative indicated each student's disability by selecting from a list of options. For Millie, she initially checked three: "Developmental Delay," "Physical Impairment," and "Speech/Language Impairment." Then Millie turned six, and she suddenly was no longer considered behind in her development. Instead, she had a "Severe/Profound Cognitive Impairment." Millie was still "cheerful and good-natured." And she still had "difficulty being understood by her peers and/or adults." But now the bureaucrats had started filing her under a new heading. She'd landed in a new slot.

At school, the shift was abrupt; outside school, it was gradual. There is a week in August when my children and Craig's sister's children differ in age in perfect one-year increments, with Ralph in the lead and Millie bringing up the rear. Craig's family began taking a yearly picture of the cousins to capture this moment when Millie was one and Ralph was four. Every summer, Craig's parents rented an unrenovated 1960s beach house a few miles from their home in Ventura. Ten of us shared a bathroom, slathered each other with sunscreen, and loudly devoured dinners that Craig and his father grilled on the deck. During the years following Craig's death, we kept up this tradition. Ralph took surfing lessons and went boogie boarding with his cousins. My mother-in-law kept an eye on Millie, and I jumped in the ocean and then warmed myself in the sun, trying to chase away the chill I still felt from the day Craig died. Later, when the light was right, we lined up the kids on a beat-up old couch facing the Pacific, and everyone tried to get Millie to smile.

I look at these photographs and watch Millie morph: Her hair grows longer, her face grows thinner, her mouth grows wider, her expression becomes less focused. In some of the pictures, she's wearing the glasses that an optometrist prescribed to treat her eye turn; in others, she's in glossy pigtails, courtesy of her cousins. During those years, I traveled solo to Ventura with the children, and on the flight back and forth, I had to gate-check Millie's stroller and carry her to our seats. On the first summer after Craig's death, the other passengers smiled at us: They saw a mother with a toddler, not a child who was nearly four. By the fifth summer, I had to ask Ralph to carry the diaper bag and my backpack so I could hoist Millie to my hip and muscle her to our row. By then, she was wearing plastic leg braces for support, and her clunky shoes dangled dangerously close to the faces of people sitting on the aisle. The woman across from us looked at her, then frowned. Millie's pigtails, which had seemed so cute, were spending way too much time in her mouth. I don't know when I stopped believing, even a little, that Millie would catch up—when that dream of the slender young woman shelving books dissolved into thin air. Was the realization traumatic? It's hard to say. Losing faith in that future was like losing a silk scarf on a crowded subway. With everything going on around me, I could barely feel it slipping away.

WHAT I DO REMEMBER is how much I liked driving to Millie's school. The trip took me through a patchwork of neighborhoods: African American, Mexican, Polish, and working-class white. There were verdant parklands, boulevards lined with row houses, and blocks and blocks of cottages with identical stone facades. I joined Blair's local school council, which was tasked with finding a replacement for the beloved principal, who was about to retire. My fellow parents on the council were Latinx women, many of them immigrants whose children were born in the United States. When the school district announced staff cuts, one of these women organized a protest. She requisitioned a school bus with a wheelchair lift, and a dozen of us descended on a school board meeting with our children. We each took a turn at the mike; our leader demanded a translator and refused to leave until one showed up. Afterward, my job was to write an angry letter, threatening legal action if the district didn't comply with our demands.

I felt more at home at Blair than I did at the Lab School. On the South Side of Chicago, where Blair was located, the population was over 90 percent African American, with a growing Latinx population. The Lab School was in the part of Hyde Park closest to the university, an enclave filled with people who looked like Craig and me. On the night of Ralph's fifth-grade band concert, I wheeled Millie into the gym and took a seat at the bottom of the bleachers. I located Ralph among the fidgeting children, then listened to them tune their instruments, staring stonily ahead, missing Craig. The woman next to me scooped up her toddler, then turned to her husband. "What do you think? Should we stick with the traveling team? Or let him try out for math camp this year?" I swallowed and pretended I hadn't heard.

A few months later, a couple with a son in Ralph's class invited the other parents to a party at the family's loft. I stood with a glass of wine, wondering what to do. (Millie wasn't the only one in the family who had "difficulty initiating, maintaining, and terminating verbal interactions.") If I talked to the men, their wives would glare at me. If I talked to the women, their eyes would glaze over and I'd run out of things to say. I wasn't thinking about math camp. I was worrying about how to get my insurance to pay for repairs to Millie's wheelchair and wondering how Ralph would fare in middle school, given his grades. At Blair, I was described as an "exemplary parent." At the Lab School, I felt like the carrier of a contagious disease. I had so much in common with those Lab parents, and yet I was beginning to find their lives inconceivable. Even without a shared language—for I spoke no Spanish—I could relate to the parents at Blair.

Millie finished kindergarten, and I attended her graduation. The school provided matching cheerleader costumes for the graduates and I posed with Millie for a picture. In it, I'm squatting beside her wheelchair jangling my necklace, and she's smiling in my direction, decked out in a red headband, red jumper, and white shirt. The adults applauded when I wheeled Millie across the stage to pick up her diploma. It was easy to pick out her classmates from among the other, more disabled students; most of them were now able to walk. My input into Millie's IEP during her final year at Blair had been modest: "Parent would like Millie to participate with students who have higher functioning skills." By this point, Millie, who was about to turn six, was "significantly below level for her age cycle (12 months)."

For first grade, the Chicago Public Schools assigned Millie to Christopher Elementary School, which had a reverse inclusion program and a heated pool. The three-story brick building featured a small number of classrooms for typical children—mostly the disabled students' siblings—side by side with stand-alone facilities for the "severe and profound." I delivered Millie on the first day of first grade, wandering the dimly lit halls until I found her classroom. All her classmates used wheelchairs; I wondered whether the staff would remember to take Millie out of hers. I silently counted the number of adults in the classroom; it looked like there were enough to keep Millie safe and to keep her hair out of her mouth.

Millie arrived at Christopher with a stack of paperwork, including a formal evaluation that ended with the following words:

> While Millie has made progress in awareness of motor control, awareness of her environment, following objects and reaching for preferred objects, she is below grade level for her age cycle. She lives with her mother and 9-year-old brother, and a care provider takes care of the children after school. There is extended family support, as well as a network of friends in the area. Ms. Rutherford is a caring parent who understands her child's needs and wants and enjoys her daughter for who she is. Millie is a content, easy-going girl who appears to enjoy school and the daily routine. She requires assistance with all activities. Millie attends weekly group sessions for play and social skills. She is attentive to the routines of the group, and during group she waits and anticipates her turn as she is approached. She appears to enjoy using a switch to participate in singing and saying her name to the group. She is cooperative and pleasant.

These words rang true. They would continue to ring true. Like a stone in a stream, Millie held steady as time flowed on.

THAT FIVE-YEAR TRANSITION from delayed toddler to disabled child brought with it other transitions. Millie's geneticist brought in a colleague he liked to work with, a pleasant man with a penchant for tough cases. Millie was a tough case. After they had dispensed with the likely explanations for her disability, they moved on to the rare. When Millie was five, they told me they needed blood from both of Millie's parents to rule out one of the syndromes they were considering. With Craig gone, the closest match was his mom or dad. Craig's father had been diagnosed with colon cancer a month before Craig died. Dick's decline had been slow but inexorable; now, he was entering the final stages of the disease. Craig's mother, who was thirteen years older than her husband, was showing signs of dementia or depression—probably both.

"I'll see if I can get her to agree," my sister-in-law told me. "But it won't be easy." Shortly after we spoke, Craig's father died. When we visited Los Angeles for Easter that year, I sat beside Craig's mother near a window while Karin's daughters sang nursery rhymes for Millie. We watched cars go by without saying a word. It felt cruel to bother her for a sample. In the end, it didn't matter; Millie's geneticist learned of new research that made that diagnosis seem less likely, and the theory didn't stick.

Some of the genetic disorders that the doctors considered comforted me; they weren't hereditary, and they weren't lethal. They conjured images of slow progress and good health. But the degenerative diseases terrified me. If I lost Millie, it would kill me, and then what would happen to Ralph? I spent hours scrolling through websites devoted to different diagnoses, wondering whether we wanted to belong to any of these clubs. Rett syndrome, the diagnosis Craig and I had pursued so eagerly, now felt like a bullet Millie had missed. Millie wasn't losing skills; she was gaining them, I told the doctors. Yes, they could test her to see whether she had that new mutation they'd discovered. But maybe not knowing was better.

In *Cat's Cradle*, a novel that Craig had loved, Kurt Vonnegut coined a pair of terms: the "granfalloon" and its counterpart, the "karass." A granfalloon is like the Lion's Club, or the Raiders, or the Class of '79: an empty assortment of people brought together by extraneous circumstances. A karass is the opposite: an invisible confederacy whose members somehow sense that they are made of the same celestial dust. I know I can't speak for others—and I'm not sure I'd say the same today—but back then, I was beginning to feel like the communities that arose around conditions like Rett syndrome might be granfalloons—"seeming team[s]" that were "meaningless."[3] By the end of our time in Chicago, I had accepted the fact that there might not be anyone like Millie anywhere in the world.

And I was getting restless. Ralph was back at the Lab School, struggling through another grade. Millie seemed to be doing okay at Christopher, although I couldn't know for sure; the days of popping in for a quick visit had ended. My therapist, who turned out to be anything but a downer, was helping me learn how to date. I took up with an old friend, a professor at Berkeley, who pointed out that it's hard to build a life with someone who lives two thousand miles away. "Don't be so goal-oriented," I sighed.

But the romance gathered momentum. The boyfriend had dimples and a pop-up camper that we took on road trips in the Sierras. I signed up with an au pair agency, and Denise, a wickedly funny young woman from a colored township in South Africa, joined us so I could fly to California once a month. Soon the boyfriend and I were applying for academic jobs that would allow us to live in the same time zone. Vermont Law School flew us out to visit. The dean fed us stew by a wood fire in a hilltop house with sweeping vistas of the mountains. We drove up the highway, with the forest closing in on both sides, to Montpelier, Vermont's tiny capital city, where we gasped at our first sight of the statehouse's pint-sized golden dome.

When the law school made the boyfriend an offer, we decided to give Vermont a try. I had a job offer from the University of California, Santa Cruz, which I put on hold; the University of Chicago gave me a year of unpaid leave, and I made plans to move Ralph and Millie east. "I want Millie to have the skills she needs to be happy," I wrote in the document I prepared for her final IEP meeting in Chicago. In Vermont, Millie was mainstreamed into a typical second-grade classroom, with one-on-one sessions with therapists throughout the day. Her teacher wrote rather different reports than the ones we received in Chicago, which focused solely on what Millie could and couldn't do. "The children were hesitant around Millie at first," he noted. "But now they all want to be her friend."

I took to Vermont, deer flies, mud season, blizzards, and all. I made friends with the local anthropologists and finished my second book. It was harder for the boyfriend, whose school-age sons had stayed in California with their mother. Ralph and I adopted an English setter puppy that barked at night and ate the woodwork; this hadn't helped.

Years later, in Santa Cruz, I struck up a conversation with another parent at one of Ralph's soccer games. By then, the relationship with the boyfriend had ended; it hadn't been strong enough to bear the weight of all of us living in one place. When I mentioned Craig to the other mother, she looked surprised. "I had no idea you had a husband. We"—she nodded at a nearby cluster of couples—"thought maybe you had the kids on your own."

I shook my head slowly, a mixture of emotions coursing through me. I knew plenty of women who had given birth solo. Unlike them, I had never had a burning desire to have children. I wasn't sure how I felt about marriage. But one thing was clear. Without Craig, there would have been no Millie and Ralph. What did these people see when they looked at us? Should I be flattered or insulted? Was I that weird? Were we that weird? Did they think we just sprang up from the ground?

I looked down at Millie, who was chewing on her scarf. The dog, eyeing her warily, was pulling on his leash, trying to judge whether Millie was close enough to reach his feathery tail. Suddenly, the other team's star player sprinted past Ralph and the other defenders and tipped the ball into the goal. The dog barked, startling Millie, who kicked and struggled in her wheelchair. I knelt beside her, rubbing her shoulders. When she noticed the string on my hoodie, her face brightened, and we both laughed.

Finally, I straightened up and resumed the conversation. "I had a husband; he was wonderful. He died a long time ago."

part II
the lessons

Proximity to Disability

When I was fifteen, I accepted an invitation from a classmate to do some charity work. I was beginning to wonder what it would take to get into the college of my choice; this classmate was the only person my age I knew who worried about such things. On Saturday mornings, the Mendota Institute, a residential treatment center for the psychotic and the neurologically impaired, opened its doors to volunteers, whose job it was to play with the younger residents. My classmate signed us up.

Besides us, only a handful of volunteers showed up that day—students from another high school—and none of them seemed very happy to be there. We loitered in the empty cafeteria, eyeing each other until a staff member opened a door at the end of the room. The children came in all shapes and sizes. I tried not to look at the ones in wheelchairs—their twisted backs and contorted faces made me uncomfortable—but the kids with Down syndrome were impossible to avoid. A cluster of boys surrounded me, all vying for my attention. Finally, the larger of them overpowered the others. He looked around twelve years old. "Come," I think he said to me, or maybe it was just a chirp—I had trouble following his speech. He took me by the hand. His palm was damp and a little sticky. He guided me away from the crowd to an empty stretch of floor where light from a narrow band of windows high on the wall filtered onto the linoleum. Then he turned to stare steadily into my eyes.

I was an awkward teenager. I babysat for money, but I hated it; I was bad at interacting with children my own age, let alone those who were younger. I always looked forward to the moment when I could finally tuck my charges in, raid the cupboard, and leaf through their parents' books. Facing off with this boy was excruciating. I had no idea what he wanted. I was afraid he would cry, or kiss me, or laugh in my face. I'm not sure how I made it through the hour I spent in that cafeteria. Maybe my classmate rescued me. Maybe I found the boy a toy and got him to play with it. Maybe he led me back and forth across the room. But I do remember how relieved I was when it was over. I never set foot in the Mendota Institute again.

I grew up in a community where disabled people like my daughter were hidden from sight. When I was in the third grade, the school board closed the elementary school in the suburb where my parents had just bought a house and enrolled the children in a nearby city school. At the hearing, my mother was one of the few parents who spoke in support of the plan. Other parents wanted to keep the neighborhood school open. They claimed to object to bussing, but their qualms went further. The city school, unlike the local school, served children in wheelchairs, and they were afraid that the stigma, like ink from a leaky pen, would rub off and stain their kids. As it happened, we rarely saw the children in wheelchairs, let alone shared a classroom with them, although once a week we got to swim in their heated pool. They arrived on different buses at different entrances.

My only sighting occurred when the teacher gave me a bathroom pass, and an aide pushed a little girl past me in the hall. We called other kids "retards" when they did something we thought was stupid. "Go back to Mendota," we'd say, when we were feeling particularly mean. My mother's relative enlightenment didn't stop me from imbibing this foul brew. I could barely stand to spend an hour with that boy with Down syndrome. Little did I know I would spend a lifetime with a daughter whose behavior, for my fifteen-year-old self, would have been even more disturbing.

PROXIMITY TO DISABILITY CAN be overwhelming. What made that boy at Mendota so unnerving, and my unresponsive daughter so distressing, is the fact I live in an age when everything from government policies to the media to conversations with family and friends tells us what to expect from our relationships: in short, an affirmed sense of who we are. "True love done correctly"—that's what the anthropologist Julienne Obadia calls this ideal.[1] Another person arrives in your presence. You see yourself through their eyes and find something unexpected: a kernel of strangeness, something you'd never really noticed about yourself. When that boy with Down syndrome stared into my eyes, I felt myself becoming someone I wasn't sure I wanted to be—not a college-bound do-gooder, but someone quite alien, an inhabitant of a world I'd been taught to fear. When Millie refused to return my gaze, the effect was just as distressing. But while I could walk away from the boy, I could not walk away from Millie—and that's where this chapter begins.

What happens when your children won't give you what you want? When Millie was three, not long after Craig died, I signed us up for Music Together. The other toddlers crawled, or walked, or scampered into the carpeted room, while their parents picked out instruments and scarves from a bucket. Millie had to be carried, and I rested her on one shoulder while I reached for a tambourine, then found a place for us in the circle. When the songs began, the other children swayed, or clapped their hands, or mouthed the words, twisting around every so often to watch their parents singing. Millie sat motionless in my lap, no more responsive than a pile of damp clothes. Gail Landsman has explored what it's like for parents like me in "the age of perfect children": the grief, the denial, the search for a cure, the medical crises, and, finally, the discovery of your loved one's secret talents and your own unrecognized strengths.[2] Much of this rings true to me. But when I look back on those difficult days and ask myself what I was feeling, one thing becomes clear. It wasn't perfection I wanted from Millie—it was connection.

I had hoped that Music Together would be something that Millie and I could share, but the classes left me feeling empty. Did Millie know where she was? Did she know we were together? Did she even know I was there? I longed for Millie to see me, to respond to me, to remind me I existed, to open a window into my soul. It's a mistake to take this kind of longing for granted, as natural as it seems. In Vietnam, for instance, it's troubling to imagine having a disabled child for all kinds of reasons.[3] Even now, the landscape is still contaminated with Agent Orange; birth defects remind people of the war. But parents also worry about having a child who will never be capable of taking care of others. The baby you fed, bathed, and diapered will someday do the same for you and your relatives; this is the way kinship is supposed to work.

The same is true for many of us in the United States. But parents also expect something more from their children: love, the kind born of lingering glances and shared smiles.[4] It's similar to the love that fuels romance and patriotism. We are taught to believe that we can discover who we really are through relationships that are both chosen and meant to be. You've seen the ads for baby products—the mother's rapture, the baby's twinkling eyes.[5] When a child's mind and body render this kind of love impossible, the stakes are high. What happens when our loved one doesn't look back? Who are we in this scenario? Are we citizens? Are we persons at all?

I kept taking Millie to Music Together, as painful as I found it. Then one day it dawned on me: Millie's failure to react was the reaction. In those days, a loud noise or a gust of wind could make Millie cry. The music steadied her, relaxed her, helped her find her place in space. I held Millie and felt her calmness seeping into me. Her expression was still blank. But her fingers brushed lightly across my jeans. Maybe she knew we were together after all.

I can't deny it—I'm a sucker for the romance of motherhood. When I imagine getting older, I think of Millie less as a failed future caregiver than as a companion, picturing us in our wheelchairs, side by side. Somehow, I've learned to look at my daughter with the love that makes a family. I'm no longer that high school student. In reaching for what others have told you to long for, you might just find yourself breaking free.

A WHOLE LOT OF history stands in the way of this outcome. Pearl Buck, who won the Pulitzer Prize in 1932 and the Nobel Prize for Literature in 1938, had a secret child, a daughter hidden from all but her closest friends. Carol Lossing Buck was born in 1920 "outside a small mud-walled town in North China" with beautiful blue eyes and an air of wisdom. It wasn't until 1950 that Buck published an essay in *Ladies Home Journal*, "The Child Who Never Grew," introducing her daughter to the world.[6] "Mine was a pretty baby, unusually so," Buck wrote. "She looked at me and me at her with mutual comprehension and I laughed."

Thanks to her Chinese friends, who were unfazed by the child's "broken speech and babyish ways," it took some time for Buck to realize there was something terribly wrong with Carol. Then one day on a street in Shanghai when Carol was four, two American women walked by. Buck wrote, "They stared at my child and when we had passed one of them said to the other, 'The kid is nuts.'"

Disturbed by the encounter, Buck traveled to the United States, where a doctor finally delivered the bad news.

> "Listen to what I tell you!" he commanded. "I tell you, madame, the child can never be normal. Do not deceive yourself. You will wear out

your life and beggar your family unless you give up hope and face the truth. . . . Find a place where she can be happy and leave her there and live your own life."

I don't know what I said or even if I said anything. I remember walking down the endless hall again alone with the child. I cannot describe my feelings. Perhaps the best way to put it is that I felt as though I were bleeding inwardly and desperately. The child, glad to be free, began capering and dancing, and when she saw my face twisted with weeping, she laughed.[7]

Carol was nine when Buck left her at the Training School in Vineland, New Jersey. When Buck turned to leave, Carol reached for her and wept. But Buck did not relent. She did what the doctor told her she must do to protect Carol from the cold eyes of strangers. She also did it because she knew that someday she would die, and when she was gone, who would take care of her child? But what disturbed her most was her daughter's inability to recognize her mother's sorrow. "It was this uncomprehending laughter which always and finally crushed my heart."[8]

There is so much in this story that strikes me to the core. Like Millie, Carol loved listening to music. She loved to run on the beach and play in the waves. But, for Buck, her daughter was a tragedy. Carol would never be a musician, an athlete, or an author like her mother. Buck didn't feel seen by Carol, and she couldn't see herself in her daughter. In the essay, Buck refers to Carol as "the child," not "my child," and she never calls her by her name. Buck was lauded as a humanitarian. She spoke out against racism. She took in orphaned children and raised them as her own. And yet her daughter was too much for her to bear.

What cruel planet was Pearl Buck living on? Let's call it America.

The history of disability in the United States is in many ways the story of sanctioned and avoided staring.[9] At the same time Buck hid her daughter from curious strangers, she offered her up to the curious researchers who ran the Training School. The two kinds of looking went hand in hand. It wasn't like this three hundred years ago. If Millie had been born in Scottish borderlands, where my ancestors are from, her fellow villagers might have mocked her. But she would have been a member, however lowly, of her family and community, her birth seen as a wonder, even a message from God.[10] But if she had been born in nineteenth-century New York, she would have been subject to the "ugly laws" of the time, city ordinances meant to clear the sidewalks of "unsightly beggars," whose mere appearance could ruin an evening stroll.

And if her family couldn't afford to keep her secret, she might have ended up in a freak show. There, her companions would have been colonized people, intersex people, and others whose bodies didn't fit the norm: "The Last of the

Aztecs," "General Tom Thumb," "The Ugliest Woman in the World." In 1860, P. T. Barnum "secured"—most likely bought—an African American boy and marketed him as "What Is It?" His name was William Henry Johnson; he had microcephaly and was intellectually impaired. "The curious creature is two thirds [the] size of Man," Barnum's advertisement for the show ran. "Laughs, but can't speak."[11] Millie wouldn't have had to face this kind of racism, but these phrases could have been describing her. "We know not & therefore do not assert whether it is human or animal," Barnum wrote of the attraction. "We leave that all to the sagacious public to decide."[12]

The fear and hatred that were the lifeblood of these ordinances and spectacles had deep roots. The love of the norm finds its origins in the mountain of data that eighteenth-century governments started collecting on their populations.[13] The idea that people were countable influenced how they thought about their identities: They were both unique individuals and regular folks. In the nineteenth century, factories treated workers the same way democracies treated voters: as so many anonymous, autonomous, interchangeable parts. Like the ideal baby, chortling and lily white, the ideal citizen was the average citizen, sound in mind and body. Freaks were the opposite; they were singular specimens—vivid pictures of what the truly human was not. Individuals like Millie were the ghosts who haunted the bell curve, a reminder that normal was a fiction—a fiction that no one lived up to, or at least not for long.

But it wasn't just that people feared becoming like the disabled; they also feared being with them. Throughout this period, medical experts—the most "sagacious" of the bunch—drummed up support for their profession by presenting the mentally "defective" as a threat to civic life.[14] Thanks to their efforts, in all likelihood, nineteenth-century Millie would have spent her life in an institution. The treatment center I visited as a teenager was founded in 1860 as the Wisconsin Hospital for the Insane. If Millie had lived in one of the colonies established at roughly the same time, she would have been labeled an "uneducable idiot." In the twentieth century, she would have been a candidate for forced sterilization, along with promiscuous women, "morons," "imbeciles," and the poor. And if I had been her mother? I'd like to think I would have followed Pearl Buck's lead, searching out the best possible home for my daughter. But I can't say I wouldn't have followed the doctors' advice. I wouldn't have had to worry about the romance of motherhood. I wouldn't have had to worry about whether Millie would ever play her part in it.

Then again, maybe I would have had a chance to worry about our relationship. During the same decades when eugenics was all the rage, reformers founded charitable societies that adopted a gentler approach aimed at making the disabled presentable. If Millie had been born in the 1960s, I might have seen the Hollywood film *The Miracle Worker*, set in that period, and been inspired to keep my daughter with me. In this, I would have been following the lead of self-help groups founded by parents in the 1930s.[15] The film would have shown me what it would take to turn an outcast into an insider—what changes needed to happen, who needed to change. For the families of children with all kinds of disabilities, the moral of the story would have been clear. At the start of the film, Helen Keller marauds through her family's beautiful home, screaming, kicking, pulling the eyes off dolls, grabbing food off her relatives' plates. Enter Annie Sullivan, fresh from Boston, where she has a position as an expert teacher for blind and deaf children. She comes to work the miracle of teaching Keller to communicate with finger-spelling—and the even bigger miracle of getting her to fold her napkin and eat with a spoon.

Sullivan, who was herself visually impaired, spent part of her childhood in an almshouse, which the film portrays in horrifying detail. Keller's parents hire Sullivan in a last-ditch effort to avoid sending Keller to such a place. Like everyone else in the theater, I would have gasped at the climax. With her hand under the pump spout, Keller spontaneously makes the sign for "water." "I love you" is one of the next things she says. The fact she says it to her mother wouldn't have escaped me. At the start of the movie, Keller's parents tolerate her bad behavior because she is their daughter. But her birth alone is not enough to save her from being sent away. It is not enough for Keller to be her parents' offspring. She must recognize herself as her mother's child. She must do true love correctly. And she must do it with words.

In telling her mother she loves her, Keller takes her first step toward becoming a public figure: someone famous enough to appear on postage stamps worldwide. The actual Helen Keller learned to write, speak, and comport herself in ways that made her interactions with others as predictable as possible. (In the course of this, she became a socialist. I approve.) If Millie had lived at the same time as Keller, I would have wished for this outcome. I still sometimes wish for it today. All those services she received as a child—they were designed to kindle this hope. Millie hasn't learned the sign for "I love you." She probably will never give speeches. Somewhere along the way, I gave up on the idea that Millie would respond to me in a typical fashion. But I gave up on it without giving up on her.

Carol Lossing Buck spent the rest of her days at the Training School in Vineland. She took trips to visit her mother a few times a year, always in the company of an aide from the school. She was happy to see her family, but after a few days, she was just as happy to go back to what she now considered her home. Carol was seventy-two years old when she died. The Training School wasn't a bad place, according to her sister. No filthy cement floors crowded with naked, shivering children. No days spent without seeing the sun. Carol became an athlete: She played Special Olympics basketball. She had hobbies and close friends. A picture taken two years before her death shows an attractive woman with a gentle smile and kind eyes. What if Pearl Buck had reacted differently to her daughter's laughter? What if she'd tried to understand Carol instead of asking Carol to understand her? What if she'd come to see her own sorrow as laughable? As a ridiculous response to someone so beautiful, vibrant, and alive?

Times are different now; doctors are no longer telling mothers like Buck to send away their daughters. Disabled activists and artists follow the lead of the late, great Harriet McBryde Johnson, who lived joyfully in her extraordinary body, sparring with photographers and setting the terms on how she would be seen.[16] In Millie's lifetime, we've seen the rise of genetic testing alongside the growing recognition that normal is a sham.[17] I've spent much more time with Millie than Buck did with Carol in what special educator Duncan Merceira would call our daughters' "zones of proximity."[18] I've had opportunities to be drawn into Millie's world, and I've seized them—mothers and daughters are supposed to be close. That day in Music Together with Millie was just the beginning. She's grown into a young woman with an excellent ear. These days, when the right kind of song is playing, it sure feels like we're together. I watch her, grinning, as her face erupts in joy at every chord change, every shuffle, every riff. I am not alone in arriving at this kind of intimacy. But the cold eyes of strangers are still hard to stare down. How do parents like me learn to look? What do we notice? How do we become the ones who have to change?

HERE'S WHAT I SEE when I look at Millie today. I see the feathery curve of her lashes, the powdery softness of her cheeks, and even though she isn't smiling—which she often isn't—I still see the glow from the last time she did. If I look at one of her eyes, and then the other, I don't notice that they point in different directions. Instead, I take in the perfect hazel of the irises, which is so close to matching the color of her hair that she looks like a doll. I admire the angle of her shoulders and the firm, smooth skin at the base of her neck. I see her long, graceful fingers, moving so expressively as they reach across to fondle my hem. I see her legs, how they are shaped exactly like mine and my mother's, with long shins and long, tapering thighs. "Perfect legs," my mom called them when I was Millie's age; she proved it by standing with her feet together and showing me the narrow gap above her knees.

I see her colorful scarves, the kind my sister and cousin like to wear, and I think of her care provider Xiaona, who grew up in a village outside Beijing and dresses Millie to match her Asian sense of youthful fashion. Occasionally, I see Millie's father's sense of humor and her brother's stubbornness, when she is in a responsive or rebellious mood. What I don't see are the crossed eyes, the drooling, the oversized, Velcro-fastened shoes, the scar on her wrist where she's been biting herself again, the gait belt around her waist, which we use to position her body, the compulsive way she flings her arms. Or I see them, but I know how to look beyond them. What I've been taught about how bodies should appear in public has attuned me to the ways my daughter falls short. What I've learned about the intimacy that should bind parents and children makes me look further, rather than looking away. In looking for the ordinary in my extraordinary daughter, I have come to see her through a new lens. It reveals her in fragments as a unique collection of traits, none of which fully defines her. I know how to look at my daughter with love.

I don't know how to look with love at other people's disabled daughters—not with the kind of love that breaks through the discomfort most "normal" people feel when someone who doesn't look, sound, or act the way they expect. In London, during the first days after Ralph was born, I once found myself inspecting him as if I were a visitor from outer space. He was lying in his bassinet, wearing oversized pajamas, a weird, ungainly bundle of reflexes, twitches, grimaces, tongue sucking, and kicks. "This is why people get so freaked out by some kinds of disability," I found myself musing, apropos of nothing. "People look past all this stuff in their newborns. But not in adults. Humans have a horror of matter out of place." As soon as Ralph caught my eye and cooed, I tucked that thought away in the back of my mind.

Now I think of that moment and wonder. I tend to throw new acquaintances in at the deep end, without much explanation of my daughter's appearance or abilities. "Come meet Millie," I tell the student or colleague visiting my home for the first time. They stand in the doorway to the parlor that serves as Millie's bedroom and take in the fireplace, the bins of toys, and the androgynous little figure sitting on the carpet, fondling the stuffed animal in her lap. I live in an ableist society, and I have internalized ableist norms, which force me to ask myself awkward questions. Would it be easier for people if we dressed and treated Millie like a person of her developmental age, somewhere around twelve months? Or is it critical to her dignity that we clothe her as a stylish teenager, in hopes they will come to see what I see? Millie's clock radio is set to a station that plays Taylor Swift. Does this really make any difference in how people experience her? You can't force strangers to look at your disabled daughter with love; you can only model how it's done.

It's hard. We're so greedy, we humans, when it comes to our interactions with others. We don't give our words freely. When we speak, we are bound and determined to get words back—at the right time, in the right tone of voice, and with the right volume, with any deviation scrutinized for hidden intent. The same goes for gestures and body language and all the other subtle ways we communicate. When we're suddenly thrown together, it's the give and take of interaction that tells us we are recognized and honored, accepted as co-proprietors of a small scrap of reality in which we have a rightful place. In the United States, as Janelle Taylor has explained, when we forget someone's name, we risk leaving the impression that we don't care about their welfare.[19] People with Alzheimer's, like Taylor's mother, pay the price of this moralism: People treat them as if they were socially dead. The famous sociologist Harold Garfinkel once did an experiment in which a group of teenagers suddenly started acting with great decorum, pretending they were their parents' boarders, rather than their daughters and sons. "One mother, infuriated when her daughter spoke to her only when she was spoken to, began to shriek in angry denunciation of the daughter for her disrespect and insubordination and refused to be calmed."[20] This woman was not an outlier. The parents in this experiment weren't just confused; they were outraged. They felt as if their children were cheating them of something they were owed.

When I dress Millie as a teenager, and talk to her as if she understands, I'm modeling a different ethic than the one that focuses on evening the score. I'm modeling a kind of giving more in line with our gifts to our newborns and our gods, giving as a sacrifice, giving as a gamble, giving as a calling out into the darkness without any hope of an echo.[21] There is a truth in these gifts that runs even deeper than the wisdom Taylor draws from all the small and subtle ways her mother cares for others, remaining socially alive to her daughter even as her cognitive abilities decline. We give these kinds of gifts because newborns are newborns, and gods are gods: Respecting this makes parents and believers who they are.

IT'S 2016, AND I'M in Santa Cruz. I've gotten a grant to explore the experiences of families like my own. Today, I'm sitting at a small dining room table with Tricia, who has agreed to talk to me about life with Jane, her twenty-four-year-old daughter. My chair faces the sun-drenched living room, where a Persian rug, a couch, and a coffee table are arranged to leave plenty of room for a wheelchair to pass.

Tricia sits across from me. Her curly hair, streaked with silver, frames a piercing gaze and a wicked smile. Just off the end of the table, where the kitchen begins, Jane and Millie sit next to each other in their wheelchairs; they are facing us, so we can keep an eye on them as we talk. Millie's longtime care provider Marilyn, an alert, no-nonsense woman who is older than she looks, sits next to her. Millie was agitated this morning, and before we left the house, Marilyn slipped a Kevlar bite guard over her arms and shoulders. Millie bites her arm when she is distressed, and the guard protects her skin from her teeth. It looks like Millie's wearing an extra pair of sleeves.

Millie and Jane are lost in their own worlds, but every so often they seem to notice one another. Jane raises her eyelids and casts a glance at Millie; Millie looks the other way but flings her arm in Jane's direction. Jane is smaller than Millie—seventy-four pounds to Millie's ninety-three—and less mobile than my mercurial daughter. Jane doesn't hold weight on her legs and rarely uses her hands. Her back is curved and twisted. She tends to hold her head tilted to the right, as if she were asking you to kiss her cheek. She's beautiful: She has porcelain skin, freckles, and a thick head of wavy auburn hair. Like Millie, Jane laughs at funny noises. When I begin speaking, Jane cracks up. When Millie follows suit, breaking out in giggles at Jane's throaty guffaw, I'm hit by a wave of pride and pleasure. Grinning uncontrollably, I look at Tricia. Tricia is grinning, too.

We've been marveling—and giggling—over all the things we have in common: views on natural childbirth ("Give me the drugs!"), wheelchair ramps (I admire hers), and navigating puberty with a disabled daughter (rough with Millie, easier with Jane). Tricia speaks quickly and confidently. But as she starts to tell me how she learned to look at her daughter with love, she slows down and leans forward in her chair. "I used to say, 'I love her, but I don't like her.' There was nothing to like about Jane."

I have asked for Jane's story, and Tricia has begun at the beginning: with a normal birth followed by the immediate recognition that "there is something wrong with this baby." Jane was unable to breastfeed. And other things struck Tricia as strange. "You know, [babies] look at you. They connect with you somehow. And Jane didn't. She was completely in her own alien experience."

Tricia takes a breath. "And then she started screaming nonstop. She literally screamed all the time. She never slept for more than half an hour. I tear up just thinking about it. Jane would scream, I mean, a blood-curdling scream, for hours and hours straight. I was like this electric wire with every nerve ending exposed."

Phil, Tricia's husband, was head of a nonprofit. Tricia worked full time as an elementary school teacher. Jane eventually learned to nurse but never learned to use a bottle. Four times a day, Tricia had to run from her classroom to Jane's day-care center to feed her so she wouldn't starve.

"We had a two-year-old," Tricia sighs, turning to Marilyn then back to me. "You have this idea of what your family life is going to be like, and you're going to go do all these things, and we would try to give our older son and us a family experience. But it was so hard. Because we'd go out for dinner, and one of us would be walking around outside with Jane while the other two hurried up and ate. It was always so stressed out and tense."

Jane's pediatrician initially made light of Tricia's concerns. Tricia rattles off the doctor's responses. "If you read her files, it's like, 'Tried to reassure her mom, explained to mom what colic is.' 'Mother is overly anxious.'"

Tricia shakes her head. "I'm not an anxious person."

Finally, when Jane was around a year old, Phil and Tricia arranged to have her seen by specialists. Tricia frowns at the memory. "The first neurologist who examined Jane was just a horror. She informed us that our daughter had a half a brain" and that there was "nothing she could do for her," but that she'd "love to do research on her."

I wince.

The next neurologist Phil and Tricia consulted ordered an MRI. Jane's brain was intact, it turned out, but it showed signs of hypomyelination, an abnormality of the white tissue that impedes development. The consensus was that Phil and Tricia should enroll Jane in services for children with what the bureaucrats called "special needs."

At the time, Tricia and Phil were barely treading water. Some of the professionals who entered their lives were helpful; others were not. Tricia chased away the speech therapist sent as part of early intervention. "She was just jiggling things in front of my daughter." Tricia raises an eyebrow. "I can jiggle things."

Instead, Tricia started taking Jane to see a pediatric neuro-osteopath twice a week. All he did was to press on Jane's cranium—"it was like hocus pocus"—but somehow this "changed her physical experience in the world."

And then it happened. One day, "Jane looked up at me and smiled." Tricia still remembers everything: the changing table, the house they were living in, the fact it was Mother's Day. It was a "real cognitive smile," Tricia tells me, and Jane made eye contact in her own "very fleeting" way.

Jane swings her head slowly from side to side and lets out a soft yelp, calling us back to the present. Tricia admires her for a moment. "It seemed to be in response to me."

Not long afterward, Tricia was in the kitchen cooking dinner and listening to music, and Jane was with her in her car seat when Paul Simon's "Graceland" came on. "She laughed out loud for the first time." Tricia's first thought was of the pediatric osteopath. "I almost sat down and wrote that guy a letter," she giggles. "You made my daughter laugh for the first time."

Marilyn catches my eye. "Let's get that doctor's number!" Then our laughter fades, and Tricia ponders the table in front of her. I hear a little catch in her voice. "Jane was the biggest heartbreak of my life. I remember saying to my mom, 'I'm never going to be happy again like I was before. I'll never have that feeling of just joy, and freedom.'"

But then Tricia pushes her hair out of her eyes and looks at Jane. Jane is smiling at the ceiling, her eyes moving behind closed lids, as if she were dreaming a pleasant dream. "And I don't know when it came back, but it did come back."

Millie starts complaining but quiets when Marilyn takes her hand. Tricia continues, her voice soft yet firm. "She's my daughter. With Jane, there's unconditional love. It's unconditional in that there's no condition for her to give it back. Because I'll tell you, I've been married for twenty-seven years and there are conditions to that love. There are. And with my son, there are conditions to that love. But with Jane, it is truly unconditional. There are no conditions to me loving her. She doesn't have to answer me back, she doesn't have to kiss me, she doesn't have to say, 'Mama.' She doesn't have to say anything. For a long time, she never looked at me or smiled or laughed. Or anything. Yet I still took care of her and was kind to her."

Tricia pauses and leans back in her chair. "My joy came back when I started really liking her. You know what I mean?" I nod, and Tricia completes her thought. "When she was fun to be around."

As if on cue, Jane chortles. "Look, she's checking Millie out!" Tricia points with her chin at my daughter, who has cheered up and is shaking her toy squid.

Then Tricia sits up in her chair and looks from Marilyn to me. "Right now, I'm in this period of life when a lot of my girlfriends are becoming grandparents. I'm really involved with their adult daughters. And their baby showers, and their babies, and decorating Christmas trees. You know, I see all these things." She searches for the right words. "We all make our lives fit. What we really want with our children are loving, intimate relationships. And I have that with Jane. I can't think of a more intimate relationship than when I'm changing Jane's diaper and feeding her." I'm nodding in agreement. Marilyn is, too. "And when I bathe her. And when I pick out her clothes for her. I still would like to have those other things. But it's what I have, and it's a very loving, intimate relationship."

Tricia has accepted that her relationship with her daughter will never involve baby showers or even her daughter's undivided attention. Jane doesn't communicate with conventional signs. But Tricia can sense what she's feeling.

"She definitely expresses agitation. She definitely expresses pleasure. She responds to things none of the rest of us even know are there."

Tricia demonstrates how Jane reacts to loud noises by pounding on the table. Startled, Jane and Millie both yelp in response.

Tricia explains, "If we're laughing, she'll laugh." We've been laughing quite a bit, and Jane and Millie both join in. Then Tricia's tone grows grave. "But I don't know how much of it is cognitive reasoning, I don't know if it's more just an innate reaction, or whether there's actually a cognitive process there. I just don't know. I don't need to, and there's no way for me to know, so I can either make things up or I can just not know."

I study Tricia's face. "Where do you stand with that?" I ask her. Overhead, a gull calls, flying fast toward the sea. I'm wondering how I would answer the same question if we were talking about Millie.

Tricia shrugs and looks at Jane, then glances at Millie. "I don't know what her cognitive ability is. My guess is that it's very low. But I think she's present. I think she knows she's loved and adored. I don't know if she knows it the way we know it. But her life has been very safe. Very comfortable. I think it's important for a human to feel touch and for a human to hear cooing words. And her life has been full of positive touching and cooing words and adoration."

As she speaks, Tricia rises from the table and walks over to stand behind Jane's wheelchair. "Jane, are we talking about you?" she says brightly, stroking Jane's arm and bending down to give her a kiss. Jane raises her face to meet her mother's lips. Marilyn, who has reached over to adjust Millie's bite guard, looks up.

Suddenly, Jane is sitting very still. "Hey, Jane," I call out. I'm concerned; is she okay?

"She's probably having an absence seizure right now," Tricia tells me. Not dangerous but disturbing: nothing to do but wait for Jane to return.

A few seconds pass, then Jane begins to move again. "Hi, Jane!" I say, relieved.

"Are you back?" Tricia chirps. Jane smiles, and Millie reaches out to touch her. We all laugh.

A FEW DAYS LATER, I interview Phil, Jane's father, who handles the lion's share of Jane's day-to-day care. We meet on a sparkling winter morning at his office on the second floor of a building owned by the harbor in Santa Cruz. The fish are running close to shore. On the way up the stairs, I watch a kayak glide past the lighthouse into a cauldron of churning water, with seabirds wheeling and shrieking overhead. Phil is a tall, solidly built man with glasses, thinning hair, and a steady manner—the kind of person you'd want skippering your yacht.

Tricia is retired now, and Phil is only working part time; they used to hire regular care providers, but now their lives revolve around Jane's daily needs. Someday, he admits, he and Tricia will be too old to care for their daughter. But, for now, life is good; they get by.

When I ask whether Phil ever has dreams in which Jane can speak, he shakes his head. "It's not even on my radar." Phil goes on to explain why this is the case. "I categorize people quickly. You know, are they worthy of my time or not? People don't show up here just to meet me, you know, just want to interact. They all want something from me. With Jane, it's different; the whole point is the interaction."

Verbal communication, as Phil sees it, is "probably not the only way of being in the world."

For Phil, as for Tricia, being close to Jane is being close to an enigma. "I'm sure Jane thinks about things. There's something that goes on in her head." Phil stares past me at a fishing boat heading to sea. "She dreams, you know, I'll hear her at night. There's things that go on in there. I don't know what they are, and that's fine." Unconditional love means not needing to know.

In my final visit to Jane's house, I come with my iPad to record Phil interacting with his daughter. Phil invites me into the family room, a comfortable space off the kitchen with a couch, a television, a gas fireplace, and a futon, laid out like a centerpiece in the middle of the floor. Jane is lying on the futon on her stomach, her most comfortable position, given her scoliosis, and she is fingering a string of big black beads. We chat about Jane's wardrobe. I admire her green sweater, knitted by Tricia, and how well it complements her hair. Phil scoops Jane up and she smiles, her eyes closed in apparent pleasure, then relaxes into his arms. Phil gently lowers her into her wheelchair, wheels it into the kitchen, then starts making her lunch. He sings a little ditty about what he is doing as he works the blender. Jane gently shakes her head from side to side, her eyes darting under her eyelids, and licks her lips in anticipation. Soon she is gulping down her lunch from the plastic cup Phil holds to her mouth.

After a shower, comfortable in fresh clothes, Jane is back on the futon. Phil turns on the fireplace to warm the room. Tricia has come home. She plops down on the couch and asks my opinion of the baby blanket she is making for a friend's daughter. I take a break to ooh and aah, then join Jane on the floor.

Phil entertains Jane by kneeling over her prone body and rhythmically patting the futon; Jane squeals with laughter. Then Tricia takes his place. "Who's the cute one?" she chirps loudly in Jane's ear, before giving her a loud, wet kiss on the cheek. I laugh at the song she sings to the tune of "Waltzing Matilda": "Jane sits in her wheelchair, cute as can be with fabulous hair." Jane coos. Neither Tricia nor Jane seem to mind the fact that they are interacting in a fashion that makes it impossible for them to look into each other's eyes.

It took some time for Jane to become comfortable in the world, but now she's learned to calm herself. Tricia has an explanation: "She's just had more experience living." And her parents have had more experience living with her. Tricia and I belong to a society that has pushed away people like Jane and Millie. But this same society has compelled us to draw our children near. We have attempted to live up to everything our modern world requires of us. In doing so, we have been overwhelmed by proximity to our remarkable daughters. We have learned to be with them in ways that are beautiful, strange, and new.

A FEW YEARS AGO, I attended an exhibition of work by Ron Mueck, a sculptor who depicts human figures in excruciatingly realistic ways.[22] His sculptures are out of scale—too big or too small—and are all the more striking as a result. Viewers are forced to reflect on the downy beard of a pubescent boy, the fine network of wrinkles around the eyes of an old woman, the faded brocade on which she sits. The figures often come in couples: The pubescent boy, for instance, is whispering to a girl.

Toward the end of the exhibit, I came upon the naked figure of a mother lying flat on her back with her newborn baby on her stomach. The umbilical cord still attached the infant to his mother. His crumpled face looked toward hers, while she looked back, resignation etched around her lips. The caption on the wall informed me that this piece was inspired by classical representations of the Madonna and child, which Mueck "reconfigures . . . for our time with extraordinary intimacy. This is his first sculpture to pair two figures, distilling the moment when an exhausted mother and her newborn infant first see each other."

Squatting, I craned my head to get a glimpse of the woman's pupils. I tried to match their orientation with the baby's, and I failed. Their eyes weren't meeting. The effect was one of disconnection, with the baby in a protective crouch and the mother's arms extended stiffly at her sides.

Another sculpture showed an aged couple at the beach, their sagging bodies leaning together. The man was using the woman's thigh as a pillow; it looked like they both were drifting off to sleep. But looking more closely I saw that the man's hand was caressing the woman's upper arm. He was staring into the distance, and she was gazing tenderly at his forehead. His face was troubled; hers was concerned. Here was "extraordinary intimacy," I thought to myself. People look at one another, Mueck's sculptures seemed to be saying. But it takes more than vision to connect.

And it takes more than speech. Yet people depend on these capacities—for eye contact, for words—which loom so large in Western accounts of what it means to be human. This is a fact that parents like Phil and Tricia cannot avoid.

"She's a pretty girl. I think that serves her well. I think people are more positive toward her because she's a pretty girl with a smile." I have just asked Tricia how strangers respond to Jane. Tricia and Phil leave people to figure out what to make of this small person in the big sunglasses and floppy hat. Little children sometimes stare—"She's a trip!" Tricia acknowledges—while their parents and babysitters try to be polite.

"If she knows them," Phil tells me later, "and they really try to tune in and talk to her, she'll react to that. If they just kind of go, 'Oh, hi, Jane,' in a way that's kind of disconnected, she just doesn't do anything."

And yet, despite her uncertain responses, Jane has managed to make friends. Every afternoon, Tricia and Phil take Jane on the same walk along a street overlooking the Pacific. People on the route have come to recognize Jane and her parents, who take turns pushing her wheelchair and singing in her ear. Even when she can't see Jane's face, Tricia can tell when she is smiling; the people walking toward them always smile back. Jane's day program is a few blocks from Santa Cruz's main shopping street. Jane makes frequent visits to Urban Outfitters, where there is always pop music playing full blast. The store clerks are happy to let her dance amid the clothing racks, laughing as her aide rolls her wheelchair back and forth to the beat. The day I shadow Jane, we pass a local music venue on a stretch of sidewalk where homeless teens often congregate, and several of the scruffy youngsters know her name. Jane's aide greets them for her as we walk by.

Some parents do more to normalize interactions between their children and the world around them. I'm taking a class on assistive and augmentative communication as part of my research. One day we have a guest lecturer: a young woman who is finishing her master's degree. In her gauzy cotton dress and ponytail, she sits at the front of the room in her wheelchair, pushing buttons on a device the size and shape of an iPad, telling us how her life has changed as a result of the machine. Our teacher has set up a projector, so we can watch as she types responses during the Q and A. The process is slow, but the visitor communicates with wisdom and humor, and her answers are well worth the wait. Her mother, who accompanies her, doesn't say a thing.

The difference between Tricia and Phil and this mother is not as stark as one might think. When parents demand access and opportunities for their children, they aren't simply expanding their ability to engage with a wider public. They are giving their children a chance to change what counts as the norm.[23] The social worlds that Jane and the young woman in the classroom have created do not exist in a vacuum. They have arisen in a setting where parents can't just love their children; they also must like them. They must make relationships gained through birth into ones ratified by choice. The pressure to conform to the ideal of true love done correctly is what inspires parents to subvert it. To be truly intimate, sometimes you have to throw away the script.

Proximity to disability can be overwhelming when one looks, or looks away, and even when one looks with love, as I've learned to do with Millie. And that's a good thing. These days, so much turns on our collective ability to open ourselves to new ways of being with one another. This is the first lesson from Millie's world: You don't have to be the same to be close.

BUT THIS INTIMACY, THIS love, can run off the rails. In 2006, the parents of a nine-year-old girl, known simply as "Ashley X," made national headlines for "the Ashley Treatment": the removal of her uterus and breast buds and the administration of high doses of estrogen designed to bring her growth to a stop. Calling Ashley their "pillow angel," and inviting parents of other "pillow angels" to follow suit, Ashley's parents defended the treatment as a necessary measure. If Ashley remained small and childlike, her family would always be able to care for her at home. Ashley had what her doctors called "static encephalopathy"—a fancy term for cerebral palsy and other chronic brain disorders—and was "non-ambulatory" and "non-communicative."[24] This wasn't forced sterilization, her parents argued, but an act of kindness. Ashley would never know the pain of menstruation and the discomfort of a heavy bustline. She wouldn't be sexualized by care providers or bothered by sexual feelings. And she'd never have to be institutionalized. All of this was what she would have wanted, her parents argued, and they knew her best. Ashley's doctors agreed. Disability activists did not. They saw the Ashley Treatment as a modern-day form of eugenics—a violation of Ashley's body and her rights.

"The stories of women with disabilities must be told, not as stories of vulnerability, but as stories of injustice." This quote from Sherene Razack forms the epigraph of a chapter that the disabled scholar Alison Kafer devotes to Ashley X.[25] Justice here would mean embracing uncertainty: No one could really predict who Ashley X would become. It would also mean acknowledging that there could be more to Ashley's desires and preferences than her parents could perceive. "I just don't know," Tricia says about what her daughter is thinking. "I don't need to, and there's no way for me to know, so I can either make things up or I can just not know." Justice requires respect for cognitive mystery. Respect for what binds us, but also what separates us. For the fact that there's only so much anyone can know of another person's feelings and thoughts.

There is a parallel story to the one I've told in this chapter, this story of intimacy and family. It's the story of how generations of disabled individuals have broken free from their parents and demanded the right to speak for themselves. The story of Ashley X haunts Kafer and for good reason: It's been hard for the disability justice movement to include people like Ashley X. When a group of intellectually disabled people joined forces in the 1990s, they called themselves "Self-Advocates Becoming Empowered."[26] What could empowerment look like for Ashley or for Millie and Jane? "The key here," Kafer concludes, "seems to be to focus on the unknowability inherent in the case. . . . How might we imagine futures that hold space and possibility for those who communicate in ways we do not yet recognize as communication, let alone understand?"[27]

This is where the question of which stories to tell gets tricky. If the stakes in the current struggle for disability justice are a matter of becoming, then they are also a matter of exposure, of how we make our presence felt within each other's lives. "We are all Ashley X," Kafer suggests.[28] But what about vulnerability? Can we dispense with it altogether? It's with this puzzle that the next lesson begins.

The Sovereignty of Vulnerability

Ralph was five when I threatened him with the long arm of the law. It wasn't one of my better moments. It had been snowing in the morning when Craig dropped us off at Ralph's school, two blocks from my office on campus. It continued through much of the afternoon: Big, fluffy flakes blanketed the dirty remnants of the previous blizzard in white. By sundown, when the storm ended, the snow was two feet deep, and the buses had stopped running. Ralph and I set off for home by foot, hand in hand in the dark.

When we came to a patch of shoveled pavement a couple of blocks from our house, Ralph pulled up short. The snowplows had kicked up a tiny mountain range along the edge of the road. It was warm enough for the salt to work, melting the snow in the gutter into a slurry. Ralph eyed the situation, then pulled me over the curb. He bunny-hopped into a puddle, sending slush flying, and cackled with pleasure when the icy water splattered my boots. Then his mitten slipped from my grip, and I watched him marching on the pavement, intrepid in his snow pants, a solo explorer in this frozen land.

A car eased by us, its wheels grinding against the ice. I was suddenly self-conscious. "Ralph, you have to get out of the street."

Silence, then a splash as Ralph stomped on another puddle. "Ralph, listen, you need to obey me."

Another splash.

I turned up the volume. "Ralph! Ralph! You need to obey me."

It finally dawned on Ralph that I was talking to him. He looked up, his eyes glinting. "Why?"

"Because I'm your mother."

Ralph considered this. "So?"

"Children are supposed to obey their mothers."

"Why?" Ralph clearly didn't trust this line of reasoning.

I sighed. "That's just the way it is."

Ralph squinted up at me warily, then delivered his verdict. "That's not fair!" Just ahead, a red light had turned green. The last driver had managed to avoid Ralph; the next one might not. Ralph was big for a kindergartener. Was I going to have to pick him up? He was heavy, and he'd fight like a demon. That wouldn't work.

A car rolled through the intersection, and I shivered. The snow on my hat had melted and fat droplets were running down my neck. Enough of this. I was cold. I was hungry. I was supposed to be in charge. "Look, Ralph, if you don't obey me, someone will call the police, and Child Protective Services will take you away."

As soon as the words slipped from my mouth, I wanted to suck them back in. Had I really said that? On the South Side of Chicago? Where mothers routinely lose their children for so much less? I was suddenly keenly aware of who I was and where I was standing. I felt like I was going to be sick. But Ralph appeared less traumatized than intrigued. He gazed up at me, eager to see where this turn in the conversation would lead us. "Child Protective Services?" he chirped. "What's that?"

Ralph let me hold his hand, but he sloshed the rest of the way home in the gutter, chatting happily. I let him. I had set off a bomb, and he had shrugged. My cheeks were on fire. What kind of parent was I? There was nothing I could do.

WHAT MADE RALPH SO powerful on that snowy evening was his vulnerability. I know that this sounds like a contradiction in terms. Ralph and I live in a world saturated with rules and structured by assumptions about who is in charge. Sovereignty is the word theorists use for the glue that keeps this world from flying apart.[1] Sovereignty can take the form of the monopoly modern states claim over the legitimate use of violence. Tribal nations define sovereignty as the outcome of a struggle to manage their own resources, maintain their own traditions, define their own identities, and determine their own fate.

A particularly good example of sovereignty is the power governments exert over parents and communities in the name of children and other vulnerable people. In India, the ritual burning of widows was a cause célèbre for the British Raj; it justified intervening in local politics.[2] In the United States and Canada, the sovereignty claimed by settler governments is what allowed missionaries to fill boarding schools with Native children, even though their communities had sovereign rights of their own.[3] Yes, Child Protective Services prevents children from being harmed. But for Black and Brown families, protection is often a form of control. When I spoke those awful words to Ralph, I pulled back the veil on this reality. There are laws that govern how parents treat their children. You are small and weak, and I'm obliged to protect you. If you don't heed me, all hell will break loose.

But in making this argument, I was also telling Ralph something more complicated: His vulnerability made me vulnerable. Of course, I was worried about him, but I was also worried about my reputation—what if the neighbors saw him walking in the street? Ralph could sense my dilemma, and it gave him an edge in the argument. I recognized the state's authority, and my own as Ralph's mother, but he did not. In the end, he prevailed, and we ended up together on the pavement, temporary inhabitants of a realm ruled by Ralph.

Millie has made me feel the grip of sovereignty particularly acutely. Fast forward to 2020, and I'm in Santa Cruz. Each night at 1 a.m., and again at 3 a.m., I head downstairs to make sure she hasn't kicked off her weighted blanket, which her care providers and I use to help keep her settled down for the night. I often find her guffawing, her feet icy cold, strangely gleeful because she's slithered out from under her covers. I do this because I love Millie, and I want her to be warm. I also do it because everyone who works with my daughter is a mandated reporter. If she consistently wakes up shivering, a higher authority might with good reason step in.[4]

I have no objection to laws that protect disabled people from neglectful care providers. But Millie herself has had little say in their creation and enforcement—no one asked her whether she wants her blankets on or off. You might expect to find reserves of fortitude in a talkative five-year-old, not in a young woman who sits placidly in her wheelchair. And yet when Millie kicks off her covers and laughs, it's a little like Ralph jumping off the curb. Are there realms ruled by Millie? I have to be paying attention to notice them, and that's the rub: These laws and my love for her ensure I do. In coming to terms with her vulnerability, I discover her power.

The Nigerian author and intellectual Bayo Akomolafe has described a trip his family took to a mall, where his five-year-old son had an "upsetting experience."[5] "I hesitate to call it a meltdown or a tantrum; I have learned not to. But at that moment, while he flailed and flapped and screamed and squirmed on the very public floor of a very public place in the full scrutinizing gaze of very public eyes, it didn't matter to my body what I called it." Akomolafe's son is autistic, and I can imagine what his father was going through: his burning cheeks, the looks on the strangers' faces, his frantic efforts to get the child to stand up.

Finally, Akomolafe's wife shooed him away, and he retreated out of earshot. Only later did he learn what she had done.

> She dove right in, literally: instead of trying to control Kyah, instead of trying to pull him into her world, she knelt and crawled up to where he lay, stretching herself out next to him. . . . I wasn't there to witness it, but I can almost see them . . . even now: mother and son lying down there; Kyah sobbing but his little inflamed body slowly acclimating to the gods who have taken up residence within; his mother reminding him in soft whispers that she was there for him and with him; many curious eyes wondering why she doesn't just pick him up from the floor.

The vigil only lasted a moment; soon enough, Kyah was ready to rejoin his father and the other shoppers. But the image of son and mother took root in Akomolafe's mind. For Akomolafe, that space on the floor where Kyah lay with his mother was a "crime scene." It was the scene of a crime against the rules that keep parents herding their children down the route to law-abiding adulthood thrown up by what Akomolafe calls "the colonial world-making machine." In the face of everything that was pressuring her to obey these rules, Kyah's mother chose to break them, drawn by love and fascination to accept an invitation into the world inhabited by her son.

When Akomolafe describes Kyah's autism as leading him to a "politics," it is this invitation he is talking about. Today's politics often looks like "war by other means."[6] Akomolafe's politics is nothing like this. It's not a fight for mastery. It's not about claiming rights or speaking truth to power. Instead, as Akomolafe describes it, it's about "opening up other spaces of power-with." It "enshrines the promise that in losing our way, straying away from the marked tarmacs of the conventional, we might find ourselves in different, surprising places." Places where we're invited "to crawl, to get down on all fours, to do something weird and—as such—come alive."[7] Without saying a word, Kyah became a political actor, a sovereign even, someone who drew others into a radical new regime. What about Millie? Can she become a political actor? How much has my understanding of politics had to change in order to allow me to say yes?

This all sounds mystical and abstract. In fact, it's quite mundane. But don't be fooled by the everydayness of the episodes I'm about to describe. In medieval Europe, kings thought of their sovereignty as absolute, all-encompassing, and self-sufficient, like the Christian God they used as their model.[8] The European thinkers whose ideas inspired the founding of liberal democracies transported these qualities into another form of sovereignty—that of the sovereign self. Citizens weren't simply supposed to be equal; they were supposed to be capable. Popular sovereignty, the kind that deposed monarchs, was the business of people with the capacity to rule themselves. When John Locke picked up his pen, he found himself writing about "lunatics," "idiots," and "drunks"—the exceptions that proved the rule. This wasn't an accident. Nor was it an accident that women fought for suffrage by making the case that they were smart and independently minded enough to vote.

The idea that disabled people are just as capable as anyone else was foundational to the struggle that culminated in the Americans with Disabilities Act in 1990. Without this struggle, Millie wouldn't be living the life she's living, and I wouldn't be writing this book. But when disability rights activists base their demand for access on this "mythical norm," they miss an opportunity to push for a politics built on different grounds. "Compulsory capacity," the political theorist Stacy Clifford Simplican notes, "ignores the ways in which people are vulnerable, unpredictable, and interdependent."[9] What if sovereignty were a force that acted between us, rather than a power some of us possessed? What if sovereignty weren't about the power to rule worlds, but the power to make them anew? What if politics were all about cognitive mystery—not about who we are, but about who we might become?

The founding fathers had in mind a particular kind of citizen when they designed my country's political system. It wasn't Millie. But if Ralph had been more like Millie, I would have walked behind him in the gutter, shielding him with my body. I would have followed him instead of being dragged. This is the lesson I'd like to share in this chapter: The very things that would seem to disqualify Millie as a political actor are what give Millie her force—this is her power-with. Sovereignty is only sovereignty if it is recognized. Power is unleashed when it is not. If only for a second, Millie can have it in her possession.

Like Kyah, she can stray. Like Kyah, she can have followers. She can even play a role in making the laws of the land.

IT'S MAY 4, 2016, and I'm in Representative Mike Ball's office on the second floor of the new wing of the California statehouse. With a starched shirt, bow tie, and an anchorman-worthy helmet of gray hair, Ball is standing at the head of a long mahogany table. Crowded around are some angry-looking women, most in their mid-forties, white, like Ball, well groomed, well heeled, articulate, strident, effortlessly presentable in their work-casual attire. "It's the Palo Alto delegation," our leader whispers to me as we creep into the room.

With our backpacks, sneakers, and sandals, the four of us representing Santa Cruz retreat to a leather couch by the window. I squeeze past the coffee table and wheel Millie's wheelchair into position next to an office chair. I seat myself, carefully assessing whether Millie is in striking distance of the desk; there might be some tasty pieces of legislation sitting on it that she would love to grab and chew.

It's a hot day, and it has already been a long one. We spent the morning in a nearby ballroom with other delegates from community advisory councils from around the state. There, we mingled with parents and other people with an interest in special education. We heard from a lobbyist, a legislator, special education administrators, and two mothers with their sons, who stole the show: the first with a moving tribute in American Sign Language to his mother's courage; the second with a hilarious description of what being a smart kid with autism was like. Millie sat on a regular conference chair, played with her scarf, and devoured her breakfast and lunch. She giggled when the crowd reacted to something a speaker said. She even clapped once or twice, a good thirty seconds after the rest of the applause had stopped.

We have come to Sacramento for Legislation Day, an event tacked on to the Special Education Liaison Administrators' annual conference, which brings together the staff members who convene the community advisory councils. In addition to Xiaona, others in our party include Lucia, our community advisory council's chair, a Latinx woman who is the parent of two disabled teens; and Jennifer Smith, a white woman who has just been hired as the director of special education oversight for Santa Cruz County. By the time we arrived for our first appointment we were late, and even though we lingered in the ballroom so Millie could use the bathroom, she was agitated. As a staffer directed us into Representative Ball's office, she whined angrily.

The woman who is talking cedes the floor to the woman on her left. I know the type, I think, taking in the pearl earrings, the tasteful makeup, the neatly trimmed eyebrows. She speaks in the tones of the self-righteously aggrieved. She is telling a horrific story. Her son (not with her), autistic but brilliant, was removed from his fourth-grade classroom and transferred to a facility for the emotionally disabled, where he is an easy mark for bullies. She describes the months she's spent trying to get him moved. The lawyers she has called, her son's deepening depression, his talk of wanting to die. He'd been disruptive, the teachers told her; now he was scarred for life.

These Palo Alto women are a class act—one taking over from another in a carefully choreographed recitation of the system's failures. This mother's testimony fills the room. None of us, by contrast, seem likely to speak. Ball glanced over when we walked in, but at that point he was busy giving a little speech touting all the good things he'd already done for the disabled community. During the Palo Alto mothers' tirade, he listens sympathetically, concentrating, nodding, his mouth curved into a gentle frown. Lucia, the other Santa Cruz mother, seems just as impressed by the performance as I am. I begin to wonder whether the Santa Cruz delegation will leave the statehouse without saying a word.

When the women are done, Ball thanks them for their insights but makes no promises, then turns to our corner of the room. Millie is getting noisier, and I worry for a second that someone is going to ask us to leave. Not sure what to say, Jennifer apologizes for being late and explains who we are. I remember the advice from the lobbyist who addressed us that morning—"Be brief, be brave, be gone"—and psych myself up to open my mouth. But Ball isn't looking at me; he is looking at Millie, who is alternating between gnawing on her right arm and lunging at one of the Palo Alto ladies' purse straps.

"This is Millie," I suddenly hear coming out of my mouth, followed by an enthusiastic, entirely unscripted bout of storytelling about all the school districts she's been through and about how Santa Cruz has been the best place for Millie since everyone accepts her as she is. Scratch that, I think to myself; I'm supposed to be complaining. Then I remember our talking points. "But she hasn't had a speech therapist for the past three months."

The room is silent as I speak, all eyes trained on Millie. No one seems to have noticed I'm on verbal autopilot. Even as I course-correct, inside I squirm. I'm embarrassed; I hate having Millie be the target of all this attention. She's clearly unhappy, and I feel guilty for putting her through this ordeal. When the representative closes the meeting a few minutes later, his remarks focus exclusively on Millie, on how brave we are in the face of her challenges, how committed he is to helping people just like us.

This is not the way I imagined the meeting ending. I felt sheepish for even mentioning Millie's brief interruption in services after hearing the horror story from Palo Alto. Some part of me might have relished the idea of Santa Cruz stealing the show. If so, that feeling evaporated the moment I opened my mouth. I think about the frazzled mother, the unresponsive bureaucrats, the suicidal fourth grader. I wouldn't want to be living this woman's life.

Before we leave, Representative Ball asks us to stay for photographs. His staffer pulls out a fancy camera, and we all hand over our iPhones: Ball, with his politician smile, straight out of central casting; Millie, dress crumpled, eyes crossed, her expression blank. The kind of sovereignty at work in state legislatures is supposed to be about having your voice heard, about making an argument and stating your reasons. "Rational-critical debate": That's what the philosopher Jürgen Habermas called this kind of talk.[10] Millie did not engage in that kind of conversation. Instead, she played the role of the innocent child, someone prioritized in the family values vision of the world.[11] Silent, Millie spoke more loudly than the vocal others. Her presence had more of an effect than that of the Palo Alto delegation, at least at that moment, even though they no doubt had the resources to push legislation through. Others would not have. A long list of people with cause to protest would never get a hearing like the one we just had.

But the moment felt peculiar, and it was. In a room where all other eyes were on him, Ball sought out the recognition of my daughter, the person who was least likely to meet his gaze, to offer him gratitude, to give him the time of day. Her failure to respond seemed both to attract and to disturb him. He felt the force of her invitation—her "power-with"—even if he ultimately turned away.

In pitying Millie, the legislator turned her into a more manageable interlocutor.[12] He overcame the awkwardness of this encounter with the mystery of Millie's mind by defining her as a beneficiary of his political largesse. Lobbying is one way in which individuals like my daughter can perform sovereignty. But there are others. Let me take you to San Lorenzo Valley High School, where Millie was enrolled for many years.

IT'S A COOL FALL day in 2016, and I am in Millie's classroom. In the back are dividers that carve out four cubicles, each equipped to meet a student's needs. There are padded sleeping benches, diapers, medical supplies, boom boxes, computers, and fans. Millie's cubicle is the most crowded, thanks to Xiaona, who has started working as her school aide: She has a desk with a lamp, a stuffed bear, and a mirror where she can see herself, with a photograph of the two of us near it. The action now is in the front of the room at the circular table where Millie's teacher holds group activities. Today the group is small; the speech therapist is here for a session with Millie and her classmate, whom I'll call Liam.

This is, believe it or not, also a setting for the performance of sovereignty. By the time Millie reached Santa Cruz from Vermont, she was numbered among the ranks of the multiply disabled. She was a "defective speaker," as the linguistic anthropologist Charles Goodwin might put it.[13] More to the point, she was a defective future citizen: someone incapable of "rational-critical debate." Yet she had spent most of her life in school, like millions of other disabled children across the nation, partaking of an extensive menu of therapies and adapted activities meant to prepare her for participation in the sovereign "we." When she reached high school, there was talk of "life skills" and "self-care." No one really expected Millie to live on her own. But I was told she'd have a job when she aged out of the school system. Petting kittens at the animal shelter was long the frontrunner. Millie has gentle hands and a passion for the tactile. I loved this idea. It showed just how far welfare reform could go.[14]

I also loved visiting Millie at school, but my presence that day brought up another way in which sovereignty is performed in this setting. School is not just a good idea; it's mandatory, and parents whose children are truant can go to jail. It's also a right, and when it comes to disabled students the relationship between education and sovereignty is particularly tight. Enacted in 1975 and updated by Congress in 2004 and 2011, the Individuals with Disabilities Education Act, as Craig learned during those early years, guarantees "a free appropriate education in the least restrictive environment."[15] Parents who suspect their children are not receiving what they are owed can sue the school districts where they are enrolled. Families with money, cultural capital, and time to learn to work the system have won settlements worth hundreds of thousands of dollars to cover the cost of private treatment centers and schools.

The community advisory councils that gathered in Sacramento are part of this system. The California Department of Education created these bodies to stem the tide of litigation: They provide "input and advisement" to their region's Special Education Local Plan Area, or SELPA, a unit in California's byzantine educational bureaucracy. SELPA administrators are responsible for ensuring local services meet federal requirements: Their job is to keep their region's school districts out of court.

The parents, teachers, and therapists who serve on a community advisory council may work together toward this end, but they have different stakes in the system. The staff members in Millie's classroom always seemed happy to see me. But I knew, and they knew, that the law was on my side. The staff represented the government, in this most governmental of endeavors, this remnant of the welfare state still in action. I potentially trumped them, having the power to go federal and take actions that could cost the school district a fortune and these employees their jobs. If I could prove they weren't providing Millie with the services she needed, I could win a big settlement. Millie's vulnerability potentially gave me access to a power much greater than theirs.

Liam's aide wheels him over for the session. Millie is already sitting, rocking gently, on a stool. Reclining in his wheelchair, Liam is beatific: glowing skin, light hair, eyes half-closed, faintly smiling. Liam's aide ties his shoes while the speech therapist gets Millie started. There is a blender in the middle of the table, along with a gray and blue switching box and a red button. There is also an iPad in a powder-blue case. The speech therapist and Millie's aide sing a song asking Millie her name; Millie swipes at the iPad and it says "Millie." Then it's Liam's turn to say his name. His aide tilts his seat forward: Five, four, three, two, one, blast-off! Everyone laughs. Smoothie making has begun.

First, the speech therapist pulls up the recipe on the iPad. Millie and Liam are supposed to hit a button on the screen in order to activate a voice conveying each step. (Add the banana. Put in the water.) Then the students make the smoothie. With the speech therapist guiding their hands, Millie puts in the banana, and Liam puts in the water. "We're making a smoothie together," the speech therapist says. For anyone used to speech therapy among the severely disabled, this is pretty standard issue. This isn't Millie's first foray with a blender, and luckily this one isn't loud.

This scene is filled with language. There are the words from the iPad—machine words that give voice to what Millie and Liam supposedly want to say. There are the many more words the speech therapist and the aides direct at Millie and Liam: "Here, friend, it's your turn!" "Way to go!" "Millie, you're going to be the next Rachael Ray." Then there are the words the three women put in Millie's and Liam's mouths. "She's like, 'I don't need your help.'" "So he's like, 'I know what to do with a banana.'" "This is an example of 'give me what I want.'" There are also the words the three staff members say to one another. "Every time you tell her you're going to help her, she does it herself." Sometimes these varieties get tossed together, as when the speech therapist talks through Liam to his aide.

SPEECH THERAPIST TO LIAM: Well, while Millie's doing her job, maybe Becky will give you another bite.

LIAM'S AIDE: I will!

SPEECH THERAPIST: I bet she will.

LIAM'S AIDE: I'm kind!

Finally, there is the language of Millie and Liam themselves. Liam sits back, head slightly cocked to one side, gently and rhythmically strumming a toy that's a bit like an overgrown abacus, with a wooden frame, metal wires, and beads. Every now and then he lets out a high-pitched mewling sound. He also occasionally, and somewhat incongruously, shakes his head no. Perched upright, Millie is as busy as Liam is still: She reaches forward, grabbing at the blender. Her sounds are equally idiosyncratic: Her hum seems to indicate interest, and another, verging on whining, suggests complaint. Then there's the biting. Every so often, Millie abruptly flings her arms around her shoulders in an awkward embrace. It looks like she's hugging herself, but if you look closely, you can see that she's bringing her bicep to her mouth. Sometimes the only way to tell that things aren't going well for Millie is to look for marks.

I call these behaviors language, but I have no way of knowing whether they are intentional. I know by now that this isn't just a phase. There are days when I think of Millie's mind as a machine in overdrive, unable to modulate its circuitry, to accomplish easily taken-for-granted tasks like holding a spoon or sitting still. There are other days when I'm convinced that she's not dropping her spoon, she's throwing it; she's not fidgeting because she's overstimulated, she's just mad. But Millie isn't the only person who presents me with this conundrum. Is my friend sighing or simply taking a deep breath?

The linguistic anthropologist Elinor Ochs has reflected on how the "incompleteness" of language shapes the experience of anyone caught up in the flow of a conversation. "Language arcs towards the place where meaning may lie," Ochs writes, quoting Toni Morrison to describe how interlocutors work together to create what will have been said.[16] Millie's speech therapy has always been characterized by the staff's insistence on the significance of gestures whose sources are far from clear. With Millie, language arcs toward a puzzle: her particular version of the uncertainty that dogs and fuels every interaction, every collaborative effort to make sense. Those of us who talk or sign may think that words can solve the problem. But they can't keep us from tripping over our tongues or hands. Cognitive mystery runs through our dealings with one another like electricity through a wire. Millie slows us down and makes us feel its charge.

In this episode, the speech therapist had a claim to sovereignty: She set the agenda and put words into the students' mouths. So did I, for all the legal reasons outlined above. And so did language with all the force of a convention; as the philosopher Martin Heidegger put it, "Language speaks."[17] But so did Millie and Liam, whose reactions determined whether the session would count as a success.

In the end, Liam earns an A in smoothie making. He hits the iPad or button within seconds of it being offered to him every time. Despite a promising start, Millie quickly loses interest. And yet when the smoothie is finished, she is all business, sucking down the purple drink through a straw, a death grip on her covered cup. The speech therapist and the aides joke about her recalcitrance. "She's like, 'This is what I want,'" quips Liam's aide. "'I wanted everybody else to do all the work.'"[18] Both women needed the illusion that they knew what Millie and Liam had in mind. And yet the staff's gentle humor belied their awareness of horizons far more strange. If a conversation is a game of ping-pong, "defective speakers" have a habit of pocketing the ball. This is one way of thinking about sovereignty—as the power to take without returning, to turn one's back and face another world, and in doing so to compel a response. A compulsion that could possibly also be an invitation into a space where we all can come alive.

PEOPLE LIKE MILLIE DON'T write legislation or run schools. The small moments I have considered here raise a question. To put it bluntly, so what? Recall the humming, the sideways glances, the rocking, and the biting with which Millie responded to the speech therapist. These behaviors foreground features of our lives together that people tend to overlook: the grain of our voices, the pleasure of repetition, the fact that our minds and bodies aren't so easy to tease apart. I still remember sitting on the floor with Millie on a sunny Sunday afternoon. It was 2009, not long after we moved to Santa Cruz, and Millie had just turned nine. We were holding hands and rocking back and forth. She said "mmmm . . . haa," and I said "mmmm . . . haa" back. Suddenly, she burst out laughing. It was the first time she'd reacted this way, and I've rarely felt a pleasure that intense. When I'm with Millie, I'm thrown off-kilter. I find myself inventing new conventions, conjuring new scenarios, perhaps even new kingdoms, that shimmer in the imagination.[19] In this sense, someone like Millie can be sovereign. When Millie addresses me, I'm called from a place I cannot name.

What kind of world would become possible if, as a society, we recognized sovereignty in such fleeting moments? One very different from the one we live in now. In this world, not many people experience the power of people like my daughter, and those who do often live lives that are very hard. During those early days in Santa Cruz, when we were settling into our house on campus, Millie stopped sleeping through the night. This went on for weeks. I spoke to her, I sang to her, I rubbed her shoulders. Nothing would soothe her; her agitation only grew. When I couldn't hold my eyes open any longer, I slipped into her bed and clasped her to my chest. Instead of melting into my arms, she popped up like a jack-in-the-box, laughing and whining. When I pulled her back down, her flailing arm whacked me in the nose. I winced and felt for blood.

One night, after I'd wrestled Millie to the mattress, an unwelcome thought tiptoed into my mind. I could be doing this for the rest of my life. Millie wasn't like other children. She wasn't getting any easier to care for. This might not be something she outgrew. I stared into the darkness. The universe owed me nothing. But was a good night's sleep too much to ask?

As it turned out, it wasn't. These days, when I don't get a good night's sleep, my daughter is rarely to blame. Most nights, Millie sleeps soundly. And when she doesn't, more often than not I'm fast asleep in Manhattan, a half-mile from my office, and her care providers are the ones who have to wake up. It's not just that I can't do this alone; I don't want to do this alone. I don't want to be the only one who stumbles downstairs at 3 a.m. to face a suffering I can't understand and have no power to stop. And I can afford to make this wish a reality.

In this world, the precarity that comes to those who care for people like Millie is not distributed evenly. It falls mostly to women, many of them immigrants from the Global South, who do the work that allows women like me to have a career, freedom, hobbies, enough rest. Rents are high in Santa Cruz, and jobs that pay a living wage are scarce. Some of the women who care for Millie are from middle-class backgrounds. Many are from working-class and poor communities at least a half-hour commute from my house. I've raised both my children with the help of women raising their own children, including children with significant needs, who only see their mothers early in the morning and late at night. Millie's care providers tell me they love Millie, but they also love their children, and they need this job to keep their family afloat.

In Millie's last year of high school, a new student joined her class. Lucas was seventeen, and he'd never been to school. His parents, who had recently immigrated from Central America to the United States, had been caring for him from birth without government help. Coming to Santa Cruz hadn't made their lives any easier. It's not easy to hire care providers at the pay rate the state covers under the few programs it funds. The social services system is intentionally impenetrable, especially to non-English speakers; it can take months and multiple trips to government offices to receive the support that your child is owed. I'm aware that my life could be different. I could be hoisting Millie in and out of her wheelchair after a day of cleaning houses, delivering fast food, feeding and bathing other people's kids. I could be up all night with Millie, then rushing her to an underfunded day program so I could make it to my low-paid job. It could be much harder for me to thrive, for both of us to survive.

When she was three, Millie had another classmate suddenly separated from his mother—a single mom, like me—who had to leave the United States to help her parents. On her way back from Mexico, she was caught by the border patrol and faced an impossible choice. Her son, Gabriel, was medically fragile. Should she bring him back to her village or leave him with acquaintances in Chicago, where he had access to the medical treatment that was keeping him alive? Where is that little boy now? A college dorm? An understaffed group home? A cemetery?

It's not these parents' fault they're so exposed, and it's no sign of virtue that I'm so sheltered. Capitalism does such a poor job of valuing the work that really matters. Neoliberalism has ripped huge holes in the safety net and impoverished the programs that remain. The savagery of the immigration system feeds the gig economy. Corporations profit from their employees' vulnerability; it's what keeps people on the job. Sexism mistakes labor for destiny and skill for instinct; racism is the linchpin that holds the entire structure in place. Soon computers will be writing our novels; they're already driving our cars. At least for now, care for my daughter, and others like her, is something only living, breathing humans can do.

To build a better world, we'd have to start with different assumptions. Hannah Arendt described the gulf between the household and the Forum in the traditions we're heir to: For the Greeks, there was nothing political, or even really human, about this kind of domestic work.[20] Simplican, the political theorist quoted above, challenges the norm of compulsory capacity. But even she retains this part of our history: Intellectually disabled people practice politics in conference rooms and restaurants, she argues—not with support staff in group homes.[21] But care is not just drudgery, when it comes to people like Millie; it's an active relationship with someone with a will of their own and desires that are often far from clear.

Eva Feder Kittay, who knows this kind of care firsthand, has criticized liberal theories of justice for privileging equality. Instead, she insists on the fact of dependency: Far more than language, it is the distinguishing mark of the human species, from our extended infancy to our protracted old age.[22] Care workers sometimes have no other options. But even those who do often have trouble quitting. It's hard to abandon someone who can't survive without your help. The philosopher Martha C. Nussbaum has insisted that everyone has the right to flourish and that political systems should be designed to ensure they do.[23] Kittay and Nussbaum both argue that care workers should be justly compensated for enduring the grip of others' needs.

I'm grateful for these insights, but I would take the argument further. This kind of care isn't just about dependency or the right to flourish; it's about using your imagination. It's about getting caught in the riptide of mysterious pains and pleasures. It's about trying to live in another person's skin. It's about holding open the possibility that there's more to all of us than we can immediately fathom. This kind of care is mutual, which means the lines of power run both ways.[24] What if sovereignty operated by way of a different relationship to vulnerability, one that had nothing to do with the violent exclusions that shape care workers' lives? What if it stemmed from the force of mutual obligation, but also of curiosity, rather than resting with whoever has the money and guns? The poet and writer Leah Lakshmi Piepzna-Samarasinha is right. In a world so mistaken in its priorities, care can be a revolutionary act.[25]

As I write this, in the few remaining hospitals in Gaza, doctors and nurses work tirelessly to save the lives of horrifically injured children. Something keeps them there beyond horror at the sheer suffering: It's the fact that each of these small people is, in the anthropologist Maura Finkelstein's words, a world.[26] I want to live in a society where care workers are richly rewarded. I also want to live in a society in which people like Millie are recognized for the power they wield. The legislator could easily have ignored Millie. The speech therapist had control over the words and the blender and could have put Millie back in her wheelchair and rolled her away. Yet they both sensed there was more to the story.

Becoming an Operating System

Craig hung the piece of foam board in the kitchen near where I sat to feed Millie, perched on a stool so I could see her in her high chair eye to eye. It was early in the fall of 2003, and Millie had started preschool. The foam board was two feet high with a blue electric-tape border, a festive touch that was clearly the work of an amateur—possibly Craig, probably me. Dots of Velcro covered it in neat rows. Affixed to the top of the array were a half-dozen two-by-two-inch squares of laminated paper, each printed with a different drawing. The first square showed a smiley face: a tan oval with two dots for eyes and a curve for a mouth. Next to it was a frowning face with the curve turned upside down. Then came a square printed with a drawing of a bright yellow banana, another with a bowl of ice cream, complete with a cherry, and another with a cup and straw. In the next row were a teddy bear, a necklace, two crackers, and, later, a toilet, added when Millie was five and her teacher told me it was time to try potty training her. Most of the dots were vacant. The therapist who asked us to begin the collection left Millie's vocabulary with plenty of room to grow.

For Millie, as for most children, with school came symbols. A parade of letters dances along the wall of a typical preschool. A is for Apple, B is for Boy, reminders for little minds getting ready to read. In Millie's preschool, the symbols were free range, ripped from one part of a felt board and stuck to another during a cheery discussion of the weather, the season, or the morning snack. Symbols were the lifeblood of early efforts to teach Millie to speak. I had high hopes for that foam board. It seemed to hold the key that would unlock Millie's mind and heart so we could return to our proper pathway through life.

In her unsparing account of her daughter's first year, the novelist Rachel Cusk describes the profound and terrifying nature of the love she felt for her baby. Her daughter's life depended on it, and Cusk was haunted by the specter of its failure. She feared the lethal reassertion of her own adult needs: for freedom, for attention, for sleep, for time to write. This changed when the child embarked on what Cusk calls her daughter's own "career in love." Cusk's daughter had received love, but now she was ready to give it. She had been an extension of her mother, but now she was a separate person, with dreams and desires, and the means to express them, a person who would someday stand on her own. At nine months, when her parents returned from a week's vacation, she reached out to embrace them. By a year, she had begun to choose between them, squirming from her mother's arms to toddle to her father's, demanding "Da," crying for "Ma." "It is in some ways profoundly relieving, the development of her preferences and moods, the slow emergence, like another birth, of her character. Her self, for so long a mystery we attempted to solve, a space we filled with guesses, is taken from us like a worrying charge."[1]

At three, Millie's self was still a space I filled with guesses. Millie didn't squirm to be released, and she didn't spread her arms to welcome my embrace. Her smile was a revelation, a ray of sunshine through the clouds. But she could barely sit, let alone take a step, and she had yet to utter a word. When I held the smiley face in front of Millie, she lowered her head coyly. My own living, breathing smiley face rarely caught Millie's eye. But Millie had potential. She would master the words she needed to embark on her own career in love. The therapists must see this, I told myself. Otherwise, they wouldn't be trying so hard.

First, the speech therapist tried PECS, the Picture Exchange Communication System, which was popular in special education circles at the time. Millie was supposed to pick up one of the squares and hand it to her teacher. This would count as a word—"banana," say—to which Millie's teacher would respond by handing her another card—a thumbs up for "okay." After that, Millie would get some banana slices as a snack. Eventually, Millie would master other symbols—the smiley face for "I like"—and the idea was that she'd be using them to communicate in sentences in no time. After her vocabulary was big enough, if she didn't learn to speak on her own, she'd graduate to assistive technologies, like the speech synthesizer used by Stephen Hawking, which would be the ticket to mainstream schooling and maybe even college and a career.

No time turned out to be a long time, given Millie's lack of hand-eye coordination. She could barely pick up a block, let alone a flimsy slip of plastic, and the speech therapist was forced to try something else. Not long after the laminated squares entered Millie's life, so did a simple communication device, a big red button called a "Big Mac." Millie's teacher asked me to use it to record messages from Millie about what she had done over the weekend. During circle time, the teacher would guide Millie's hand to the Big Mac, and together they would hit it to play my voice uttering what were supposedly Millie's words. The next step was to stick a square on the button and make the recording correspond with the symbol on it; if the drawing was of a banana, the Big Mac would say "I want a banana" when pressed. Velcro was the magic: With a dot on the device and a dot on the square, Millie would learn to associate pictures with words, and words with things.

This theory was subject to periodic testing. "Tell me something Millie really loves," her speech therapist asked me one day when Millie was four and I dropped by to see her at school. "And something she really hates," she added. These were easy questions to answer: She loved anything stringy and detested cold air in her face. The therapist went home to her computer and generated a new pair of squares. She put dots of Velcro on a new device—a Twin Talk, it was called—which had two square play buttons, instead of one round one, which opened up new possibilities. She put a picture of Mardi Gras beads on the blue play button, and a picture of a fan on the yellow one. Then she made the recordings. The blue one played "I want Mardi Gras beads" and the yellow one played "I want the fan."

I was there when Millie navigated this ordeal. The therapist dangled a string of Mardi Gras beads in front of Millie. It took a minute for Millie to notice them, but when she did, she crooned softly, her face breaking out into a grin. Then came the "dispreferred item": a handheld fan, which the therapist used to blast cold air into Millie's face. Millie's smile folded in on itself, like a balled-up piece of paper; her eyelids fluttered in surprise. Out came the Twin Talk. The fan and beads lay on the table, just beyond Millie's reach. "Which do you want, Millie?" Millie's eyelids were still fluttering when she lunged at the Twin Talk. She was either after the Mardi Gras beads, or she was agitated, or both; it was hard to tell. "I want the fan" squeaked the recorded voice. Another blast of cold air. It was like watching a film in slow motion. Millie recoiled, blinking rapidly. Her chin began to quiver. A tear squeezed from the corner of her eye. A beat later, she began to wail, as if finally realizing the world could be unkind. The therapist winced as I pulled Millie from her chair.

As the years went by, new strategies came and went. With each attempt, my spirits sank another notch. I got tired. Then I got cynical. When Millie was seven, her therapist asked me to send her pictures of Millie, her brother, her father—by then long gone—and me, which she made into laminated squares of paper. I'm pretty sure she used the images in an activity involving family trees. But I imagined her setting up the Twin Talk so she could ask Millie, "Who do you like better: your brother or your mom?" Another therapist experimented with textures in an effort to make it easier for Millie to grasp the meaning of symbols. The symbol that had pictured a teddy bear became one, a three-dimensional figure covered in plush fur. I can't remember whether they tried using real Mardi Gras beads that time; if so, Millie surely would have passed the preference test, but her skills may have ended there. It was impossible to tell whether even the most alluring symbols were sinking in.

When Millie was nine, and it came time for us to move from Vermont to Santa Cruz, I threw away the foam board. It had been years since we had added any more laminated squares, and several of the ones we had were lost. Our English setter chewed up one of them and would have eaten more if I hadn't hidden the board in the closet where I kept the humidifiers. Millie had just been diagnosed with cortical visual impairment. It wasn't clear she could even see the little squares of laminated paper, let alone understand what they were supposed to mean.

Thinking back, I'm surprised I was so hasty to discard this reminder of those early, naïve days. I still have the alligator Halloween costume Ralph made in nursery school with cardboard, colored paper, and green tin foil. I've framed just about every piece of artwork Millie and her aides have ever made. Maybe I should have kept that foam board. But by then, I had soured on symbols. The whole business smacked of cruelty. I wanted to put it in the past. Millie's "career in love" would have nothing to do with words. Or at least that's what I thought.

WHAT IS COMMUNICATED IN communication? I used to think I knew. But when you live in the company of someone like Millie, you quickly come to see that there isn't a clear answer to this question. I was raised in the United States, where I learned to take for granted a distinctive family of assumptions about words and why people use them. Communication is supposed to describe the world and reveal hidden thoughts—that's what we Americans are taught to think. We picture the passage of meaning from one side to another: a matter of tongues, ears, and an urge that becomes an utterance, articulated by a speaker who has something to say to a listener who can grasp it.[2] But what travels is often less a meaning than an energy, conveyed in an instant of experience that somehow feels as if it could be shared. The sheer fact of contact can matter more than content. Millie has taught me that communication is just as much a matter of surfaces as the hidden messages behind them: the looks on our faces, her posture, the warmth of my hand, the sensations that swirl around a touch, sound, or sight.

It would be wrong to think that this insight came easily or has held steady. A little pilot light of longing burns inside me—not always noticed, but always there. On the desk in front of me are several pictures of Millie. I was cleaning out my studio and rediscovered a box of old photographs; I couldn't help but pull a few out. Two of them were taken seconds apart on the day after Christmas when Millie was five. Millie is sitting on the carpet. Tendrils of hair have escaped her ponytail, and she's wearing a raspberry pink shirt. In one of the pictures, she's gently smiling at the toy piano she's just been given. In the other, her lips are parted, her eyes unfocused, her attention withdrawn. I keep looking from one photograph to the other. Which Millie is real? There's another picture on my desk, taken when Millie was even younger. She's sitting on my lap, taking great interest in a picture book I'm showing her. These are the photographs I've always thought of as wishful, as false, as not reflecting the young girl who was my daughter. Now I'm wondering if I made a terrible mistake. It looks like Millie had something to say about that piano. Did she? Should I have tried harder to find out?

Ralph James Savarese and his wife, Emily, labeled everything in their household in hopes that their son, D.J., a nonverbal first grader, would learn to recognize language. They spent hours showing D.J. sentences and helping him fill in the blanks. From the laminated slips of paper, they graduated to a label maker, then a laptop. They steadied D.J.'s hand so he could type. When the school district resisted them, they fought like wildcats. Emily gave up her job to make sure D.J. was included in a typical classroom, volunteering to adapt the curriculum to D.J.'s needs. Today, D.J. Savarese is an essayist and poet. Could Millie have been an essayist and poet? Where does acceptance end and betrayal begin?

It's important to keep this question open. I remember my first silent retreat and how I reveled in the sense of communion I felt with my fellow meditators, freed from the buzz of conversation. We would either smile or ignore each other in line for the bathroom. I felt like I knew who they were—how wise, how kind, how preoccupied, how caught up in the drama of their lives. Then the retreat ended, and the talk started, and I quickly discovered, for better or worse, that they were nothing like the people I thought they might be. Could the same be true of Millie? I wake up from a dream in which Millie chimes in during a heated discussion at the dinner table. When we look at her in wonder, she sighs and says, "Of course, I can talk! You just never asked me what I thought!" When I was in elementary school, a friend and I found a book in the library that explained how to make a hot air balloon using crepe paper and glue. We signed up to march with it in the Fourth of July parade. The result was a fiasco, a mess of torn parchment and split seams, which we carried while holding back tears. What if we had used different materials? Followed different instructions? Would we have made something that could actually float?

This chapter is about a do-over. It's about trying out a different kind of contraption. About trying to reach Millie through different means. Speakers communicate, as the philosopher Jacques Derrida pointed out, but so do hotel rooms when they are connected by a door.[3] What passes through the door can be anything: a suitcase, a worried mother, a breath of fresh air. It's the meeting point that matters, not what moves across the threshold. One such meeting point is a remarkable experiment in communication called PODD. I thought I was over communication systems. But PODD made me think again. Here's what I learned when Millie and I tried it out.

CASSIDY HAS LONG AMBER hair pulled back from her face. She is slender, and her back curves to the left, while her shoulders twist to the right. She is in a wheelchair, which is slightly reclined to support her trunk. Her eyes are a clear, light blue and ringed with short, dark lashes. She has a turned-up nose, covered with freckles, and slightly parted lips. Her face is motionless, at rest in an expression that lies somewhere between disdain and faint amusement. I later learn she is fourteen. She is wearing a fancy pink dress, which is partially covered by a patchwork quilt arranged on her lap. Someone dressed her this way for a reason, I think to myself. The dress carries the ambience of a senior prom into the trade show. It tells those who meet Cassidy that she is a person with allies. The effect is not frivolous; it's ethical. Whoever chose the outfit is saying something about the young woman—who she is and why she matters—and about themselves.

I am at Closing the Gap, a national conference on assistive and augmentative communication that is held every year in the same airport hotel in Minneapolis. Sue, a mentor for other parents attending the conference, is showing me around the crowded exhibit hall when she catches sight of Cassidy coming through the door. "Hey, it's Cassidy!" she says as the wheelchair approaches. "How's it going? I love your dress!" Unsure if Cassidy sees me, I smile and introduce myself; only then do I notice Cassidy's mother. She sighs when Sue turns to her. The two women are fellow Minnesotans, and they know each other well.

Cassidy's mother raises an eyebrow. "It's been a long day."

She does look tired. "I didn't want to come," she is explaining to Sue. "But Cassidy was dying to show off her new power chair. Hopefully we'll run into Linda." Sue turns to me to explain. Linda is Linda Burkhart, the communication consultant who gave Cassidy's mother the courage to lobby her school district to pay for the machine. I take in the wheelchair's bulk, and then it dawns on me: Cassidy doesn't drive it. Power chairs offer independence to wheelchair users; they no longer have to depend on others to push them. But for Cassidy, mobility isn't the point; rather, her power chair charges the equipment that allows her to speak. The power chair's battery is attached to a tablet mounted on Cassidy's wheelchair: It's a speech-generating device from Tobii Dynavox, a major producer of assistive communication technologies. "Cassidy is such a chatterbox," her mother says, grinning. "She's definitely the social butterfly of the family." Meanwhile, Cassidy is staring at a distant corner of the ceiling.

When I meet Cassidy, I've just spent two days learning about the communication system she is using. I've watched videos in which Linda Burkhart works with children whose capacities seem as limited as Cassidy's do to me, or Millie's would to the average stranger on the street. A friendly woman with a toothy grin and a head of curly hair, Linda is a trainer—and evangelist—for PODD.

PODD stands for Pragmatically Organized Dynamic Display. This name, Linda explained at the preconference workshop I attended, captures what makes the system so powerful. Unlike many communication systems, which demand that their users have a grasp of abstract categories, PODD, as its name insists, is "pragmatically organized." This means that the symbols it uses are grouped according to the practical purposes of speaking, such as commenting, demanding, admiring, and shooting the breeze. The "display" is "dynamic," to quote PODD's name again, in that you can move along "pragmatic branches" through multiple levels to gain access to a wide range of things someone might want or need to say. PODD is structured in a way that makes visible what linguistic anthropologists have identified as the functions fulfilled by utterances.[4] "PODD is a fully fledged language," Linda told us. "It gives people all the functions of speech." With PODD, they can say whatever they want to say, whenever they want to say it, not simply to others who are adept in the system but to anyone they meet.

PODD is as different from that Twin Talk with the Velcro dots as nylon is from crepe paper. An Australian speech pathologist named Gayle Porter invented PODD to allow people like Millie to communicate what she referred to as

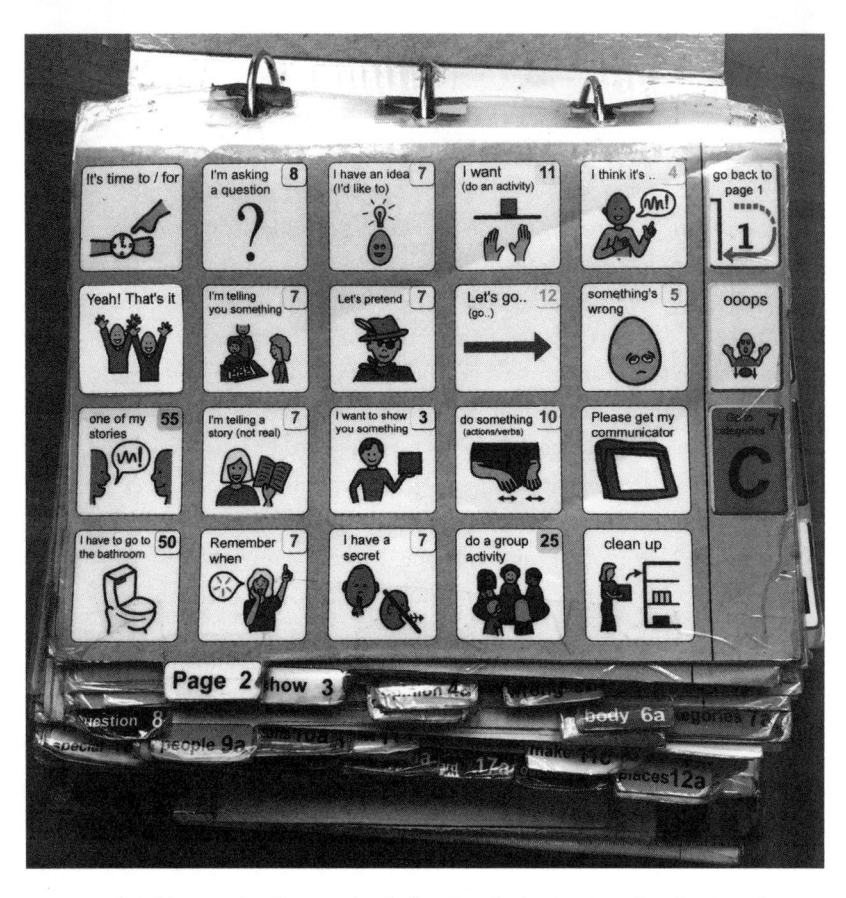

FIGURE 1. A "direct select" PODD book showing the beginning of a selection of pragmatic branches. "Something's wrong" is in the fifth column, one row down. (Danilyn Rutherford)

"autonomous thoughts and ideas." Picture yourself in front of your computer with your browser opened to a website. You select an option from the menu, and you're taken to another page, then another, traveling along a pathway the designers put in place. Some websites are hard to navigate—designers can mess up—but in principle there should be a trail of breadcrumbs leading you to what you want to know. Now take away the electricity and imagine that the website is a book of symbols (fig. 1). Here, the breadcrumbs are numbered tabs taking you from page to page to lead you to what you want to say. This is the magic of PODD. The communication devices Millie encountered in the classroom were like posters; they had no depth. They gave students a limited set of options—juice or a cracker, a fan or beads; what they could say was constrained. PODD

114 BEAUTIFUL MYSTERY

offers its users freedom. It allows them to do more than choose a snack. They can use the book of symbols to complain of a headache. They can tell stories, pass judgment, even swear.

Porter designed the system to be taught through something called "aided language stimulation"—a strategy very different from the ones tried with Millie.[5] People learn PODD the same way babies learn language: by immersion. Like babies do, PODD newcomers spend months in rooms filled with talking people long before they are ready to talk back. In the case of PODD, these talking people aren't using their hands or vocal cords to communicate. Instead, they converse by way of fat binders of laminated, color-coded sheets. The sheets are divided, checkerboard style, into square cells, each of which holds a simple drawing meant to represent the word or phrase printed above it. The sheets and cells are arranged according to the various things an utterance might do; new PODD users must work to master this structure.

The disabled person's partner, usually a parent or care provider, both speaks through the PODD book and explains how they are speaking. Let's say you want to say to your son, "Hey, let's go to the store." You would act like the book was a website. You would point to the icon for "let's go!" and then turn (or "link") to a page of likely destinations and choose a drawing of a shop. As you did so, you would describe the route through the book you were taking as you made your way to the utterance, which you would then speak out loud. Over time, these routes would become second nature to both you and your son. If, like Millie, your son couldn't point or flip through the pages, you would find another way for him to indicate his choice—with a body movement or turn of the head. Eventually, your son would learn to use the book to tell you and anyone else in the vicinity what he wanted to say.

Some disabled people use advanced communication books or modified iPads equipped for the system; these provide them with access to the full complex syntax of English or whatever language they wish to speak. In high-tech devices, the screen automatically changes when the user selects an icon, and the device itself does the talking. (Again, think Stephen Hawking. He's delivering a lecture. He twitches a cheek muscle to select words that his computer then speaks out loud; his colleagues don't have to understand how the software works to follow along.) In the light-tech version, the "operating system" is the PODD user's human partner: A human plays the computer's role. This human voice generator might be a parent or a paid care worker, or, in the ideal case envisioned by PODD's advocates, everyone the PODD user works with in a day program or at school. The user picks the symbols, either by pointing at them directly or by selecting from an array of options by nodding or shaking their head.

Instead of a computer speaking for a person, a person speaks for a computer. The partner turns the pages, names the icons, and serves as the user's voice.

I listened to Linda with the ear of an anthropologist. My grant included funding to learn about assistive communication and other interventions directed at people like Millie; that's how I ended up in Linda's audience of parents and professionals. The workshop was meant to teach us to serve as communication partners. Linda showed us how a PODD book works. "I have something to say!" she called out from the front of the conference room, smiling broadly and waving her hand. Then she opened the book she had projected onto a screen and pointed to an icon. "Something's wrong," she groaned, reading the caption with an exaggerated frown. "Go to page 5," she added more softly and neutrally, pointing to the number on the icon's upper-right corner. She turned to a page marked by a tab of the same number, and an array of whimsical oval faces filled the screen: "My head hurts," "My stomach hurts," "I'm angry," "I'm sad." "Go to the next page," she read out in the same soft, neutral voice, pointing to one of the narrow icons that had been added to the right edge of the page to use in navigating through the rest of the book. On the next page, she pointed to still another icon in the middle of the display. "I'm hungry," she loudly announced. "Something's wrong! I'm hungry!" she said, repeating the entire turn at talk, giving voice to what the icons had to say.

We quickly got down to the business of learning to use PODD. Linda began by teaching us how to use "chat words," commonly used expressions like "uh-oh," "hurry up," "more," "done," "help," or "just kidding," which appear at the start of every PODD book. Then she explained how to use the next set of icons, which had numbers corresponding to pages in the book that would enable us to complete an utterance. "I want [to do an activity]," for instance, led us to a set of icons symbolizing common things someone like Millie might want to do, like listen to music or have an aide read them a book.

We each found a buddy, and soon the room was filled with chattering voices, some dull, some animated, as we practiced our role. We were not only becoming operating systems. We were also becoming interlocutors, which is to say fellow PODD users, and that was why it was so important for us to practice. In *Gulliver's Travels*, the hero encounters an imaginary world in which people use objects as words and haul them around like a tinker carries his wares.[6] PODD books come with straps, so a user's partner can wear them like a purse. PODD partners carry their loved one's language over their shoulders and in their throats.

As the conference continues, I find myself thinking of Millie. It's not just children who can learn to communicate using PODD, as Linda and other parents in the workshop explained to me. So can young adults, once they find themselves immersed in a PODD-using social world. Linda later explained to me what she meant in referring to PODD as a language. "I often define communication as connection with another person," she said. "Language is just a shared set of agreed-upon symbols, patterns, and rules that enable a community of individuals to communicate more specifically with each other."[7] If PODD is a language, it is one that thrives in the company of others: Its distinctive visual language is modeled next to a verbal language, and there are versions in Danish, English, German, Norwegian, and Swedish. The distinct way that Millie uses her muscles has arguably prevented her from expressing herself in conventional ways, but when it comes to spoken language, who can say how much she understands?

I go to a presentation in which Linda shows a video of a mother making brownies with her severely disabled son and his typically abled little sister. A big metal bowl propped under her arm, the mother uses her PODD book to explain what she is doing; the sister reaches out for the book so she can chime in. The whole family has learned the system, using the icons to come up with an utterance, then voicing what they've said, soaking the boy in PODD-generated talk. Another presentation features a different mother in a video describing her battle to get her school district to view her son as capable of communication. Midway through the saga, I glance at the woman next to me; there are tears in her eyes. I remember the language that school districts use in documents on disabled students. If parents honestly evaluated their newborns' "present levels," the reigning euphemism for abilities, or lack thereof, would children ever learn to talk? I think of Cassidy's party dress and the videotaped mother's struggle to get the authorities to recognize her son as a future speaker. Suddenly, I feel inadequate. Am I a bad mom?

I run into Cassidy and her mother again at a gathering for parents held in the hotel on the final evening of the conference. We are meeting near the pool in the hotel atrium, a vast, empty shell of a courtyard ringed by five stories of guest rooms. "I have a story," a young woman's voice chirps as soon as Cassidy and her mother settle in. It's coming from Cassidy's device. A man's voice lists two options, repeats them, and then stops. "She wants to talk about this thing that happened at the dog park this morning," Cassidy's mother explains. But the machine is only giving her two options: "It happened long ago" and "It's going to happen in the future." Cassidy needs "It happened earlier today."

Another PODD user, Caleb, who is seventeen but looks younger, has been walking in circles; now he comes over to investigate. Caleb's mom reaches into his backpack and pulls out his device. She fiddles with the screen, then gives it to him. "I'm Caleb," says a digital man's voice. "I live with my mom and my cat." As I reach for a cookie, Cassidy's mom is helping her daughter. "I'm Cassidy" comes from her device. Sue, the parent mentor, turns to me with a grin. "They're having a conversation!" I notice something I missed the first time I met Cassidy. There are flat silver plates mounted a few inches from each of Cassidy's ears; I see now that she is activating the device by moving her head slightly to the right. Sue explains that Linda helped Cassidy pick out these switches; they spent hours watching music videos together, giggling, and testing out the various types. It took years for Cassidy's mom to screw up the courage to try out PODD. Now, she's a trainer. "I'm the shy one. I never pictured myself as a teacher. Cassidy is much more suited to the job."

Later that evening, when the party is over, Cassidy and her mother will drive me to my hotel. In that short ride, I will get to know both of them better. Cassidy's mother lost her own mother and her marriage during the same year I lost my husband; she is trying to get her house ready to sell, and the burden is killing her. To make matters worse, Cassidy is recovering from major surgery. She wakes up every night at 2 a.m. in pain. I couldn't do what you do, I find myself thinking, and I sense that Cassidy's mother is thinking the same thing about me. But back in the atrium, she gazes proudly at her daughter. I glance over at Cassidy, and for a brief moment, I see her meet her mother's eyes. Before she looks away, I see her smile. Again, I think of Cassidy's party dress. Was I wrong to assume someone else picked it? Who knows? Maybe Cassidy likes to wear pink.

I RETURNED FROM CLOSING the Gap exhilarated and confused. The parents I met were taking a leap of faith. They were betting time and not a little money that PODD would help them discover what their children were thinking: their secret desires, stories about their school day, the jokes they would tell if they had a chance. I worried that this dream might come at a cost. It could make their existing relationships with their children seem lacking—as if sharing a look, a touch, a hug, or pleasure in a strange sound were less worthy than sharing an idea. But, in the end, that old longing crept past my defenses. Yes, this was research, but I wouldn't be doing it if it didn't hit close to home. Was I seeing everything there was to see, when it came to Millie? Could I know her better? I imagined what it would be like to hear Millie speak to me through an iPad. Even if she just said something as simple as "hi," my heart would explode. In the end, my curiosity won out. I contacted Linda and asked if she would be willing to meet Millie. We set up a daylong consultation for a week when Linda was planning to be in the East Bay.

The windshield wipers beat a rhythm on the wet glass as we cruised up the interstate through the foothills on the appointed day. I was chatting with Greta, one of Millie's care providers, who was riding shotgun; Xiaona was napping in the back. When Millie started complaining in that irritated, wordless drone she uses to express displeasure, Xiaona woke up. "She needs to go to the bathroom." Ten minutes later we were pulling up a steep driveway to a small cottage. Linda's husband answered the door. "I'm Danilyn," I told him, and I introduced Greta and Xiaona as they sped by with Millie, who was kicking her legs and biting her arm. Linda greeted Millie with a smile, which faded as Xiaona wheeled Millie across the carpet toward the bathroom, leaving a line of leaves and mud. Millie was wet and hungry. Greta rummaged in Millie's backpack for food as Xiaona sat Millie on the toilet and wrestled her out of her diaper.

I asked Linda for some paper towels and apologized for the carpet. Amid the chaos, she had grabbed a dish towel and started dabbing at the lines. "No problem. Do you think she'd like a banana?" I was paying Linda for this day-long consultation, but so far we were swept up in that welter of complications that accompanies Millie when she ventures into unfamiliar terrain. But Linda quickly recovered her composure. Xiaona and Greta brought Millie from the bathroom and seated her in a wooden chair. As Millie wolfed down her sandwich, biting her forearm between bites and spraying crumbs on the floor, Linda pondered her. Then she turned to the table and grabbed two thick binders.

I had seen these PODD books at the workshop; now I had a chance to examine them more closely. The binders were black and bound with plastic coils. One was eight and a half by eleven inches; the other, half that size. As Xiaona and Greta looked on, Linda explained their key attributes. Both books featured the same icons, stylized drawings from Boardmaker, the same company that made the pictures on the foam board. The icons were in bright colors—the face that indicated "I'm sick" was olive green; they were designed to stand out against a dark background, making it easy for people with low vision to pick them out.

The icons were printed on rip-proof sheets of paper that were attached with Velcro to the black pages. The smaller, thicker book had one large symbol on each page (fig. 2). The larger one had nine smaller symbols (fig. 3). Both books had numbered tabs. Linda pointed out the "chat words" on the first page of the larger book and showed us how the smaller book presented them one by one on the first few pages. Flipping through the smaller book, I took in the postcard-sized symbols for "more," "stop," "finished," and "hurry up." The book with nine icons on each page, Linda reminded me, was a "direct select," meant to be used by the communication partner for direct modeling. It could also be used by disabled people who were able to point. The book with a single icon on each page was the

FIGURE 2. A scanning PODD book designed for users with cortical visual impairment. (Danilyn Rutherford)

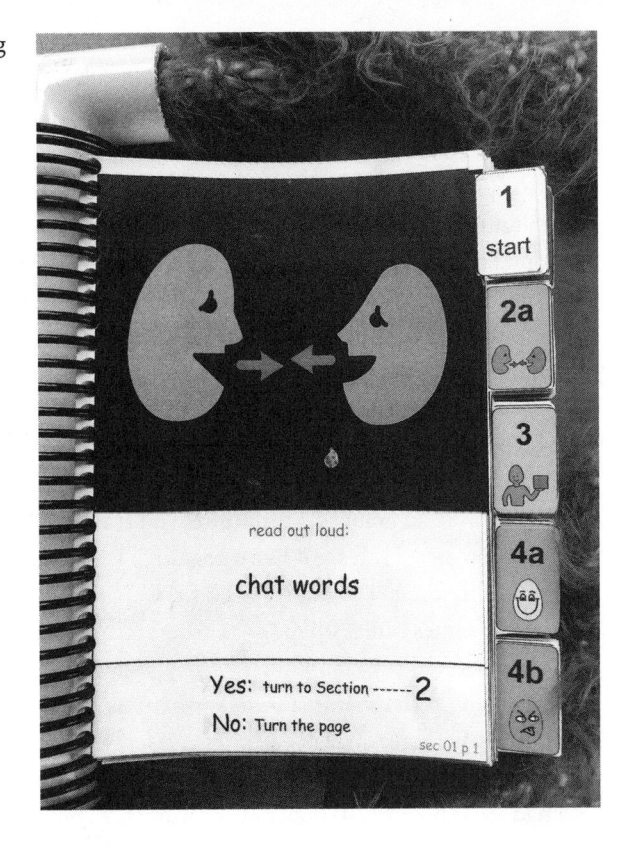

"scanning" version. In this case, the partner presented the options one by one, and the disabled person acted in a way that indicated their choice; they might nod, move their head, or lean in. During the session, Linda would introduce Millie to both. These books would be the first leg in Millie's journey toward the high-tech access to language that Cassidy enjoyed. At first, we would be her voice generator. Then, armed with an iPad, she would be able to go out in public and generate spoken language on her own.

Linda took a seat on the floor in front of Millie, took up the bigger book, and waved her hand in Millie's face. "I have something to say!" she called out. Millie had finally gotten a fix on the straw to her juice, and she was slurping intently. She stopped when she heard Linda's voice. It was rich and cheerful, the opposite of a monotone—the voice of a Sesame Street host or a television clown. *Rip* went the Velcro as Linda pulled one of the small paper squares off the first page. "You like it!" she said, with the emphasis on "like." "Go to page 6," she said more softly and dully, then flipped to the middle of the book, where she found

FIGURE 3. A large direct select PODD book designed for users with cortical visual impairment. (Danilyn Rutherford)

another icon and pulled it free. *Rip.* Linda gently shook the slip of paper and moved it slowly into Millie's field of vision. "It's yummy!"

Linda encouraged Xiaona to try using the book to offer Millie more juice. "I have something to say," Xiaona called out, gamely. *Rip.* "Use quick chat," Linda instructed her. "Quick chat," Xiaona announced, and then turned to the appropriate page. "I want more," she blurted out, pulling off the icon that voiced what she thought Millie might say, which pictured two hands making the "more" sign in American Sign Language. "You want more," Linda corrected her. "At this point, we're talking to Millie. Not for her. We're not trying to make her say anything herself."

After Xiaona practiced using the books, Linda announced, "Let's try the computer." On the table, she set up a laptop and two small switches. One of the switches was red, and the other was green; the first operated the cursor, and the second clicked the selection, working something like a mouse. A few days earlier, Linda had asked for some pictures of Millie and some of the important people in her life; I'd sent her headshots of her brother, her four regular care providers, and the dog. I soon discovered what Linda wanted them for; she had incorporated these images into a game in which the computer showed Millie a picture, then partially hid it behind a colored block. Linda wanted to use this game to determine what kind of switch access Millie might be able to use when she graduated to the high-tech version of PODD.

I was eager to see how this would work. But when I reached to lift Millie out of her chair, Linda stopped me; we had to use the PODD book to tell her what we were going to do. "I have something to say," Linda exclaimed, reaching for the single-icon book, which she used to speak to Millie. "Chat words. No. Something wrong. No. I want something. No," she ran through a series of options, swiftly turning the pages before arriving at the one she wanted. "I want to do something," she said to Millie with more emphasis. "Yes!" She moved the book into Millie's field of vision, then turned to another page and went through a new list of alternatives. Finally, she arrived at the icon of a yellow chair. "Yes." Then she put it all together. "I want you to sit down over there."

I took a seat beside the laptop so I could record the experiment with my iPad. I couldn't see the screen. But I could see Millie's face, and Linda's, with her broad smile, twinkling eyes, and halo of curly hair. On my flight from New York, I'd spent some time with two babies, one eighteen months, the other six months old. I had surprised myself with the pleasure I took in attracting and holding the attention of these small, nonspeaking humans. "I'm good at this," I thought to myself as the younger one locked eyes with me, smiling in pleasure at my happy voice and animated face. "Linda is even better," I thought to myself now. Millie smiled shyly as Linda spoke to her and glanced quickly at the book. By the end of the session, I noticed Millie looking at the book when Linda was silent, as if she thought that this would encourage Linda to speak.

Now Millie looked at the screen as our familiar faces floated in and out of view. Linda used the book to encourage her to try out the switches. She held one in front of her, then in her lap, then close enough that Millie's smallest movement activated it, then waited for Millie to take the initiative to hit it herself. Millie sat primly, her hands folded in her lap, her eyes glued to the screen. Linda let several long moments go by as we watched her, in silence, waiting for her to move.

Eventually, Linda gave up and moved on to another activity, in which she used the single-icon book to invite Millie to talk with it. This time she lingered over each option, watching Millie closely, waiting for her to move her head. When Millie turned away—in frustration or boredom—to give her upper arm a nip, Linda took this as rejection. When Millie rocked forward, Linda waited; if she didn't follow this up by turning away, she took it as an affirmation: This was what Millie wanted to say. "We're just babbling," she explained to us. "I'm not thinking she understands what is going on." But Millie seemed to take pleasure in the experience. Indeed, the entire session at the computer went on far longer than I would have expected Millie to tolerate without whining, flinging her arms about, or becoming obsessed with the cord.

Clearly, we were in the presence of genius, and I couldn't help but feel a bit jealous. Earlier, I'd made the mistake of mentioning an activity I'd described in the paperwork for Linda—the one where Millie and I sit on the floor together and I imitate her sounds. "Let's try that now," Linda said, and I got up to move Millie. "Wait!" said Linda, waving the book at me. I was supposed to be using it with Millie now. She demonstrated the sequence—"I have something to say," "I want to do something," "I want to change your position," "Let's sit on the floor"—and we settled on the carpet. With all eyes on us, and the cameras rolling, I tried to get Millie's attention. I blushed. No dice. Millie's lips had curled back into a snarl, and her teeth were clicking as she bit at her arm. Linda thrust the book into my hand. My early alarm was catching up with me. "I have something to say," I muttered softly, then realized I did not. Somehow I found the pathway that allowed me to tell Millie I had no idea what was wrong. "Maybe it's lunch time," Linda concluded. After some discussion, we set out for Whole Foods to fetch some salads, leaving Xiaona and Greta behind to feed Millie another sandwich.

As we ate, Linda shared her conclusions. Or, rather, she invited Xiaona, Greta, and me to offer observations, then commented on what we said. A moment passed, and I wondered whether I should tell Linda what I was really thinking: "Millie just loves your voice." Instead, I settled on a more technical observation. "I was impressed by how closely she watched the screen." There ensued a long discussion about the advantages of hand switches versus head switches, like the ones Cassidy was using. "She has good control of her head," Linda noted. "But then she is so mobile. It's hard to know how you could set one up." Linda mentioned the Rett syndrome girls she has worked with, who also had trouble with motor planning.

I chimed in: "When Millie is really into something, she doesn't have any trouble reaching for it."

"Yes," Linda replied, "that's like the Rett syndrome girls. When you ask them to perform, they can't."

When it came time to leave, Linda had me practice one more time with the nine-icon PODD book. "I have something to say," I chirped loudly, waving my hand in front of Millie. Food had helped us both. Millie glanced at the piece

BECOMING AN OPERATING SYSTEM

of paper, then looked down, softly smiling. The next day, Linda and I had the following exchange of emails:

> DANILYN: Thank you for spending the day with all of us. It was amazing. I look forward to staying in touch! P.S. Millie was in a very good mood this evening!
>
> LINDA: Glad she was in a good mood... maybe she likes having more say and not being told so much about what to do—like most teenagers.
>
> DANILYN: :) A lesson my son has tried to teach me for years!

Linda would say that Millie has a mind of her own, a mind that her method could reveal. And she could be right. Perhaps Millie is a stubborn teenager, just like Cassidy is a prom queen in the social world made possible by PODD. And yet I also sense that what Millie found most seductive about PODD was the sound of Linda talking, the rip of Velcro, and the fluttering of paper under her nose. This communication contraption affirms the personhood of its users. Like Cassidy's prom dress, PODD conjures familiar American figures: free thinkers and rebellious teens, the stuff of situation comedies and domestic dramas, the characters Americans expect to meet in everyday life. But there may be more to what PODD communicates than one might think.[8]

I'M SITTING ON A leather chair, to the right of my new acquaintances Luisa and Ana, a fellow mother and her disabled daughter, who are nestled together on an overstuffed beige couch. Xiaona is leaning into another couch to my left, holding her bangs away from her forehead, relaxed but attentive. Millie is perched next to her on the edge of her seat, head down, absorbed in the fringe of her scarf. Occasionally, a slight smile comes to her face. A few minutes earlier, when I was midway through asking Luisa a question, Millie interrupted me with a little humming noise. "Millie, are you laughing at your mother?" She didn't meet my eyes, but her smile grew slightly broader.

Ana, by contrast, has a laserlike focus on her mother. Her glossy mop of dark hair is pressed against Luisa's shirt, and her eyes slowly track between her mother's face and mine as we converse. Luisa has an arm draped around Ana's shoulder, and she's gently scratching Ana's scalp, keeping time with her daughter's subtly shifting mood. With Luisa's other hand, she's drawing a figure in the air.

"But many times she wants to be with Dad, too." Luisa points at Ana's head. "So, she'll go back and forth between beds." Luisa gestures back and forth, tracing her daughter's movement through the house, then throws up both her hands: What to do?

Ana looks up at her mother, grinning.

"Yes." Luisa raises her eyebrows, then plants two quick kisses on Ana's forehead to end the tale.

Luisa speaks with a slight accent, a reminder of her childhood in the Dominican Republic. And she speaks with her body. Luisa's husband, a dentist, grew up in Lebanon; Ana is their fourth child. Luisa's Spanish-speaking mother and her Arabic-speaking mother-in-law were both living with the family when Ana was born. Ana and her mother are both short, a bit stocky, and striking, with the openness of Luisa's sparkling eyes matched by the intensity of Ana's smoky gaze. "We're very attached," Luisa tells me. No kidding. The two are joined at the hip.

We made the trip to this suburban ranch house two hours from Santa Cruz so I could interview Luisa, whom Xiaona met at a PODD training several months before. Luisa told me Ana's story over lunch, amid the scramble involved in feeding our daughters—walking them to their seats; getting out bibs, tumblers, and sippy cups; spooning appropriate portions onto plates; keeping their hands out of the food. Like Millie, Ana is seventeen. She doesn't use a communication system or any conventional signs. Unlike Millie, Ana has a diagnosis: Angelman syndrome, once pejoratively known as happy puppet syndrome, a genetic condition characterized by seizures, low muscle tone, intellectual disability—and smiling. People with Angelman syndrome are known for being affectionate. In the entrance hall, when Xiaona was getting Millie out of her wheelchair, Ana lumbered over to me, beaming, and gave me a big hug.

Over lunch, we also talked about PODD. Luisa had borrowed a twenty-icon book, but she was having trouble getting going with it. "I'm stuck." She demonstrated the difficulty. "I mean like this," Luisa said, gesturing toward the platter of fried chicken and sweet potatoes. "I don't know how to slow down and use my communication book. It's easier just to say, 'Honey, here are some sweet potatoes.' Instead of"—Luisa pantomimed pointing at a PODD book and flipping through it to find the right icons to capture what she wanted to say to her daughter—"'Honey, here are some sweet potatoes.'"

In the living room, I bring the conversation back to PODD. "So, what attracted you to PODD in the first place?"

Luisa weighs her answer. "Because it makes sense," she finally says, with a sweep of her arm. Ana snuggles up against her mother more tightly; she's been squirming, but now she grows still.

"Because you are having the child choose." She opens her palms in a welcoming gesture. "You're basically having a conversation through pictures."

Over Ana's head, Luisa waves one finger, then responds with another, pointing at an array of imaginary icons. "And it's slowing you down to communicate, which allows the person you're talking to to digest what you're trying to say. So it's kind of a win-win."

Luisa was inspired by a video that Linda showed at the training. It followed the progress of several of her clients. "You could see where they started and how far they had come. It was motivating. You know, it is something that you can look forward to."

What is she looking forward to? I wonder. "What are your hopes for Ana?"

"Oh my gosh." Luisa speaks slowly, letting the ideas come to her. "Oh, just so she can be able to tell us how she's feeling." Luisa rests her hand on her forehead, pushing her hair back from her eyes. "What hurts her. What she doesn't want, what she wants." She sighs. "Just to have that."

I think of Millie: I'd love all that, too. And yet I feel a twinge in my stomach. My worry seeps out. "I got interested in PODD through this research, and I've felt very attracted to it. But Millie has her own way of being with us, and I wouldn't want to devalue it."

"Yes." It sounds like she's agreeing with me, but she's going in a different direction. "And the thing is, we ourselves are able to communicate in a variety of ways." Luisa gently strokes her daughter's hair out of her eyes. At the same time, she talks with her free hand, flexing her wrist, then opening her fingers to show "variety." "Why can't we do the same thing with the kids, too? With you, I use body language." She raises her eyebrows. "And you get what I'm trying to say."

I nod. As if to confirm what her mother has just told me, Ana raises her head slightly and looks at me, then scratches behind her right ear.

Luisa pauses to see what Ana is doing, then reaches down to hold her hand. "You OK?" She's talking softly.

"You got something in your ear." I smile at Ana.

"Yeah," Luisa coos.

"Yeah," I repeat in the same gentle, high-pitched tone.

"Yeah," Luisa says again. She has found the itchy spot on Ana's scalp and is gently scratching it. Ana settles again, soothed by our caresses and the sound of our voices.

"And so," Luisa's voice is firmer. She sweeps her free arm though the air. "What is to say they can't do the same thing?"

Later that afternoon, as we drive home through the mist, I will reflect on what Luisa has told me. I will think of the phone call Luisa received in the middle of lunch from her second daughter. "How are you?" Luisa had frowned into the receiver, unsatisfied with her daughter's answer. "Are you okay? Tell me. No, no, tell me." The story had tumbled out—Luisa's daughter's best friend's mother was in the ICU with end-stage cancer, and Luisa's daughter was distraught. I will think of another parent I interviewed who has a twenty-two-year-old daughter named Helene, a graceful, cognitively atypical woman who lives in a group home on the other side of town. Helene is verbal. "She's always telling me she has a stomachache," Pauline sighed. "But I never really know whether her stomach is hurting. She needs something, but I can't tell what it is." And I will think of a moment, late in our visit, when Ana suddenly left her mother's lap and lunged at me, frowning, her hands reaching for my hair. Parents of children with Angelman syndrome are among PODD's most vocal proponents. I can see why. Ana seems so transparent, but this impression is misleading. Luisa is right: Touch and words are both insufficient. One way of communicating is never enough.

THE DAY AFTER MILLIE'S first PODD session, Linda sent me a follow-up email about a consent form I had sent her. "Just so you know," she wrote back to me, "I'm a special educator, not a speech therapist." The distinction Linda drew opens onto a wider story than the one I've told here: The debate over nontraditional communication methods has driven a wedge between experts, pitting psychologists and speech and language pathologists against special educators and occupational therapists. At issue is the question whether people like Cassidy or D.J. Savarese are actually using these systems to speak: The psychologists and speech and language pathologists tend to be skeptical. In the class I took on assistive and augmentative communication, our teacher spoke favorably of alternative approaches. My fellow students had imbibed the opposing view in their other classes. During the break, they scoffed at the administrators of a local school district, who had taken the unusual step of promoting PODD.

This wider story is about power, professional authority, and resources. It is but the latest installment in a long series of struggles over whether certain persons are in fact persons. In 1772, the masters of Phillis Wheatley, an enslaved African in Boston, had trouble raising the funds they needed to publish a collection of the young poet's verses. In 1892, Helen Keller and Annie Sullivan had to face a panel of judges to prove that Keller had really written a short story. Writers from groups seen as inherently incapable of literacy have long been cast as parrots and frauds.[9]

The debates over facilitated communication are particularly fraught. People with poor motor control have trouble selecting letters and typing, and some alternative communication methods, like the one Savarese uses, involve an assistant gently stabilizing the user's hand or arm. A team of researchers recently used eye tracking to show that autistic letterboard users, who also depend on partners, are the authors of their own utterances. The users consistently looked for the next letter of the word they were spelling before pointing with a pencil to indicate their choice. The study offered strong evidence in support of the method, but it couldn't make a dent in the opposition to this way of speaking.[10] In calling herself a special educator, Linda is telling me what side she's on in this battle. For all kinds of important reasons, it's a side I share. The lives of disabled people, and the livelihoods of those who make a living as their allies and advocates, depend on our willingness to challenge those who refuse to acknowledge the agency of people like Millie. And yet my relationship with Millie has alerted me to questions that the debate leaves out.

Neither the dominant view of communication nor the alternative that I have discussed here is monolithic: They form an unstable pair.[11] Luisa voiced a concern common among parents with disabled children about the danger of low expectations, the danger of letting others tell us what our loved ones can or can't do. She was rightly critical of the school system, with its lack of services, and the need for her daughter to be offered more. I could see why Luisa wanted to try PODD. I could also sense that she shared my ambivalence. No matter who we're talking to, we're always broadcasting on multiple channels.[12] The pitch of our voice, a shrug of the shoulders, a touch—mere words are never enough. If communication is multimodal, it's because none of our modes are adequate. It's not just the mothers of disabled daughters who dream of closing the gap. From the language of the body to the language of PODD, there moves the desire for a communion so perfect that there would be no need for signs. Deep inside me, that little pilot light of longing burns for this.

To make sense of this desire, it helps to turn from what people dream of to what they do. The anthropologist Patrick McKearney did research in an English care home for the severely disabled.[13] There, when care providers gather to chat in the kitchen or sitting room, they never speak of the residents in the third person if the people they're discussing are present; instead, they include them in the conversation, whether they seem to be listening or not. "You were really happy when you moved here from Manchester," a seasoned staff member might say to a nonverbal resident who walks by while he's explaining the man's life history to a new volunteer. Care providers don't need a theory about what's running through a resident's mind to engage in this kind of interaction. Rather, they just need to trust the resident—trust in their status as a worthy interlocutor: a "you" to be addressed rather than just a "they" to be described. To speak to them in the second person, rather than about them in the third, is to accept them without needing to understand everything that is happening in their heads. This is not just true of the care providers McKearney spent time with. Most people worry a lot less about other people's thoughts than some psychologists seem to believe.

And when people do worry, that's not good news. As McKearney sees it, it signals a breakdown, rather than the smooth functioning of relationships. For Luisa and me, and other parents who have experimented with PODD, this breakdown comes when something happens that casts doubt on our bonds with the people we care for. We bump up against American norms concerning what it is to be a person. We find ourselves wondering whether we've been missing something key. It suddenly seems like an ethical violation not to seek out every possible avenue to help our loved ones make their intentions known. In practice, PODD leaves these desires and doubts behind in a flutter of turned pages and waved paper icons and the syncopated rhythm of animated and monotonous words. The model is language development, and the pace is leisurely. We tell ourselves that we are doing the right thing. Every time we reach for the book of icons, we are respecting the limits of our understanding without giving up on the dream of knowing more. Both the dream and its abandonment are essential to PODD. And to communication wherever it occurs.

In the end, PODD is not just a strategy for knowing another's thoughts; it's a mechanism for creating shared experience. In this, there is an equally strong ethic involved. I'm watching YouTube.[14] A neatly dressed brunette in her thirties stands at a podium. She is speaking stridently. The special educator Erin Sheldon is exhorting the parents in her audience to rethink what a communication system is and can be.

The stakes are high.

> I dare you to go into wherever you go, McDonalds, Starbucks, wherever you go, with your child's system and order something to eat. And just experience that. Experience that silence that happens around you. And then think about what that must feel like for our kids every time the stars align and they actually manage to reach out and say something with a system. How many times they must actually feel like a freak. Being the only person who has to talk with an iPad, the only person who has to talk with a paper book or a PECS symbol. If we do it, too.

She pauses, mastering her emotion.

> If we argue with our spouses with it, if we make our "honey do" list and nag them with their communication system, then we're making our child

not alone. We're surrounding them with a whole community that says, "We so value your communication that we're willing to communicate with it, too." If we can do that for our kids, then we've really changed things."

Not being alone: This is the gift that PODD promises to disabled people. But it is also the gift it promises to their care providers—their operating systems—who can look forward to a community that they can also make their own as they step into their loved one's shoes. The labor of PODD—the hard work it takes to incorporate PODD into one's daily life—is the glue that holds this world in place.

A friend who uses PODD with her daughter told me about a mother she knows who has gotten in the habit of speaking PODD without the book. "I have something to say!" she'll call out cheerfully, while driving her minivan with her children in tow. Then comes the neutral mutter: "More to say. Let's go. Places." Triumphant, she completes the utterance with a flourish. "We're going to the store!" PODD is special but not unique: Every communication system feeds pleasures and spawns dreams. And every communication system relies on what lies beyond its limits. That mother is right. There is always "more to say."

YOU NEVER KNOW. Beth Harry's daughter, Melanie, her first child, was born in Trinidad, small, weak, and terribly sick.[15] Her skin was "ash gray," according to her father, Clive, and her cry was "a tiny hooting sound" so feeble that her mother could barely hear it.[16] For over a month, she lay in an incubator, muscles rigid, her head twisted to one side. Clive was an economist. Originally from Jamaica, Beth was a lecturer at the University of the West Indies; she'd met her husband in Toronto. She called their daughter "Baby Bird."

Melanie had soulful brown eyes. But she couldn't suck or swallow, and she seemed to lack the capacity for peristalsis, the involuntary constriction and relaxation of the muscles involved in digestion. Beth and Clive took their daughter to specialists. Eventually, they ended up back in Toronto, where Beth had family and Clive's agency had an office. With hard work and prayer, Beth succeeded in getting food to stay in Melanie's stomach. She and the doctors also began noticing some remarkable things about her child. Melanie couldn't move her pupils, but she did look at people—it seemed like she was turning away from them, but she was really peering at them out of the corner of her eye. She wasn't capable of forming words, but she vocalized in meaningful ways; when people talked to her, she seemed to understand. In the mid-1970s, CT scans were new and considered somewhat unreliable. But when Melanie was four, a doctor talked Beth and Clive into having her brain examined.

"Gross global brain damage with severe mental retardation"—that had been the original assessment.[17] It turned out that the little girl was almost entirely missing her cerebellum, but her cerebral cortex was intact. Without a cerebellum, Melanie had difficulties keeping her balance and controlling the muscles in her eyes, hands, throat, and face. But her cognitive abilities were unaffected. One thing was certain: Melanie had lots of things to say.

Millie was ten months old when she had her brain scanned. By 2001, the technology of choice was an MRI. I sat beside the technician in the dark, windowless studio, as the machinery whirred and whined around my anesthetized little daughter. I watched the pinpoints of light form into shapes on the screen and wondered if something was missing. Nothing was. My sister, who is a geneticist, thinks Millie must have a condition that affects myelination, the process that fixes the neural circuitry that comes into being when children develop new habits of thought and action. This sounds right to me; Millie learns, but at her own pace. There's no magic bullet. No secret truth that could be exposed to a camera. I don't know if Millie has anything to say. And I can't deny that this makes me sad.

Beth Harry writes with pride and disarming clarity about her daughter. Melanie learned to walk with support, and she was learning to read when she choked on a piece of bread. Melanie was six at the time, and Beth had left her with a friend while she ran an errand. She tried to explain the Heimlich maneuver on the phone, but it was too late. A dark, shuddering dread descended on me as I read of Beth's flight across the crowded city to her dying daughter: the traffic lights that turned red right as she was approaching them, the snarl of cars and trucks on the side streets, the ticking time bomb that was her heart. Sorrow has many stories to tell.

Proprioceptive Sociality

"Hand over hand." In Millie's huge stack of Individualized Education Programs (IEPs), this kind of assistance pops up the most. The language in these texts is rarely pretty. Here's how one of Millie's short-term objectives reads: "By January 2019, student will participate in enjoyable and challenging activities, signing 'finished' with gentle tactile prompt/hand over hand assistance at elbows from behind when finished or when needs to leave activity due to showing signs of overstimulation or discomfort." The document quantifies this achievement: "2/5 trials on 4/5 trial days." Translation: Millie will put up with an adult grabbing her elbows and making her hands make the sign for "done" when she starts acting in ways that look unhappy. Millie has been offered this kind of help for years.

When Millie was little, it was all about picking up small blocks and dropping them into buckets. On a visit to Blair, I watched a therapist wrap her adult hands around Millie's toddler hands, easing her fist open, then closing it around a cube of wood. Together, the two of them lifted the load together. Pivoting like a crane on a building site, they swung the block into position. I held my breath, waiting for Millie to complete the deed. A perennial goal was to get Millie to relinquish the block without having to pry her fingers off the prize.

Giving Millie help and having her accept it isn't as easy as it might seem. I reach for Millie's hand in hopes of guiding it to the magic marker I've laid out for us to draw with. She welcomes my touch for a second, then seems to realize I have designs on her appendage and snatches it away. Ralph and my dad used to love to play this game in which Ralph stood with his feet on his grandfather's, and they walked together around my parents' living room in Wisconsin. You can only do this sort of thing with a willing partner—someone ready to relax into the experience of two bodies acting as one. At first, I was skeptical of hand-over-hand assistance. It took me back to the tea parties I used to hold for my stuffed animals—the action, the characters, even the tea were make-believe. No amount of play-acting can bring a toy to life. Could play-acting really teach Millie to act on her own?

The answer turned out to be yes. Millie did learn to perform some of the feats listed on her IEPs. It's Millie's last year in school, and Xiaona spears a chunk of apple, then eases the fork into Millie's hand. Millie's motions are jerky, but she seems to get the concept. She opens her mouth. The piece of silverware begins its unsteady journey. The tines are akimbo when the fork arrives, but somehow the apple survives the trip. Then comes a bang as the fork hits the floor near Millie's feet. Xiaona sighs. "She won't give it back to me." I imagine Millie's reasoning: Now that the fork has served its purpose, it no longer exists. Teeth brushing works a bit better. Millie maintains a death grip on the brush as she chews the bristles, her lips glistening with spit and foam. To get her teeth really clean, the dentist has to anesthetize her. She's not going to get a job as a dental hygienist. But she seems to get the general idea.

For the therapists, hand-over-hand assistance has always been a means toward an end. I'm not sure it feels that way for Millie. It has stopped feeling that way for me. I got Millie up on a Saturday morning not long ago. When it was time to feed her breakfast, I took the easy route and wielded the silverware myself. As I was bringing a spoonful of oatmeal to Millie's mouth, she reached out to grab my wrist. But she didn't want me to give her the spoon. When I released it, it clattered to the floor. Millie's face was placid, but there was an expectant gleam in her eye. Did Millie want to help me? I fetched a fresh spoon, and when I loaded it for the trip to Millie's mouth, her hand shot out again. She cooed with pleasure as her fist closed over mine. I could be wrong but I swear she wanted to give me a hand-over-hand assist.

It's been a long time since I worried about Millie meeting her goals and objectives. As I am writing this, Millie is about to age out of the school system.

Over the years, a long parade of teachers and therapists has worked with Millie. I wonder whether she'll miss all those hands wrapped around hers. I know I will. Having all these adults so invested in my daughter made me feel much less alone. But as it turns out, the lessons aren't over—Millie will be giving them herself. Once or twice a week, she'll visit one of the local kindergartens and play the children a story on her laptop. Her work experience specialist is pulling together documents so the school district can hire her for this job. She won't be pushing the button to start the recording. She'll be working with hand-over-hand assistance from one of her aides. I no longer think of this as play-acting. Everyone everywhere works in concert with others. No human anywhere ever achieves anything on their own. Millie is uniquely attuned to this feature of our species. Why shouldn't she be paid to model it for the kids?

TOUCH PROVIDES MILLIE WITH a way of connecting with other people. I should have noticed this much earlier in Millie's childhood, but I was obsessed with the fact that she wouldn't look me in the eye. The ability to perceive what another person is perceiving is the first step toward understanding what another person is saying, according to most accounts of normal language development.[1] Sight and sound loom large in this scholarship. One camp holds that people's relationships with one another begin with the visual ability to picture the world as another person sees it. Another describes how speech helps us imagine the impression we make on others because we can hear ourselves talk.[2] But Millie has taught me there are other senses that people come to share when they use minds and bodies in different ways.

One of the main ways in which touch becomes social for Millie is through "proprioception," the feeling of one's own body in space. Proprioception is what enables a figure skater to soar through the air, twirl three times, and land gracefully on her feet. For years, it allowed my father to watch football and drink lemonade without ever pouring it down his shirt. A close look at proprioception, as Millie and others like her seem to experience it, puts a new spin on how the senses make us humans into the social creatures we are. Narrowly speaking, touch differs from proprioception. The English neurophysiologist Charles Scott Sherrington distinguished proprioception from "exteroception," the perception of what's outside us, and "interoception," which includes sensations like a stomachache or burning lungs. I'm using touch metaphorically to capture how all these abilities involve feeling and being felt.[3] Understood this way, proprioception has the potential to do with touch what a mirror does with vision or a recording does with voices: It can put us in conversation with our own bodies. In doing so, it can also help us develop what I can only call fellow feeling: a sense of connection with other people. Every time I interact with Millie, we enter into a "communion of mutual engagement"; proprioception helps us perform this feat.[4]

I find it helpful to draw comparisons. At the age of nineteen, a British man named Ian Waterman permanently lost his sense of proprioception. In May 1971, the young butcher was apprenticing in a shop in Southampton, England, when he cut his finger.[5] The accident was followed by an infection that set off a chain reaction. A rare disease destroyed the part of his nervous system that controls proprioception and forced him to develop new strategies for accomplishing basic tasks, like walking, sitting down, and driving a car. Millie, by contrast, is what physical therapists call "proprioception seeking": The feeling doesn't come naturally to her, but she still wants it. If Millie were sitting in front of you, you'd see that her trunk is in constant motion. This is one of the ways she seeks this feeling out.

The neurological differences that shape Waterman's and Millie's experiences of the world affect some very basic bodily functions. Proprioception controls muscle tone and motor coordination, which you may be using to sit still while you're reading this, and, most relevant here, the sense you have of where your body is located in relation to the floor and chair. For Waterman, proprioception is impossible. For Millie, proprioception is a challenge, a pleasure, and a collaborative project involving her other senses and other persons, including me, who help provide her with the input she lacks. Technologies are features of our daily lives that only jut into awareness when they malfunction: The skillful hand becomes one with the chisel until the blade breaks.[6] Proprioception is like that. It's not a sense people make much of until they are in situations that force them to experience it directly—perhaps in meditation; definitely when neurological disease or difference puts it on the agenda of their awareness as something they must actively do. Waterman completely lost his chisel, as it were, and was forced to fashion another with the ingredients of his intact senses. Millie was born with a curved tool, which she has learned to hold steady with the help of partners who enable her to enjoy its use in an active way. Millie has learned to dance the dance of proprioception with others. Waterman simply stopped going to the ball.

I'm not the first anthropologist to explore how touch can become a vehicle for forming relationships. The linguistic anthropologist Terra Edwards has done pathbreaking research with DeafBlind people in Seattle.[7] Most members of the community learned American Sign Language as children, then lost their sight as adults. Over time, they have developed ways to use touch without the aid of intermediaries to do the linguistic work that other speakers accomplish with sound and sight. Instead of seeing language, they learned to feel it taking shape as they tap each other's hands and guide each other's limbs into forms conveying the meaning of words. Millie may not use her fingers to speak, but a current of warmth and interest passes between us whenever she rests her hand on mine. Touch foregrounds how beings affect and are affected by one another, simultaneously. One can see without being seen, but one cannot touch without being touched, at least in the absence of the machineries of distancing and emotional hardening involved in drone warfare, police violence, and domestic abuse. Touch binds us, whether it results in communication, care, control, or harm.[8]

Perhaps not surprisingly, proprioception plays a key role in conversations among DeafBlind people. To describe a lollipop, a DeafBlind speaker will take her partner's fingers, fold them into a fist, and raise them so that his hand and arm take the shape of the candy.[9] For the conversation to continue, the speaker's partner has to be able to feel not just her fingers, but also how his own hand is positioned and posed. It's common to think of touch as involving persons bounded by the surface of their skin. Proprioception goes deeper, to the place where humans and other vertebrates touch and are touched by their own bodies in a fashion that places them viscerally in the world. Like sound or sight, proprioception is an affordance, a resource that can connect people. Like the noise that becomes a word, or the sight that becomes a sign, proprioception requires framing—it must be perceived in a certain way to become instrumental in the forging of social ties.[10] When perceived in the fashion Millie and Waterman bring to light, proprioception invites reflection on how people build social worlds within and beyond the normalizing regimes of speech and sight.

FOR IAN WATERMAN, IT all began with a bad case of the flu—so bad that after a week of growing weakness and exhaustion, he checked himself into the hospital. He woke up the next morning on the ward unable to move his arms, legs, and trunk. He could shift his gaze, and he could raise his head, but he had no voluntary control over the parts of his body that would have gotten him out of bed and into the bathroom to brush his teeth. With a great deal of concentration, he found he could raise his arm. But he could not direct it, and it ended up hitting him in the face. Other than a faint tingling, he had no feeling from the neck down.

Jonathan Cole, Waterman's neurologist, describes what happened in his biography of his patient. Waterman was suffering from Guillain-Barré syndrome, a rare condition that attacks the peripheral nervous system. The infection had caused a reaction that destroyed the circuitry involved in two kinds of sense perception: what neurologists call "light touch," which is felt on the surface of the skin, and "deep touch," which delivers input from the muscles. Waterman had no access to information from his fingertips. But equally importantly, he had no access to information from what lay below them: the tendons, ligaments, and delicate motor structures involved in carving or picking up a coin. Cole describes what is involved in these actions: "Within the muscles are tiny nerve endings which respond to stretch and so to active contraction and passive stretching of the muscle. There are 20,000 of these muscle spindles, and they give information about limb position and movement."[11] An impulse in a motor neuron contracts a muscle, and the muscle ignites a spindle, which leads to an impulse conveying information to the brain. This leads to further motor impulses that adjust the muscle and the joints and tendons that surround it, whose receptors fire in turn, allowing the brain to feel where these body parts are and what they're doing. Proprioception is the sense that results from this interplay of touching and being touched.

In 1934, the American philosopher George Herbert Mead coined the phrase "the conversation of gestures." He used it to describe what happens in the course of an interaction: Those involved constantly send each other subtle little updates that capture who they are and what's going on. Let's picture what this means. It's 2005, and I'm pushing Millie on the baby swing in the park down the street from our house. The mother of the toddler in the swing next to us strikes up a conversation. "How old is your daughter?" she asks. Millie has settled peacefully into the motion, looking cute in the pale pink sweater my mother gave her for her birthday. I grin. "She just turned five." The mother's smile stiffens. In her eyes, her next question takes shape, the one she doesn't want to ask: What the hell is wrong with this child?

"She's developmentally delayed," I explain, a bit too brightly. "Oh," she answers, then turns to straighten her son's collar. She can't think of anything else to say. And neither can I. When I speak, I anticipate the way you will view the world and me as a result of my utterance. Your subtlest reaction—a tiny smirk, a glance over my shoulder—can lead me to rethink what's happening and adjust my approach. Are you mocking me? My words trail off into embarrassment. Are you thinking of something else? I lean in and try to catch your eye. What I get back from you determines what I give next and what I make of the whole encounter after it's done. And you, of course, are doing the same thing. Social action is only social when it occurs in the light and warmth of another person's response. The conversation of gestures continually defines and redefines what, in the wake of the interaction, we will imagine we've been doing: arguing, agreeing, or maybe acting like fools.

Proprioception is critical to the conversation of gestures: To talk, smile, or watch for a frown requires the coordination of delicate movements in one's lips, throat, eyes, and posture. It's no accident that the highest concentration of muscle spindles is found in the neck.[12] In this sense, social life is proprioceptive. But at the same time, on a deeper level, proprioception is social. I'm not simply referring to the lesson the French sociologist Marcel Mauss taught anthropologists long ago, when he explained the social origins of bodily habits: why Parisians, say, swim differently than New Yorkers do—in Mauss's day, gulping water and spitting it back out—and have a different gait when they walk.[13] Rather I have in mind the fact that, by virtue of this capacity, movement, like meaning, is emergent. Through constant, minute adjustments, we vertebrates accommodate movement to touch, and touch to movement. In this sense, proprioception is sociality incarnated. Adjustments in position inspire further adjustments: To reach for a jar is no less interactional than to converse. In proprioceptive sociality, to borrow the anthropologist Kamala Russell's words, "The way one is near others is the key issue."[14] Proprioception creates a space where the brain is other to the limbs, and the muscles are other to the nerves. Our first partner in the conversation of gestures lies within.

I'm speaking metaphorically. But not entirely. It's a truism of cognitive research that children are slow to grasp that others have their own mental states; even toddlers don't have a fully developed "theory of mind." The developmental psychologist Vasudevi Reddy had absorbed this wisdom. Then she had a baby of her own. Now she is certain: "Any bridge across the so-called gap between self and other must involve bodies, not just brains."[15] This means it must involve proprioception. Studies have shown that infants as young as two weeks old have a visceral reaction when others fix them with their gaze. They experience the connection between the "looking eyes" and their object, that is, themselves, as "perceptual, emotional, and proprioceptive."[16] When an adult smiles at a typical newborn, the baby can feel it from head to toe. Reddy's account is dotted with seeing, but sight isn't essential to her argument. Cradled in my arms on our roof deck in Chicago, Millie wouldn't have looked if I had pointed out the parakeets. But she may well have felt the attention I was paying her, with our hearts beating together and my words vibrating in her ear.

Waterman did not lose all his peripheral functions, and this turned out to be helpful. He could feel pressure and exhaustion, which helped him compensate for what he had lost. Cole's book describes how Waterman taught himself to move again through sheer force of will by using his vision to locate his limbs and control their movements. If he could see a part of his body, he could use that part of his body, and he managed to achieve a level of function that allowed him three years later, at the age of twenty-two, to walk, drive, climb stairs, and hold down a desk job. (Butchering was out.) But he was completely dependent on his eyesight to accomplish these feats. Dark hallways were a problem, and if the lights suddenly went out while he was standing, he would crumple to the floor. Unlike stroke victims, who often regenerate neural circuits, Waterman never recovered from his condition. The name of his biography, *Pride and a Daily Marathon*, is apt: "Pride, bloody pride, and a daily marathon" are what helped him get by.

Waterman learned to move skillfully enough to pass as "normal." But this came at a cost. If Waterman's fortitude is one theme in Cole's book, his solitude is another. No one he knew could imagine what he was going through. At the beginning of the ordeal, friends who visited him in the hospital had no idea why he was paralyzed. Later, when they met him on the street, all they could see was that he walked with a limp. "To feel that someone somewhere had an understanding of the problem would have been comforting," Waterman told Cole. "I was on the scrap heap, deserted."[17] To make matters worse, the mental effort it took to keep the conversation between his brain and his limbs going smoothly left him exhausted. "To cope, I have become selfish with my time and energy. . . . This makes me misanthropic, though I try hard not to be."[18] Waterman enjoyed two significant relationships over the course of twenty years—one with his first wife, who died young, and the second with his second wife, who was his companion in early retirement. But in his effort to be self-reliant, he turned other people away. "I feel I have been too quick to rebuff their help. To accept it would probably have helped to build a bond particularly with my family, but possibly I have built a barrier instead."[19] Without that most intimate of companions, the feeling of his limbs in space, Waterman found himself alone.

All this might seem merely circumstantial. But it's not. Touch, as the philosopher Judith Butler once wrote, "reminds us we are undone by one another."[20] It's more than a mere figure of speech to say we've lost touch with a friend. Scholars think of vision and cognition as affordances that make social life possible, and they're not wrong. But there's a basis for relationships that works at a deeper level. Waterman's problem was clearly practical—a matter of cognitive load. But I would like to suggest a further dimension of his predicament. The same interchange of activity and passivity that characterizes proprioception is critical to the creation of social relationships. This is not to say that Waterman lost the capacity to be social because he was without proprioception. Rather, he had to be willing to take advantage of the flexibility that characterizes our species to learn new ways to connect. And, equally importantly, he had to be willing to act in ways that the "normal" people around him would have found deeply strange. Waterman chose not to pursue this strategy. As he saw it, there was no middle ground: He could either be entirely "self-reliant" (entirely active) or entirely dependent (entirely passive). Waterman ran a daily marathon to stave off the prospect of spending his life in a manual wheelchair, unable to move without another person's help.

It took the absence of proprioception for Waterman to appreciate its value; you don't know what you've got until it's gone. Many of Terra Edwards's Deaf-Blind collaborators have had to face a similar change in the channels through which they access the world. Unlike Waterman, they haven't just compensated for what's missing; they've traded eyesight for touch in a fashion that allows them to communicate directly with one another, without having to rely on support staff. They aren't ashamed to act in ways sighted people might find weird. A protactile leader invites newcomers to leave the old ways behind: If they want to know whether someone is eating, they should feel free to feel their face and hands. There is no celebration of difference in Waterman's story—he loathed the idea of being identified with people who were born disabled. He had internalized his society's ableism, but that's not all; the severity of his condition also came into play. Waterman had lost both light touch and deep touch as a result of his illness. Without the pressure to conform, and the loss of surface sensation, he might have been able to accept the touch of others. Having feeling in his hands and fingers would have enabled him to use the world of objects and others to locate himself in space. *Pride and a Daily Marathon* offers one picture of life lived with a neurological difference. Let's consider another, in which a body isn't lost but shared.

MILLIE HAS JUST TURNED twenty and I'm in Santa Cruz, with her in her bathroom, which was originally built to be a study in the Victorian where we live. There are heavy red curtains and honey-colored oak floors, mahogany woodwork, and a chandelier fitted with orange lights. Bookcases border tall windows opening onto the front drive; at their base sits a large tub, still damp from Millie's bath.

Among other bathroom things, the study's bookcases store diapers; I reach for two from the shelf nearest the bath chair, where Millie is perched. I have just pulled Millie out of the tub, grabbing her under the armpits and easing her slippery form over the lip of the tub onto the towel that cushions the plastic. The bath chair is a cheap but sturdy aluminum and plastic bench I found in a back aisle at CVS. Once Millie's weight is on it, I reach for her slender legs, lifting her knees and swiveling her so her feet are on the floor. Now I tip Millie onto her back. Millie flexes her knees and holds her core taut to help me, and when I'm done drying her off, I lower her feet back onto the floor. After rubbing lotion onto her back and applying deodorant, I ease her shirt over her head; again, she helps me, raising her arms so I can slide them into the sleeves. I thank Millie, who has a grave look of concentration on her face. When I make a raspberry noise with my lips, she makes a humming noise that shows she's pleased. She holds still as I comb her short wet hair. Next comes the double layer of diapers, and the leggings, and the socks and ankle braces, and the sports sandals Millie usually wears in the house. And then it's time for Millie to set out for the dining room, where dinner awaits.

As you know by now, the list of typical things Millie cannot do is long. She is legally blind, due to difficulties organizing her visual field. She doesn't talk, feed herself, or reliably use a toilet. She has a wheelchair and rides in an adaptive van. She is a few years older than Waterman was when he lost proprioception, and she is the embodiment of his fears—at least when I describe her in these broad strokes. The truth of the matter, as you have gathered, is that Millie actually can do all of these things, but she does them in her own way. She can use her peripheral vision to pick out an electrical cord or a ribbon on the other side of her bedroom. She will laugh at the sound of a joke. She does pretty well with the toilet if you keep her on a schedule. And, if you help her, she can walk.

Back in the bathroom, I clip Millie's gait belt around her waist; it's made of a wide strip of nylon, equipped with loops. Standing in front of her, I reach for the loops and pull Millie gently onto her feet. Pushing the bath chair out of the way, I ease around her so we're facing in the same direction. Her feet are firmly planted, and her knees are slightly bent. When I nudge her left buttock gently with my left leg, she shifts her right foot slightly forward. "Take a step, Millie," I softly say. I wait to see if she'll move her left foot on her own, before using the same motion to prompt her. This time, she raises her knee and extends her foot further, warming to the task.

The next step, with her right foot, comes unbidden, and it's a big one. She raises her knee high, like a drum majorette leading a band, allowing her foot to waver mid-air before lunging forward into the hall. I'm caught off-guard, and we sway a moment, before I regain my balance and help her regain hers. Millie seems happy. She loves a nice meal. She's also excited to be moving; her next step, with her left leg, is more labored and timid, but it is followed by a huge stride, and she giggles in pleasure as she lands two feet closer to her goal.[21] The evening light is shining through the bank of windows and doors that lead onto the deck from the dining room. Little gray birds rise like glitter from the quaking branches of an olive tree. We both can smell the pasta I just made. We're engaged in a joint project, an unsteady adventure, and I imagine Millie sharing my sense of accomplishment. In front of a heavy ceramic stool, I use my upper body strength to swivel Millie into position. Our journey is complete.

It wasn't until Millie was a teenager that one of her therapists gave me a name for the strange way Millie moves: She was the one who told me that Millie is proprioception seeking. Unlike Waterman, Millie doesn't lack the neural circuitry that would allow her to get feedback from her joints, tendons, and muscles, but the feedback isn't delivered in a reliable way. What she has experienced, when it comes to motor coordination, muscle tone, and the range of capacities associated with "deep touch" is not an absence but a meandering. Millie's development has been slow and singular, and it's left her with a unique set of abilities. Her nervous system makes connections that foreground embodied experiences that might otherwise pass unremarked.

Although I can't know for sure, Millie seems to feel trunk rotation and muscle tone to a degree most people don't. She also feels texture and treasures that sensation: Nothing makes her happier than a chenille scarf. And she feels that form of feeling that is proprioception—she seeks it out. When she pauses mid-air, with her foot waving in the air, she is reaching for a sense of her foot in space. When she sits on her ceramic stool, rocking back and forth and swaying side to side, she is feeling for the position of her trunk. She's not weak; she's as strong as a horse, with plenty of force packed into her slender frame. But she's embodied in a way that amplifies proprioception's conversation of gestures. She is like a tennis pro who has broken down a serve into discrete gestures: The ability to do this may be counterproductive, when it comes to hitting the ball fast and hard, but it reveals very clearly just how to make a complicated stroke. Millie plays a version of the game of locomotion in which winning is beside the point.

Like a tennis pro, Millie brings others into her game. Among Millie's care workers, those of us who have been with her the longest take the lead in training new hires. There are various things to learn, some of them quite standard: medication doses and schedules, food preferences and preparation, bathing and toileting routines. But when it comes to working with Millie, the most challenging and important part of the job involves skills that Millie alone can teach. Andrea has just started working with Millie. Marilyn, who is shadowing her, reports back to me on her progress: "She did great today! Walking is still a challenge, but she's getting the hang of it!" Locomotion Millie-style is the hardest thing to learn.

I can describe it. You shift your weight and wait for her to shift hers, then pull upward on her gait belt, and give her a chance to take a step spontaneously; if she doesn't, you press your knee or thigh against her left buttock to prompt her to lift her right foot. I'm 5′10″ and Millie's much shorter; this method works for me, but it doesn't work the same way for Xiaona, who has a much lower center of gravity because she is roughly Millie's height. Everyone has to learn their own method for sharing in Millie's conversation of gestures: blending their body's circuitries with hers, touching and being touched by Millie as she touches and is touched by herself, allowing themselves to be propelled unsteadily forward in a deliberate dance. Millie loves this dance; I've heard her squeal with glee at the pleasure of being upright and in motion. Just as she loves the dance of the senses involved in sitting in front of my friend when she plays her cello, or when I wave a ribbon in front of her face. Waterman, for his own reasons, couldn't make proprioception into a project involving friends and family: He turned inward and relied on his own brain and eyes. Millie has no objection to living her embodied life collectively. I feel closest to Millie when we are sitting hand in hand, or moving together stride by stride.

This is life lived with a difference, as Waterman's is a life lived with a difference—a difference that slows us down. A difference that brings to our attention those aspects of our embodiment that not only suit us but condemn us to lives lived in concert. Judith Butler was right: We are undone by one another. But in the same conversation of gestures, we are made.

IT COULD HAVE GONE otherwise for Millie. In an alternate reality, she might be moving on her own. In 2008, when Millie was eight and we were living in Vermont, the physical therapist at her school heard about a specialist who had designed a device she thought might help Millie. On a Saturday when Ralph had a play date, I loaded Millie into the car and drove to Burlington for the appointment. I was joined by Iryna, who had arrived from the Russian-speaking part of Ukraine after Danielle's tour of duty had ended. It turned out that the device was a full-length brace, a plastic suit of armor, designed to hold people with poor motor control upright so they could learn what it was like to walk. I looked at Millie, who was leaning back in her stroller watching the ceiling fan, then caught Iryna's eye. She quickly shook her head. Millie wouldn't like this at all. We thanked the specialist and left.

One warm fall day during the same year, when I was with Millie on the enclosed porch in Montpelier, I did an experiment. It turned out that Millie could stand on her own under close supervision, as long as she was leaning against a wall. I stood her against the paneling, her legs firmly planted, and placed my hands on either side of her shoulders. Millie swayed slightly, and I was there to catch her, but she corrected herself before I touched her. She was clearly concentrating. Her spine was erect, and she was looking past my shoulder toward the trees beyond our gravel driveway, not whining, not grimacing, not ducking her head to nip her arm. She remained in place for fifteen minutes without complaining. I was amazed.

I found a different physical therapist, one who lived in Montpelier and shared my aversion to equipment. She convinced Millie's social worker to incorporate this trick into her Vermont IEP. At the meeting, the physical therapist insisted that the exercise could help prepare Millie to walk independently. I nodded; that would be nice. But I was no longer all that obsessed with this milestone. I was more interested in making sure Millie had something fun to do at school. I told myself that Millie enjoyed being on her feet. Standing was good. Standing might be enough. If Millie had learned to walk on her own, new horizons would have opened for her. But we both would have lost the pleasure of walking together.

This pleasure is akin to the embodied pleasures involved in all forms of human interaction. "Don't touch," Linda Burkhart warned us at a recent workshop for parents and care providers that I attended. She went on to explain why we shouldn't physically assist our nonverbal children and clients in using Pragmatically Organized Dynamic Display (PODD). "Otherwise, no one will believe the disabled person can speak."[22] I understand what is gained through this policy: an opportunity for the severely disabled to showcase their humanity by saying "what they want, to whomever they want, however and whenever they want to say it," as Linda Burkhart put it. I appreciate how this kind of communication torques more familiar ways of engaging in speech. PODD, like other methods, slows down the conversation of gestures, teasing apart its elements and logic.[23] It demands patience and an acceptance of bodily rhythms that don't match what many people are used to in this era of shallow sound bites and hasty repartee. But this kind of communion is not the only kind there is. Autistic writers and activists have said as much. "Normal" people try to find symbolism in the distinctive things autistic people do with their bodies. But when people hum, sway, or hand flap, what's really meaningful is a bodily experience of sensory engagement: with things, with other people, and with the world.[24]

There is not just an ethics to these questions; there is also a politics. The Black feminist philosopher Alexander Weheliye has built on the experience of enslaved Africans and their descendants, and other victims of Western violence, to call for a rethinking of what it means to be human.[25] For European thinkers in the eighteenth and nineteenth centuries, enslavement was warranted: They believed that Black people weren't simply lesser humans; they weren't really human at all. To qualify for human status, non-Europeans had to fulfill certain requirements having to do with how they spoke, behaved, and looked. If you were Black or colonized or, I would add, severely disabled like Millie, you were protected by the law only if you acted like someone you were not. A truer understanding of humanity, Weheliye insists, would have little to do with legal litmus tests. It would spring from the acknowledgment that should be accorded anyone who inhabits a body—in Weheliye's words, anyone "enfleshed." Here, Weheliye parts ways with the Italian theorist Giorgio Agamben, who has been popular among anthropologists. Agamben used the term "bare life" to describe people like Millie—people reduced to nothing more than their physical needs.[26] For Weheliye, there is nothing bare about bare life because flesh itself is relational. People in shackles have suffered, but they have also hungered and loved, developed friendships, and dreamed of freedom. The powers that be may strip people of their liberty and their language, but they can't strip them of their ability to touch and be touched.

Proprioception should figure centrally in this new conception of humanity and the political struggles that spring from it. How people navigate together is particularly urgent today when the ground is shifting under everyone's feet.[27] An understanding of how, like Millie, we are dancing whenever we move forces us to confront all the ways we are touched by others.[28] Millie, like all of us, owes her life to strangers: The privilege she enjoys by virtue of the color of her skin has its roots in Atlantic slavery; the struggles of disability activists contributed to creating the government programs she attends each day; her very existence is evidence of lives led and lost by beings of all kinds. Waterman presented himself as autonomous, but the same was true for him.

These connections aren't always obvious. It can take actual contact to bring these links to life. When the Pope kissed the feet of Sudanese negotiators, the faithful argued over whether this meant the Church was ceding power.[29] When Waterman refused to grasp a friend's arm and let her help him up the stairs, he sent a different message: He wasn't going to let anyone else take control. It's easy to be selfish when you have a child like Millie; other people's needs pale in comparison, and all that matters is what's good for her, which, by extension, is good for you. But when Millie strokes my hand, the walls around me crumble, and I feel myself dissolving into a universe that extends beyond anyone or anything I could ever know.

In the end, proprioception is just one thread in the connective tissue of social life. Research on cognitive disability has brought many others to the fore.³⁰ Some are the outcome of the evolutionary history that gave us humans the embodied capacities and limits we are endowed with. Others spring from the histories that gave us the institutions that shape and constrain us and all the other life forms with which we share the earth. Proprioceptive sociality puts all sociality in a new light. We move together before we think together, as the French sociologist Émile Durkheim insisted long ago.³¹ Touch begins in the body. But that's never where touch ends.

"MILLIE'S SUCH A CREATIVE communicator!" Ricky, Millie's new speech therapist, grins at me; I grin back. I just met Ricky, and I already know I like them. They are friendly and cheerful, and the pronouns on their nametag strike me as a good omen. I'm always on the lookout for comrades in arms—people who know that "normal" is overrated. I'm not expecting Ricky to grab Millie's elbows and force her to make the sign for "done."

It's September 2022. Three months have passed since Millie's graduation ceremony in a parking lot next to the Santa Cruz County Office of Education. I sat with three of Millie's care providers, surrounded by her classmates' families and friends. Birds chirped in the nearby forest. Armed with flowers, we listened to speeches about each graduate: who they were, what they liked, and what their teachers would miss about them. We also learned about what they would be doing next: going to a day program, volunteering at the animal shelter, working for Pizza My Heart or one of the handful of other local businesses that hire disabled people. A few had already started bussing tables and stocking shelves.

At this point, Millie is well into her postschool life. She goes to a day program on Tuesdays and Thursdays, where she rides horses; she also rides horses on Wednesday and Saturday afternoons. I was anxious for months—actually years—about what would happen after Millie aged out of the school system. I was sure she would lose access to services as soon as the state no longer had a legal interest in what she learned. Faye Ginsburg and Rayna Rapp have described the dread many of us feel as our children approach adulthood.³² I feared falling off this cliff, but the landing has been soft. Much to my amazement, Millie qualifies to see a new crop of therapists: occupational, physical, and now speech. Ricky works at a clinic, not a school, and their services are covered by Medicare. Speech therapy in a medical setting is not just for stroke victims, it turns out. The government, at least until the next round of budget cuts, is willing to pay for weekly sessions.

It's our first appointment, an evaluation, and Ricky is using the time to get to know Millie. We're sitting on a sunny sidewalk in front of the waiting room; COVID restrictions remain, but it's a nice day, and Millie has trouble wearing a mask. Marilyn is sitting next to me; Vanessa, who just started working with Millie, is in the next chair. Ricky is talking with Millie and taking note of how she reacts: leaning toward Ricky, leaning away from them, smiling faintly, furrowing her brow, shifting her weight, gingerly touching Ricky's sleeve. "I hear you like ribbons!" Ricky announces and dangles a shiny blue one just out of Millie's reach. When Millie grabs for Ricky's hand, their assistant jots something down on a clipboard. I chuckle. "Millie's pretty good at telling you what she wants."

At the end of the session, Ricky turns to me. "What are your goals for Millie?" I glance at Marilyn and Vanessa; they are waiting to hear what I say. I decide to be honest. "My goals are more for us. We need to get better at understanding Millie." Ricky smiles; they get it. Then another thought takes root in my mind. "But it would also be great if she could learn to nod or shake her head. You know, so someone who doesn't know her could get the point?" I think again of all the times I've acted like I know what Millie's feeling. How many times have I been wrong? The right to refuse—the right not to comply—isn't that what "independent living" should really mean? It sure would be nice if Millie could tell me and her other care providers to go to hell.

On Wednesday mornings, Millie visits classrooms. The first story she plays is about a boy who disobeys his teacher during art class and ends up getting trapped in an enormous puddle of glue. Millie's job is to introduce the book and ask the kindergarteners what they think of it when it's over. She is parked in front of the class holding hands with her care provider, Julie; when everyone is settled, electronic talk fills the air. "My name is Millie Best, and I love stories." Later, the class will hear, "Did you like this story? Would you like to hear it again?" It's my voice in the recording, and when I'm in town I'm responsible for connecting the computer to the screen. Marilyn manages the switch device, and Julie holds the button within Millie's reach. Sometimes Millie reaches out to hit it; sometimes she turns away. Millie is teaching the students that it's okay to be dependent. But she's also teaching them it's okay to say no.

part III
millie's flock

Cross Country

I stepped from the van and looked downhill at the dark blue lake and the two-lane state highway that ran beside it. Golden hills, dotted with live oaks, surrounded us. The air smelled of dust, sunshine, and creosote; a hawk circled overhead. It was June 2011, and Millie was ten; we'd been living in Santa Cruz for almost two years. I was midway across the southernmost spur of the Sierras at a truck stop, if you could call it that, on our way from California to Vermont. Two dingy structures stood next to a ridge above the road. Beside the abandoned gas pumps, the gas station windows were plastered with advertisements for sodas that no longer existed. A padlock dangled on the door of the building marked "Café." The parking lot, a huge field of concrete that reached from the buildings to the road, was vacant, other than my Honda Odyssey.

Our family's other car, my Prius, had been visible in my rearview mirror most of the way from Bakersfield, California, the dusty Central Valley city where we'd stopped for gas. When we slowed to a crawl at a construction zone after another hour of driving, I'd caught a glimpse of Ralph and Amy, one of Millie's care providers, a college student who had just graduated and was off to China in the fall. But the beauty of this stretch of highway had distracted me. By the time I remembered to check the rearview mirror again, the Prius was gone. Stop and call each other: That was the plan for if we got separated. I checked my cell phone. No messages. One bar. Then nothing. I glanced back at the road. Still empty. But the Prius could be coming. The driveway was steep—too steep to park on—and we had stopped at the first flat spot. They wouldn't notice us up here. I was going to have to get out and flag them down.

I climbed back into the driver's seat, turned the key so I could roll down the windows, then swung around to talk to Millie, who was sitting in her wheelchair in the middle of the van where a normal Odyssey would have a row of passenger seats.

"Hey, Millie! What are you up to?"

"Mmmm?" She wasn't looking, but, at the sound of my voice, she hummed softly, a smile spreading on her face.

Millie was tugging on the shoestring I'd tied to her shoulder strap. It was one of the curly ones her aunt had given her for Christmas; after pulling it straight, Millie giggled, before letting it snap back into a coil.

I considered lowering the ramp and getting her out, then thought better of it. She was happy. I reached back and patted her thigh, before opening my door again.

"Biak and I will be right back."

Ralph had named Biak the Dog after Biak the Island, where I did field work. The English setter was riding shotgun. He sat at attention while I fastened his leash, then scrambled down from the van, all spots and tufts and silky white fur. Together we headed downhill across the pavement at a trot. At the entrance, while he raised his leg, I looked back up the road we'd just driven down, stretching west for a half a mile before the highway curved out of view, hugging the water as it rounded a peninsula. No Prius. Where could they be?

Amy would be driving, of course; Ralph was still too young. I thought of everything I'd packed into their car. The Prius's back seats were flipped down, and a small cooler was lodged in the crevice behind the driver's seat next to a shopping bag carrying snacks. Millie's disassembled bath chair filled the same space on the passenger side. The cargo compartment held an even layer of luggage and a fold-out mattress arranged to hide my brand new road bike, which I was riding to stay in shape for a rowing marathon later that summer. A cool breeze grazed my shoulders. A lone cloud blocked the sun. The faded green dinosaur sign that marked the truck stop clanged softly as it swung on its chain.

I hadn't seen a car go by, but then again, there were moments when I wasn't looking. Could they have passed us? Would they know to stop? Amy was smart and efficient, but she wasn't an experienced traveler. Ralph was an experienced traveler, but he was only fourteen. From the van, I heard Millie chirp; her giggling was getting louder and taking on a tone of urgency. She needed a bathroom. I could keep driving, but by the time we reached another gas station we would be out of the foothills, and it would be too hot to leave Biak in the car. I would have cell coverage, but who knows how long I'd have to wait until Amy did, too?

I stepped off the road. The cloud had passed, and the wind had died down. All was still. It was the kind of silence that invited crazy musings. When I was a child, on those rare occasions when my mother was late picking me up at school, I passed the time by picturing myself miraculously transported into a different life, in which I was secretly an orphan. Now I found myself playing a version of this game. What if the Prius didn't exist? I imagined what it would be like crossing the country with Millie and Biak solo. Not fun. Maybe not possible. We were two days in, and Millie had slept fitfully, apparently amused by the sounds and smells of the cheap hotel rooms where we were staying. We'd had to stop for every meal—Millie couldn't eat in the car—and each of these interludes had lasted for more than an hour. Amy and I took turns with Millie; Ralph walked the dog. It was only with their help that I managed to fill the gas tanks, go to the bathroom, and get something to eat myself.

I took a deep breath and looked down at Biak, who was nuzzling my leg. I remembered that trip in the Volvo wagon we'd taken with some friends when Millie was five. One of the children wanted to see the Badlands, and Millie had a messy diaper after we turned off the interstate. I had to clean her up at the side of the highway, propped against the passenger door, doing my best to shield her from the tourist traffic whizzing by. At that moment, all I had wanted was to be alone with Millie. A mother-daughter road trip, with no one to help and no one to watch.

Now it looked like I was getting my wish. We could be waiting here forever. We could drink lake water, but how long would we last without food? And how many diapers and wipes had I squirreled away in the back? Would we starve before or after we ran out of those? I pictured a passerby coming across the rusted-out van, shreds of soiled fluff strewn around it, our bleached bones scattered inside. Millie chirped again, pulling me back into the cold reality of my predicament. In the years following Craig's death, I learned to tell myself that I was indestructible and that trouble couldn't touch me. I still wanted to believe this. Except now I wasn't. Except now it could.

I climbed back up the pavement to the van, sat back down in the driver's seat, and looked at my watch. An hour had passed. Three p.m. I took a deep breath and stared through the windshield. The lake water had gone from blue to gray, and the wind had returned and was stirring up ominous little waves. I'd wait for another half-hour, and then we'd drive back up the road and look for the car. The mind game had stopped being fun. My mother had always shown up. But losing Craig had taught me that my loved ones could disappear for good. The Prius existed. Ralph and Amy were in it, and there was a chance they were dead. Their car could have left the road. They could be at the bottom of the lake. The scenario suddenly seemed plausible. Would I never see them again?

Five minutes ticked by, and then I heard it. A faint buzzing, barely audible over the sound of the wind rustling the trees. I walked down the hill, breaking into a jog as the sound grew louder. A blue smudge topped with a black line was approaching. A Prius with a surf rack. It had to be ours. I waved. But it wasn't until the tires crunched through the gravel on the edge of the parking lot that I felt real relief.

The Prius followed me up to the van, and Amy rolled down her window. "We were in an accident."

My breath caught. But Amy seemed fine.

Not to be outdone, Ralph leaned over to chime in. "Someone rear-ended us."

"I have zero cell coverage. I couldn't call. We had to wait for the police. Ralph fixed the bumper with string."

There it was, the panel of plastic, wrenched free from the rest of the car, held in place with a piece of twine.

I looked up from the damage at Ralph's and Amy's excited faces. "I'm so glad to see you guys! Were you hurt?"

Amy smiled. "We're fine. And your bike is fine. But that string isn't going to last. Is this place open?"

DOWN THE ROAD WAS an open gas station with a mini-market and a patch of lawn for walking the dog. Amy took Biak, and I changed Millie. Before heading into the ladies' room, I gave Ralph some money. He used it to buy three rolls of duct tape, which he wound around the damaged bumper, turning the back of the car into a lumpy gray mass. With occasional refreshing, the tape held for the rest of the way across the country, and the rest of the summer, and even for the drive back to Santa Cruz, where I finally had the bumper replaced. I still have nightmares about what would have happened if Ralph and Amy hadn't pulled into that parking lot. The thought of driving farther and looking for help never crossed my mind. Without our quirky little caravan—a rolling residence for my daughter's world—there could be no forward progress. Left to our own devices, Millie and I would still be on the side of that road.

THESE SUMMER ROAD TRIPS from California to Vermont made absolutely no sense. But I still loved Montpelier and the house I had co-owned with the boyfriend. Ralph loved Montpelier, too. As a newcomer, he was a minor celebrity with a gang of loyal friends. Millie was also a celebrity. I couldn't walk with her down Main Street without little girls dragging their mothers over to say hi. Our house was a three-story structure on the edge of acres of undeveloped land, just a mile uphill from Vermont's statehouse. It had custom woodwork, a vintage fireplace, and cathedral ceilings and skylights through which you could see distant mountains and forests coated with snow. Even if we could have sold the house—which proved impossible during the Great Recession—Vermont seemed too good to let go. After I took the position in Santa Cruz, I bought out the boyfriend and found one of Millie's school care providers to take care of the house between our visits. And so began several years in which we led a bicoastal existence, packing up our two cars every June and migrating across the country to spend the summer in Montpelier. I'd always liked to drive, and I was a warrior. I relished the challenges—and the challenges were great.

There was the trip in which I got separated from Marilyn, who got lost on a foggy night in the mountains between Montana and Idaho. I was in the Prius, and I turned right at a fork. Marilyn was in the van with Millie, and she turned left. Once again, I had no cell service. It was a miracle that we found each other. There was Marilyn, standing outside the van in the glow of a gas station where she'd stopped to fill up, not far from the junction where the two roads came back together. She was visibly shaken when I pulled in. I leapt from the Prius without a word, and we hugged each other hard, our eyes filling with tears.

There were the meals at roadside restaurants, where Millie overturned bowls of pasta and spewed breadcrumbs all over the carpet. I would be at the ready with a napkin to catch the scraps. While Millie's care provider for the summer took her to the bathroom, I'd kneel on my hands and knees to clean up the debris, my neck burning from embarrassment. I always left a huge tip.

There was always the nightmare of toileting. I was desperate to have Millie pee in the toilet, so she wouldn't wet herself in the van. Her care provider and I spent long hours waiting for her to do the deed. We often stopped in gas stations that had only one restroom. Long lines formed while one of us sat with Millie, singing to keep her occupied. When it was me, people didn't make eye contact when I finally opened the door and rolled Millie past them, but I sensed their irritation. When Millie's care provider was with her, and I needed to use the bathroom, I sometimes joined the line myself and got to witness the anger firsthand. It was bad, but so was the alternative: If we gave up and she peed in her diaper fifteen minutes down the road, we had to stop again before we had really had a chance to start.

Throughout these adventures, I tried not to imagine what other people were thinking. In restaurants, I sometimes smiled apologetically at nearby diners, but mostly I pretended they didn't exist. But I couldn't help but feel the pressure of their gazes—curious, critical, friendly, empathetic. I avoided looking at them long enough to tell which. I could not avoid talking to some of them, and it was hard to know what to do with their reactions. "I don't know how you do it," the woman at the next basin tells me when I'm washing my hands in a Denny's. "You're a saint." I liked the idea of being Superwoman—I should have gotten the cape—but did she really think that life with Millie was such a drag? Breadcrumbs, sloshed soup, and filthy diapers aside, I loved these trips. And, so, we did our best to travel through America's heartland in a bubble, like songbirds on a flyway thousands of feet in the air. I imagined us soaring past the public, which barely took notice of our strange squad: a beautiful dog, a beautiful boy, two women of varying ages, and a spritely, squirming figure in a wheelchair. We turned our backs on the onlookers. When we struggled, we made it clear we wanted to struggle alone.

Our bubble afforded us moments of beauty and serenity. Crossing Nevada in the late afternoon light, across a landscape of endless possibility: purple mountains lining the route, the desert ablaze, the highway a silver ribbon to the horizon. Spending hours listening to Lucinda Williams, petting the dog as I drove, catching a glimpse of Millie smiling in the rearview mirror. Stopping at Pipestone National Monument and taking the disabled access trail with a friendly Native American ranger who showed us how to see the chiefs' faces in the rocks. Long bike rides on icy highways in Colorado or speeding through dusty red canyons in Arches National Park. Ralph lost in conversation with Amy or whichever young woman accompanied us on that trip—about hip-hop, television shows, movie music, surfing, skating, George Bush. Ralph learning to drive in Nebraska on lonely state highways, then the interstate, supervised by Marilyn, who gave him good marks for his nerves of steel.

For his admissions essay to Lewis and Clark, Ralph wrote about an evening we spent in a small Iowa town, many miles from the interstate. The only place open was a tavern, empty but for two men in overalls who nodded at us when we entered, then turned back to their beers. We ordered burgers, and Millie's care provider and I wheeled Millie to the tiny ladies' room. Ralph ventured out to walk the dog. With the last rays of daylight fading into crimson, he made his way along a street with neat lawns and houses with porches. A tiny light twinkled, then another, and soon the air was glowing with fireflies. Ralph never forgot that night. He found magic in our migrations through other people's landscapes and lives.

MILLIE USED TO HAVE one care provider; now she has a team. In the years since we moved to Santa Cruz, a growing group of companions have learned to thrive in Millie's bubble. One afternoon Marilyn, who has been with Millie the longest, read aloud the text that Millie's former aide, Adri, had sent her from Miami. "Want to move back to Santa Cruz. Think Dani has shifts?" I immediately texted Adri back. I offered her the choice of coming directly to Santa Cruz or joining us in Vermont and then flying back with us to California. "Or none of the above. Your choice, sweetie! Ralph btw is doing great. Got a 5 on his AP world history exam. Barely passed the class."

By that point, Adri and I had been through a lot together. A straight-talking Puerto Rican woman from a military family in Miami, she joined our household by way of another of Millie's care providers, her best friend, Grace, a woman as diplomatic as Adri was blunt, who liked to write poetry and was studying to be a firefighter. We all quickly became tangled up in each other's lives. It began when I paid for the funeral expenses after Grace's mother died suddenly. Shortly afterward, Grace moved back to Florida. But Adri stuck around. Adri and I spent hours in my kitchen, strategizing on what I should do to get Ralph to study and what she should do to ensure that her father was treating her autistic brother right. She found me a gym—Santa Cruz Power Fitness—where she'd made friends with the body builders. I found her a massage therapist, after a car accident messed up her hip. She lives in Puerto Rico now, but she still takes pleasure in bossing me around. "DANI!!!" she shouts into the phone. "How's Ralph? Tell him if he doesn't obey you, I'll kick his butt."

Millie's care providers are my employees, but they have always felt like so much more. I have helped them choose classes, and I have talked to them about their sick grandparents. Many have been first-generation college students, and I have attended their graduations, sitting next to their little brothers on folded chairs in a field. I got myself ordained in the American Marriage Ministries when one of them asked me to officiate at her wedding. I even offered to host the ceremony in my backyard. I pay them as much as I can afford, and sometimes more. In return, they keep me company in the morning, when they arrive to make Millie's breakfast, and in the evening, when I join them in the kitchen to cook. I try to remember that inequality runs like a seam through these relationships and that it's easy for me to be informal because I'm in charge. I'm deeply grateful. Millie's care providers have allowed me to build a life.

IT'S A LIFE THAT'S been enriched by a remarkably diverse group of people. There was Scott, the first person I hired in Santa Cruz, an earnest young man with a BA in literature, who was taking time off from nursing school. He didn't have child-care references, so he had me call his ex-girlfriend, who cheerfully told me how great Scott was with kids.

There was Adriana, the daughter of undocumented farmworkers and the first in her family to go to college. Adriana came to my house every morning at 5 a.m., bleary eyed and wearing a sorority sweatshirt, with an endless appetite for happy chatter. She quizzed me on my family and was delighted to discover a connection. "Get out! Your mom is a Kappa, too?" Her verdict on the Greek economist I'd made friends with: "He's perfect!" "He talks too much," I complained. "That's okay! Take him running so he's out of breath and he'll be fine!" We laughed about her cop boyfriend, who owned a Pomeranian but wouldn't admit it. "Carlos's friends all think that dog is mine!" Adriana and I got tattoos together on the last day of one of the summers she spent with us in Vermont. Adriana wanted an angel wing, stretched across her left shoulder blade. I asked for a small dandelion, which is only visible when I'm wearing a bathing suit. I think of her every time I go for a swim.

There have been others. Izzy, the runway model whose goal in life was to do development work in Africa. Mike, the drummer and waiter, a white kid raised by progressive parents in San Francisco, who couldn't drive, spoke perfect Chinese, and smoked a lot of pot. Annie, the cheerleading coach and Fresno valley girl, with a Russian boyfriend and a wicked sense of humor, who wanted to be a history teacher and got all A's. Aniek, who was Dutch, easygoing, and dependable, and the best friend of another care provider, Leia, a talented Asian American artist and curator. Katy, a friend of Leia's, with purple hair and kilts, cropped bangs, and thigh-high combat boots, who got a degree in environmental studies and moved to Montana to study taxidermy. Xiaona, who was studying to become a nurse in order to overcome her fear of blood and went on to finish first in her class. Marilyn, who began her career at Pacific Bell back when farmers in the Central Valley still used party lines and who has become my surrogate mom.

MY REAL MOM OFTEN chatted with Millie on the phone. "Tickle, tickle," I could hear her saying, and I watched Millie's passive face for a response; when I came back on, my mother laughed with pleasure. "She's doing so well!" I lost Craig's mother in 2011, five years after Craig's father passed away. My own father died in 2012. The last of my children's grandparents, my mother lived out her life in a memory care unit not far from my sister's house in Providence. She went swimming, wrote poetry, and invented a fantasy life that she lived with passion and gusto. For years, we had the same conversation every time we talked. Then the talk trailed off, and when I was with her, she just smiled.

My mother's dementia was emotionally less difficult for me than it was for my siblings. Millie has taught me that there are things more important than coherent speech when it comes to our ability to connect. From the kitchen, I hear one of Millie's care providers interact with her. "Take a step, Millie." Julie's voice is light and gentle. "She smells what you're cooking!" she shouts, and Millie does. She's paused a few paces into her journey to the toilet, and I can hear her sounds of happy anticipation. "Mmm, mmm, mmm." "Come on, Millie, we have to go to the bathroom before we eat." I smile, remembering what happened at bedtime the night before. On the way from the bathroom, Millie refused to make the turn into her bedroom. Instead, she dragged me to the dining room, where I sat her down in her chair. She smacked her lips and rocked forward. I was not going to get away without giving her dessert.

Jeanette asks me to fill in for her. From the kitchen, I glance into the living room, where Millie is sitting on the couch. She has a toy—a squiggly green cord of soft plastic—and she's shaking and squeezing it when I approach her, swaying back and forth and side to side. She doesn't look up, but she recognizes my footfall and freezes. "What are you doing, Millie?" I ask her. She grins.

I'm sitting next to Millie in a rocking chair, holding her hand, while my partner—who is not the Greek economist—is getting set up to play the electric guitar for her. She's swaying and humming again, with the same small smile on her face. When my partner plays a lick, she goes silent, her face suddenly grave. She swings her head slowly from side to side, trying to get a grasp on what she's experiencing. "She's listening," I whisper. And she is, apparently fascinated by this resonant, unfamiliar sound. Other friends also play instruments, and they all like practicing under her supervision. They watch her respond to the music, alert to what captures her attention. Wendy has discovered that if she scrapes her bow down the neck of her cello, Millie will erupt in hilarity. Diana likes to play her acoustic guitar with Millie sitting on the floor in front of her. She's learned that Millie will scoot toward her so she can touch her knee and feel the vibrations of the song. Cameron has Millie on the piano with her hitting the keys.

Those of us who care for Millie have learned to read a wide array of facial expressions. Some, such as Millie's toothy smile, are easily interpretable, although a grin can turn into a grimace in an instant. Others, such as Millie's look of absorption, can pass as vacancy: Is she thinking about something, or is it lights out, nobody home? Millie's moods pass through her like so many clouds crossing the sun. The way she looks always seems to imply that there's both more and less to her than meets the eye. The same goes for her vocalizations, with all their subtle shifts in timber and tone. When she laughs, really laughs, I feel like I get her. Laughter can be a symptom of an anomalous brain. But when Millie finds something funny, I still grin like a clown. I've been told that working with Millie is "rewarding"; if so, it's her joy that's the prize. Adri has a high, squeaky voice she uses to amuse Millie. I repeat the noises I hear Millie making, in hopes she'll echo me. "She's all smiles and giggles today," Cameron texts me when her shift is over. Julie writes in the log: "Happy girl. Good day."

Other days, like the ones when Millie bites herself, are painful. "Danilyn, can you come down?" Cameron calls up the stairs, her voice tight with concern, and I arrive in the dining room to find Millie snarling. I try to catch my daughter's attention, but she turns her head away from me, her arms reaching and waving, her graceful fingers feeling the air as if they were searching for relief. Her sadness spreads as easily as her happiness, and it ties us in interpretive knots. Is she tired? Or mad? In the end, it doesn't really matter—no more than it really mattered whether my mother's imaginary boyfriends were made of flesh and blood, and not just memory and desire.

Either way, we are there for her. Millie is at the center of her bubble, exerting a gravitational pull on all those who make it their business to worry about what she might be feeling and thinking. We come together around Millie like so many starlings in a murmuration. We copy each other's motions, and we try to beat our wings in time with hers. We make strange and shifting shapes that pose a mystery to those who see us from the ground. If Millie could talk, I don't believe any of us would feel that much closer to her. We certainly wouldn't feel that much closer to one another. Millie has forced us to cultivate an ability to notice and to respond. We get Millie—which means we get what it takes to care deeply about someone we will never fully understand. Someone like me, or like you, or like all the someones whose lives are entangled with ours, whether we are willing to acknowledge them or not.

HELEN MACDONALD, WHO WRITES with heartbreaking beauty of the natural world, has described what it's like being at a pond when huge flocks of migrating waterfowl land. "There is boiling confusion over the lake as flocks come from all directions to join the mass on the water.... Suddenly it is almost too much to bear."[1] Macdonald finds relief when she adjusts her binoculars and zooms in: "I am watching stately groups of cranes in greyscale, landing, drinking, shaking their loose feathers, greeting one another and getting on with the business of finding a place to sleep.... I marvel at how confusion can be resolved by focusing on the things from which it is made. The magic of the flocks is this simple switch between geometry and family."[2] Macdonald goes on to draw a comparison between flocks of birds and the refugees pouring into Europe at the time she wrote the essay. The lesson she learned at the pond has allowed her to see the refugees not as a "singular entity strange and uncontrollable and chaotic," but "as people just like us . . . individuals and small family groups wanting the simplest things: freedom from fear, food, a place to safely sleep." I love Macdonald's prose, but I'm unsatisfied by this conclusion. Can we only open our lives to others who are "just like us"? Birds flock together to protect one another. The murmuration is also a space of care.

There are two ways of looking at my daughter, two ways of perceiving her situation. On the surface, Millie is a severely disabled person who is legally owed a certain level of support, which her shifting cast of care providers is paid to provide. She exists within a hierarchy bound by rules, and I have a prominent place in it as her mother and conservator. She has a fixed place within an edifice of laws and policies designed to provide disabled Americans with "freedom from fear, food, a place to safely sleep." But Millie is also the lure drawing those who attend to her into a very different space of care. A space where conventions are emergent, fragile, and often short-lived. A tiny murmuration with a mystery at its heart.

What Social Worlds Are Made Of

Max sends Millie cards. They arrive in our mailbox in brightly colored envelopes festooned with stickers. Some are invitations, some are holiday cards, but they all contain a message just for her. "Happy Valentine's Day! I want to thank you for coming to my house to visit. I really enjoyed seeing you. We should do it again soon. Maybe we could make some new toys together (ribbons with bells?). Keep in touch." "Happy holidays to you, my friend. I'm so happy you made it to my Halloween party. Your Ghostbuster costume was really cool. Let's stay in touch and enjoy listening to some Christmas music."

Max is in his late twenties. He's small in stature with piercing brown eyes and a sober set to his jaw. He lives in a small house a couple of blocks from ours with his mother, who is a nurse for the county health department. At Max's sixteenth birthday party, his mother showed me the lift system she'd just installed. With tracks and a seating system that dangled from the ceiling, it looked like one of the rides at the Santa Cruz Boardwalk. I watched Max float in a harness from his recliner in the living room, where he sits listening to children's books, to his bedroom and bathroom, a few yards away. Like Millie, Max is multiply disabled. Like Millie, Max doesn't speak, although he hums along happily when he hears a good rhyme. Max's care provider, a different Amy than the one who worked with Millie, has been with Max since he was born. She says he's the best friend she's ever had. "I can tell him anything, and he never judges me." Amy is Max's social secretary. She plans his parties. Her neat handwriting fills his cards to his friends.

During one of his visits to our house, Max reclined on the floor next to Millie, while our friend Diana strummed her guitar and belted out a rousing version of "House of the Rising Sun." Millie giggled, Max whooped, and Amy and Julie, Millie's care provider, flushed with pleasure. The Christmas card from Max contained a handout with all the words to "The Twelve Days of Christmas." I sang the song to Millie, and she cackled with glee. In South Africa, the Xhosa people have a proverb "Umuntu ngumuntu ngabantu," which means "A person is a person by means of other people." Max is a person by means of Amy. Millie is a person by means of Max. And those of us who care for and about Max and Millie are persons by means of them.

Umuntu ngumuntu ngabantu. The Black consciousness leader Steve Biko, who gave his life in the battle against apartheid, traced his official first name—the Xhosa term Bantu—to that proverb. He said this to his followers, "Man, you are okay as you are. Begin to look upon yourself as a human being."[1] On one hand, Biko endorsed the idea that people only exist due to their relationships. On the other, he insisted on the humanity of the people he fought for. Biko and other Black intellectuals have had to struggle against the weight of an entire tradition of Western thought to develop what the poet and politician Aimé Césaire called "a humanism made to the measure of the world."[2] For disabled people, the lure of this kind of humanism is just as strong. The same goes for people like me, who try to be their allies. But a question remains. How far beyond mainstream assumptions would I have to travel to find a place for Millie's kind of body and mind?

In superficial respects, not so far at all. Americans like Millie live in two kinds of social worlds. One is devoted to "humanizing" people like my daughter. Max doesn't write, and Millie doesn't read. But this kind of world cloaks them in normalcy. The goal is to encourage others to see them as typical members of their society: people who send Christmas cards, visit friends, go to school, hold down jobs. The impulse is understandable. Not so long ago, people like my daughter fell into the Nazi category of "life unworthy of life."[3] If Millie had grown up in the 1920s in Dortmund, Germany, where her father's grandparents lived, there's a good chance she would have been killed. The special education programs Millie has attended, the postgraduate activities she takes part in now: They're built as a bulwark against this nightmare. This bulwark is built of love—a love that is genuine. It is also built of fear—a fear that is justified, given what has happened, and is still happening, to people whose humanity is in doubt.

But alongside these worlds and running through them is another variety: built not of love and fear, but of love and that other sentiment, curiosity. The anthropologist Laurence Ralph tells the story of a mother driven mad by the brutal murder of her son in a low-income Black neighborhood in Chicago.[4] Her son was shot through the head, and afterward she insisted that everyone she encountered cover their heads to protect themselves—and when they didn't (or even when they did), she screamed. Instead of ostracizing her, her neighbors accepted her. They changed their habits to meet her needs—they only appeared before her wearing a helmet, a hood, a headscarf, or a hat. Instead of curing her, they built a world around her—a social world infused with a sense of both grief and grievance at the structural violence that besets Black communities. They didn't try to control her or explain away her behavior. Instead, they let her shape their daily lives. The impulse here is adventurous. Instead of worrying about who qualifies for full membership in the species, those who inhabit this second kind of social world live in wonder at the people they share them with, and at the people they've become. I've discussed what it takes to make social worlds in which Max and Millie appear as normal: activism, legislation, paperwork, and funding, all focused on individuals and their capacities. But what about the social worlds that Max and Millie have made?

You don't have to be human to make a social world—bees, dogs, and many other creatures survive by living in an organized fashion. But the social worlds that humans inhabit have specific traits. Chimps have to rebuild their social identities and hierarchies every time they interact: That's what all that teeth baring and chest thumping is about.[5] People do not. We can depend on our memories, and things like uniforms and post office counters, to tell us who we are and where we stand. Our social worlds are made of houses and roads, recipes and poetry, nail files and computers, pets and houseplants, and a mess of other things whose origins we cannot fully fathom. Our social worlds are made by gods and ghosts. All those things scholars have identified as hallmarks of the human, from speech to the burial of the dead, turn on our ability to imagine sharing the experiences of absent others, the ones who will someday read our tombstones, people whose minds we can imagine but never fully share. As a species, we don't just allow for cognitive mystery; we depend on it. Humanity lives in the spaces we reach across in order to meet.

A humanism big enough to hold Max and Millie would have less to do with who we are than with how we come together. It would rest on our willingness to touch and be touched without having to pin each other down. But I'm still afraid of the violence that lurks in this exercise. My mother was rejected when she tried to join my father's Presbyterian church. The minister asked her whether she took Christ as her only lord and savior. "No," she said. "There could be others." Maybe that's a better motto for this exercise: "There could be others." Other ways of thinking about who qualifies for our care and attention. Other ways of being a person. Ultimately, the question isn't what makes Millie human. The question is what allows us to live together. It's what matters in the making of social worlds.

ONCE UPON A TIME, I thought what mattered was language. I was a dreamy child. I remember spending hours lying in the grass, staring up at the clouds. I was only five, but I already had burning questions. Where did all this come from? How did I get here? What would it feel like to be someone else? When I landed in graduate school, after two years on Java teaching English, speaking Indonesian, and doing my best to fit in, I was naturally drawn to grand explanations. When it came to explaining human experience, accounts that focused on language seemed the grandest of all.

I was a fledgling radical in college, and I thought I knew all about ideology. It was one thing to think that the stories told by the powerful had given me a mistaken view of reality; it was quite another to realize that everything I knew had been filtered through the words I used. It was a heady discovery. I devoured texts that described cultures as being like languages, systems of symbols, like a stop sign, an internet meme, or the Cross, built out of the kinds of conventions that Millie doesn't seem to have access to. Even music, I thought, only made sense if you had a label for what you heard. Now I shudder when I read the passage from Clifford Geertz, where he describes "men without culture," by which he really means men who don't use symbols, as "unworkable monstrosities with very few useable instincts, fewer recognizable sentiments, and no intellect: mental basket cases."[6] At the time Millie was born, I believed every word of this. But now I know—things other than language are critical to our ability to live together, love each other, and somehow connect. These things compel us even when, like Millie, we can't give them a name.

One of these things is a home. Millie's life has centered on the locations where she has resided: from the small apartment she came home to from the hospital to the sprawling Victorian where she lives now. These dwellings have acted as a hook connecting her to government agencies in Illinois, Vermont, and now California. The fact that Millie has an address has qualified her for services and opened her (and me) to surveillance by the protective arm of the state. Filled with equipment, strange playthings, and repurposed pieces of furniture, they have also born witness to Millie's grip on the people around her, who have molded her surroundings to meet her needs. Even the most dispossessed strive to create a space that somehow feels like their own: a scrap of cardboard under the scaffolding on a wide New York sidewalk, a bed in a nursing home with the pillow angled just so to relieve an aching neck.

A home is an anchor for social relationships. Millie's care providers have spent hours sharing space with Millie, in her bedroom, her bathroom, our living room, the kitchen where we cook her meals. In caring for Millie, they've left their mark on her surroundings; they've become part of her intimate circle, much more so than Millie's cousins, whom she sees no more than once a year. For Millie, as for people in every corner of the globe, social life revolves around residences and all they contain: sleeping compartments and hearths, birth certificates and Korans, silverware and ceremonial daggers, wedding dresses and precious cloaks made of feathers and cloth. As anyone who has moved to the other side of a city or a country can tell you, where you live shapes how you place yourself in the grand scheme of things. As anyone who has been stripped of their possessions can attest, without belongings, it's hard to tell who you are and where you fit.

It took me some time to arrive at this understanding. I was an anxious graduate student, keenly aware of what I didn't know—and that was a lot. In college, I studied biology and European history. I had never taken an anthropology class, and now I was getting a PhD in it. What did anthropologists actually do? My advisor, Jim Siegel, accidentally helped me out. Jim taught us about thinkers from the early twentieth century who insisted there is nothing outside of language. We called them structuralists. Jim didn't seem to like them much.[7] But they wrote about societies in Eastern Indonesia, where I thought I might work. Eager to learn more, I did some independent reading. These writers obsessed over everything: which cousins people married, what cuts of beef different relatives ate at feasts, the difference between what people named their race horses and their dogs. Supposedly, people did all these things in a logical fashion, and without words there could be no thoughts. I'd just picked out a field site and was applying for grants. Going to weddings and collecting the words for "great aunt" and "brother's daughter"—I could fill lots of notebooks with that.

Six months later I was in West Papua. While I was searching for marriage patterns, my Biak friends were trying to tell me what really mattered: a village neighborhood filled with friends and bathed in mottled sunlight; that cool spring for bathing, a hundred yards down the path; the breeze under a coconut palm someone's grandfather had planted; the stars overhead and the sound of waves crashing nearby on the sandy path that led from choir practice home. People explained these things on front porches, when I arrived as a visitor, and out back in their kitchens, after they accepted me as a fixture in their lives. They spoke of them in cities, where even Biaks with advanced degrees and high-powered jobs dreamt of retiring and opening garden plots on their ancestors' land. The house was quite simply where social life lived.

It turned out that this view was much more in line with contemporary anthropology than mine was, weighed down as it was with charts and abstractions.[8] But Millie has forced me to take it to heart. A few years ago, a geneticist, who was testing Millie for yet another new syndrome, observed that she seemed to be more interested in objects than people. I let her words bother me for a minute, then thought again. What's wrong with a person having a passion for things? Millie is unlikely to marry, and she doesn't use kin terms, as much as I would love to hear her call me "Mom." She is one of many people—people who are trans, gay, polyamorous, or asexual—who don't seem to have a place in the theories I took so much trouble to learn. People come to life through objects, and objects come to life through people. Millie's personhood is embodied in her room, her bed, an antique print of a girl holding a kitten, framed photographs of her father, her chair.

But this isn't the last word. Day in and day out, Millie's house accumulates history, the history of her life within it. This history overlays other histories, associated with everyone who has lived here, from the nineteenth-century widow who built the residence to the Native people who were the owners of the land where it stands. Millie's life here and the lives of all those others are embedded in this place. So is her father's. I bought the house with the insurance money and savings Craig left us when he died. Someday, all this will be forgotten. Buildings crumble. Memories fade. I only know about the widow because her name is on a plaque next to our front door.

Shortly after we moved into Millie's house, I had to have the roof replaced. One day, one of the workers called me outside. He had discovered the rotted-out remains of a turret top under the eaves. It looked like a jester's hat; I was charmed. On a whim, I took it to a woodworker and had it rebuilt. I also picked out a placard and had it engraved; the woodworker attached it to the base. When the work was done, I gathered our friends and held a little ceremony. I have a photograph of Xiaona and me holding Millie upright next to the turret top; she's reaching out to feel the ball on top. Here's the message we left for strangers to find:

> This turret top is dedicated to Millie Best, who moved here on June 16, 2015, with her brother, Ralph, and her mother, Danilyn, with the help

of Marilyn, Xiaona, Yosselin, Senia, Eszter, Ashley, Marlis, Jack, Karin, Ron, Wendy, Jan, Curt, and Steve. Millie was born on August 9, 2000. She cannot walk without assistance, and she cannot talk, but she has already filled this house with sunshine. May Millie's house always be filled with laughter, wisdom, and peace.

Will the next set of roofers notice this little piece of metal? I hope so. I want them to know Millie was loved. I want her to be remembered. I want this with an urgency that aches and burns. So many people like her were institutionalized and forgotten. There's little sign they ever lived. Millie's social world is made of more than abstract categories. It is rooted in people and things her companions can see, smell, hear, and feel. But it is only when we register and react to their presence that Millie's world becomes real.

A FEW YEARS AGO, my sister-in-law, bitten by the genealogy bug, self-published two books of family history for her daughters, which she shared with my siblings and me. One traced our ancestors on my mother's side, the other on my father's side, across generations of bearded men, corseted women, and solemn-looking babies, leading up to my father, a tow-haired toddler in a sailor's costume, and my mother, a lithe and winsome teenager near the pool on the Jersey shore where we later learned to swim. To be someone's child is to take one's place in a lineage. From the earliest humans to those dour great-grandparents to my parents to me: Millie belongs to the species by virtue of where she came from, not as a reward for what she can do.

But it's not just Millie's ancestry that's at stake here. As humans, we were all once small and weak, like those infants in the photographs. Left to their own devices, none of my forebears would have made it, and Millie wouldn't be here today. Then there's the linguistic relationship implied by the fact of having a mother. Motherhood implies childhood in its very meaning. Millie is as dependent on me for her recognized status as a daughter as she is for a roof over her head. Relationships are the lifeblood of Millie's social worlds—the typical ones I link her to, as her legal guardian, and those realms, more speculative and strange, which flicker into focus whenever we connect. But relationships are not just genealogical, nor are they only linguistic. There's more to relationships than one might think.

Where did the capacity to form relationships come from? As an anthropologist, I've always been interested in this question—even more so, now, as Millie's mom. It's easy to laugh at the just-so stories I came across in graduate school, but they did offer an explanation. Picture yourself standing on that fuzzy, mythical stage set they call prehistory. There aren't any grocery stores, and money doesn't exist. What do you do? You give away whatever you have. Gifts create obligations. Obligations create bonds between people, and these bonds help get people fed. Nature is bountiful but fickle. Food is perishable, much more so than the memory of someone given a few of your extra berries in hopes she will share hers with you at some future date. This may sound silly, but at stake is a profound truth: Human beings are vulnerable, and relationships help them survive. Millie, who is so dependent on others, could very well be Exhibit A.

But that's not the only thing relationships do. Who you are depends on your relationships with others: the ones to which you give everything from dinner parties to sidelong glances, and the ones who give such things to you. Some relationships are institutionalized, like those involving national governments, which issue identity cards and collect taxes. Others are temporary and fragile—say, with that stranger who seems to recognize you on the street. Here in the United States, some of us like to think of ourselves as free agents. We're not—we're as dependent on others for our sense of ourselves as our children are for food.

This holds for Millie as much as for the rest of us. I used to think relationships happen when two individuals come together and decide to form a bond. In fact, the bond comes first. At any particular moment, we have the potential to become any number of kinds of people. Then a stern look from across the classroom, or a funding appeal from a major charity, conjures up one of these possibilities, and, for the moment, that becomes who we are. The other day, one of Millie's care providers sent me a voice memo of Millie giggling, which consisted of an eerie mixture of gurgling, humming, and moaning. I wouldn't have recognized it as laughter if I didn't know Millie so well. My recognition makes her into a person. But when Millie responds to me, she also creates me as her interlocutor—I feel myself becoming someone new through her touch.

I'm not just talking about talk. Nor am I only talking about people. A baseline receptivity opens humans to forming relationships with one another—a receptivity that springs from the impermanence and interconnectedness of all things. The same receptivity that opens me to Millie, and Millie to me, characterizes beings as different from one another as a protozoan and a rock. Out of an infinite array of possibilities, one part of the world takes the measure of another, carving it into shape and making it relevant and real. Blood calls forth hearts; hammers call forth nails: These things would not exist in one another's absence. Words like "here," "there," and "I" are equally creative. Depending on who is speaking, "I" could be me, Danilyn Rutherford, but it could also be the ghost of Boris Yeltsin. "Here" could be the East Village or the South Pole;

"there" could be the other side of the galaxy or the other side of the couch. Funding appeals often begin with a salutation, "Dear Friend," in hopes you will act like one.[9] But this linguistic conjuring is just one instance of a much broader phenomenon. Everything that's real, from Half Dome to a gnat, comes into being in this way. I thought of the world as filled with substances, but it's really filled with interactions. Big or small, the question to ask about something is not what it is but what it does by virtue of how it connects.

Of course, the interactions that make social life possible take particular forms. But these forms are not as limited as one might think. People use their senses in a plethora of ways to engage with those around them. A DeafBlind man on a bus helps a friend reach her destination. He uses the vehicle's vibrations to tell him when the right stop is coming up.[10] On a veranda in Oman, young women sit near the front door at a distance from their household's guests.[11] This allows them to joke with the visitors comfortably. For them, interaction is not simply a matter of speech, it's a matter of sensation; they use the built environment and their bodies to strike the right balance between feeling too hidden and too exposed. Michele Friedner makes the point adroitly: "Sensory normality, as a desired goal and outcome, results in a contraction rather than an expansion of ways of engaging with the world."[12] In graduate school, I learned a lot about the formation of identity. About how people derive a sense of themselves from the stories others tell about them. About how these stories lead them to see themselves through new eyes. With Millie, there's no need for a story. Our becoming together is felt, not said.

Millie is a person because she's in relation. At that moment when her father and I looked at the pregnancy test and saw that blue line come into focus, we called Millie into being and made her ours. Human relationships take form in different ways, for different reasons, within an interconnected universe; as the feminist physicist and philosopher Karen Barad puts it so elegantly, "Humans are part of the configuration and ongoing reconfiguration of the world."[13] But there's still another direction to take this exploration. In searching for a place for Millie in theories of the social, I have bumped up against difference. Indeed, it may be difference that matters the most.

WHEN I TAUGHT KINSHIP in Santa Cruz before accepting my current job, I launched a frontal attack on the institution of marriage. Or at least that might be how some of my students experienced the course. We started the quarter by reading the chapter in *The Trouble with Normal* where Michael Warner criticizes the movement for marriage equality for demonizing people who don't live or mate in pairs. Each week, students watched an episode from *Big Love*, a television show about a polygamous Mormon family trying to "pass" in the suburbs and talked about how the series related to the themes we discussed in class. You might think you are learning about kinship, I told my students. But this class is actually about sex, money, life, and death—and all those ways of living and loving that mainstream ideas about humanity have left out.

By the time Millie was born, I should have been convinced of the trouble with normal. I have a talent for multiple-choice tests; I can always smell a rat. When I received the results from my first college entrance exam, I was proud as a peacock. But I kept it to myself. In my high school in the 1970s, nerds were low in the pecking order. The cheerleaders and football players who clustered by the cafeteria, surveying the ordinary mortals, already had me pegged as a weirdo. Why make matters worse? Millie, who scores at the tip of the other tail in aptitude tests, has given me a stronger sense of the violence that comes with the demand to conform. But this is not the only way that difference matters. Difference, not sameness, is where social life begins.

Shortly after I left Chicago, my colleague Marshall Sahlins published a small but influential book, *What Kinship Is—and Is Not*. I was immediately struck by how he addressed this problem of sameness and difference. "The specific quality of kinship," he told his readers, "is 'mutuality of being.'" Kinfolk are persons who "participate intrinsically in each other's existence: they are members of each other."[14] Weddings, baptisms, and funerals enhance this feeling of unity. At my husband's memorial service, Craig's parents and siblings sat with my children and me in the front of the chapel; our friends and my own relatives sat in the back. Indigenous people in the Amazon stage rituals in which in-laws play the role of enemies or even prey. This feeling of unity is grounded in a more pervasive sense of sameness. Whenever someone speaks with someone, or gives them a present, or simply wonders how they are feeling, they imagine themselves in their position. For that brief instant, they are alike. Biology is only part of the picture. People arrive at mutuality through multiple routes.

But in getting there, they are driven by the force of difference. My graduate training left me with plenty of examples that make this point. Young children, for instance, tend to see other children as rivals.[15] In this case, sameness leads to hostility (think evil twins). Who gets the last cookie can feel like a matter of life and death. By teaching children to share, care providers guide them away from this precipice. I let you play with my toy, you let me play with yours. But at the end of the play date, we part in peace. The twin is no longer evil. Gift exchange brings security by way of a different kind of sameness, the sameness expressed as mutual love.

How difference matters becomes even more obvious when you explore what social life looks like for people like Millie. Consider Andrew Solomon's bestseller *Far from the Tree*. "There is no such thing as reproduction," Solomon starts out.

> When two people decide to have a baby, they engage in an act of production, and the widespread use of the word reproduction for this activity, with its implication that two people are but braiding themselves together, is at best a euphemism to comfort prospective parents before they get in over their heads. In the subconscious fantasies that make conception look so alluring, it is often ourselves that we would like to see live forever, not someone with a personality of his own. . . . Children whose defining quality annihilates that fantasy of immortality are a particular insult; we must love them for themselves, and that is a great deal harder to do.[16]

Solomon takes as his starting point his experience as a gay man with parents who could not accept him. He continues with chapters on children whose parents struggled to accept them as well: from deaf people and little people to children with Down syndrome, autism, and schizophrenia, to prodigies, children born of rape, criminals, and people who are trans. In each case, Solomon depicts parents searching for a basis for mutuality—a search that can lead them to attempt to "fix" their children's bodies and behavior or, in the best instances, to learn to love them as they are. Solomon starts with difference—with the fact that reproduction is an impossible goal—and shows the difficulty it causes within a model of kinship that privileges sameness. But as he also shows, love can thrive in the pleasure of reaching beyond the limits of what parents can know.

I still think that Millie looks a bit like her father. But for the geneticists she saw as a child, Millie's fair skin, wide grin, and the gap between her teeth were symptoms. Their tests all came back negative, and the experts still don't know what is wrong. Millie goes bowling and takes art classes with other disabled people. But she's not much like any of them either. By Solomon's measure, she is far from everybody's tree.

This is not for lack of trying. One summer on our way back to Santa Cruz from Vermont, I ran into a Mennonite family at Niagara Falls. The mother and father were traveling with six children. The women wore prairie skirts and bonnets; the father wore a beard, suspenders, and a suit. The couple approached me and Marilyn. Millie reminded them of their daughter; she had died a year earlier, and they clearly missed her. She had had a rare genetic condition. Maybe Millie had it, too. (She didn't, I learned by looking up the syndrome on my phone after we got back into the car.) I felt a rush of affection for this family, so different from my own, yet united by shared experience. We exchanged addresses and phone numbers—they didn't use email—and pledged to stay in touch. Yet while I flirt with the kind of fellowship this family was grasping for, Millie's real kin group is in fact much more unlikely. For Millie, mutuality is not given in some recognizable commonality. Its emergence involves a leap of faith.

At 8 a.m. I walk into Millie's bedroom, where she is lying fast asleep, splayed out on her back, her face turned away from me. On weekends, whoever has the morning shift arrives at 7:30 a.m. to empty the dishwasher and make oatmeal. On Saturdays, that's sometimes me. I lean over the rail to whisper in Millie's ear. "Good morning, Millie," I say softly. Millie's eyes are still closed, but her lips curl into a gentle smile. When I say it again, she grins. I say it once more in a funny voice—"Good MORNING!!"—and she laughs in that mischievous, contagious, slightly wicked cackle she seems to have inherited from her dad. She still hasn't looked at me, but finally she casts a glance in my direction. She meets my eyes for a fleeting instant. Then she looks away.

As you know by now, Millie doesn't like faces. Instead, she loves looking at and, often quite perilously, playing with straps, ribbons, belts, headphone wires, and electrical cords. She's a fan of toy octopi, you'll recall, but also toy jellyfish and dolls with dangling locks—anything stringy she can shake and watch move. "Are you happy to see me or my zipper?" I'm tempted to ask her when I walk in the room wearing my favorite fleece vest. Well-meaning strangers approach Millie in airports. They lean over and get in her face. "Hello!" they announce. "What's your name?" Millie's face goes blank. But when the person walks away, Millie bursts into a grin, reaching out to gently fondle the tag on their suitcase as it rolls by.

Those of us who live with Millie on a daily basis go through routines that approximate "normal" interactions: facsimiles of conversation. I chatter ceaselessly when I'm with Millie, consulting her on all kinds of large and small decisions; sometimes she ignores me, sometimes she acts like she's listening. Sometimes she laughs when I'm talking; I tease her for making fun of me, even though I never know whether she understood a word of what I said. "Any social contact entails an appeal, an appeal which is a hope for a response."[17] Claude Lévi-Strauss, who wrote this, was the most famous of the structuralists. On this point, they were right. Hope is the infrastructure of Millie's social world.

My most pleasurable interactions with Millie are those in which she takes the lead. She vocalizes, choosing from her repertoire of chirps, trills, groans, and giggles. I copy her. She bursts out laughing; sometimes she repeats herself, copying me. When I hand her a stuffed animal, she seems to get the same pleasure out of throwing it back. She doesn't follow my gaze. But she does take turns, however tenuously, in a way that seems to indicate that she can imagine being me, although it's always possible she's simply having trouble keeping the toy in her grip. I do something and an eternity seems to pass; the stimulus hangs in the air, waiting for the response. When it comes, the effect is electric, heightened intensity, heightened mutuality, born of the recognition of something that could be an accident but is legible as a social act. Millie is at once my most intimate and my most alien interlocutor. Millie shows me every day how difference impinges and incites. There *is* something outside of language. That's what Jim Siegel was really trying to teach us. But he warned us that we can't say what it is. We may suppress it, ignore it, domesticate it, or fight to wipe it out. But difference spurs the creation of social worlds.

BY NOW IT SHOULD be clear: Millie's world is also built of privilege, the privilege that affords her a home, excellent services, plenty of sunshine, fresh air, good food, and the companionship of well-paid care providers. I enjoyed this kind of security when I was Millie's age, and I know it made me oblivious, even stupid, just when I thought I was being smart. I played with it like a puzzle, this question of being human. Today, I feel its urgency every time I look Millie in the face. But at the same time, this entire train of thought leaves me queasy. Why is this a question at all?

There are so few of us, so few people with loved ones like Millie. I just finished reading *Narrowed Lives: Meaning, Moral Value, and Profound Intellectual Disability*, a study by a team of Finnish philosophers who did field work in group homes in Helsinki. Much about the book struck me as true and useful. But the statistics hit me the hardest of all. Somewhere between 1 and 3 percent of the world's population is intellectually disabled.[18] Between 2 and 4 percent of that small share of our species could be classified as severely and profoundly impaired. Do the math. You'd need to meet as many as fifty thousand people to run into anyone like Millie. It's no wonder I was so happy to talk to the Mennonite family at Niagara Falls.

During the year we spent in Princeton, I joined a discussion group on humanitarianism run by a famous political theorist. As it turned out, he wasn't particularly interested in my opinion. As he saw it, my findings from Biak were irrelevant; the population was too tiny and exotic to count in the search for truth. My experiences with Millie would seem even more exceptional and, by this view, unenlightening. I've argued that Millie has expanded my understanding of what it is to be a person. That she has taught me something about the making of social worlds. But what kinds of social worlds actually exist for people like Millie, a population that is rare, deeply unusual, and scattered across the globe?

Narrow ones, as the authors of the Finnish study point out. The people in some of the group homes where they did their field work had "little genuine opportunities for social interaction."[19] Their days dissolved into the endless grind of personal care—being woken, being dressed, being taken to the toilet, being fed, being left to rest once again. By prioritizing the routine tending of bodily needs, these institutions failed to "contribute to people with PIMD [profound intellectual and multiple disabilities] being recognized as fellow human beings worthy of dignity."[20] But it doesn't have to be that way. There are solutions on offer. One, endorsed by the authors of *Narrowed Lives*, involves taking residents out of their group homes to cafés, concerts, and shopping malls, where they can mix and mingle like everyone else.

It's February 2018, and someone has set up a red carpet on the sidewalk leading into the cafeteria on the campus of a massive evangelical church. Xiaona is on her tiptoes, craning to get a glimpse through the crowd. "I think Millie should go to the prom," Marilyn announced one spring morning when I came to the kitchen to make a cup of tea. "It's called Night to Shine. They hold it every year in San Jose." She signed Millie up, and a fancy invitation arrived in our mailbox. We found a maroon satin gown online and bought it in two sizes, in hopes that one of them would fit her. Marilyn, Jeanette, and Xiaona offered to join Millie and me for the trip over the mountains to the venue. When we arrived, a volunteer snatched Millie away to prepare her for her grand entrance; the nice woman at the registration table directed us to the pavement in front of the next building, where a crowd of "fans" was gathering. And so here we are.

A limo pulls up and a couple emerges. She's in her thirties, I would guess; he looks like he's in his forties. They both have Down syndrome, and they're dressed to the nines: silky blue full-length dress, powder-blue suit, corsages on their wrist and lapel. Beaming like a starlet, the woman takes the man's arm, and they strut up the carpet. They wave; the onlookers cheer. Before the door to the next limo opens, someone hoists a sign. It says, "Quiet please," so instead of clapping, we wiggle our fingers in approval as a young man in leg braces and a tuxedo passes by. Then we see Millie. She materializes at the curb in her wheelchair, along with her date, a blonde speech therapist from the small army of helpers running the dance. The speech therapist is wearing sequins and a bright smile. Millie is wearing her gown and a look of desperation. Marilyn raises an eyebrow. She's the one who insisted on adding a silver bite sleeve to Millie's outfit. I'm glad to see she has it on. Without this protective layer, Millie would be sinking her teeth into her bicep deeply enough to draw blood. We call out to Millie as the speech therapist wheels her past, but she's too agitated to notice us. The noise, the flashing cameras, the commotion—it's clearly a bit much for my girl.

Later, we sit down in a small dining room with the parents, friends, and aides of the other "honored guests." We eat donated lasagna and watch a closed-circuit television trained on the dance floor, where shadowy figures are swaying. I'm wearing a nice outfit, and I was looking forward to dancing with Millie, who would stand leaning into me for balance. But we're not allowed inside. The football player Tim Tebow, who is known for thanking the Lord after every touchdown, created Night to Shine to provide intellectually disabled people with "an unforgettable prom night experience centered on God's love."[21] The event is designed to mimic a "normal" rite of passage. No one goes to the prom with their mom.[22] No one goes to the prom in their forties either, but that hasn't stopped some of the honored guests from coming back year after year.

At the end of the evening, the blonde speech therapist returns Millie. She seems no worse for the wear. She spent most of the evening in a quiet room away from the noise. The souvenir picture from the evening shows the two of them together. The speech therapist smiles into the camera. Millie's gaze is unfocused, her mouth slack. Night to Shine welcomes people like Millie into a world of glamour and adventure. Intellectually disabled people don't get many opportunities to be celebrated, to be applauded, to shine. The couple with Down syndrome will no doubt remember the dance with pleasure and look forward to the next one. Seeing them so happy stirred me. But in the end, who was this unforgettable experience for? For the parents and care providers who got to watch their loved ones being "normal"? For Tim Tebow? For God?

Could it be that the bonds forged in the endless grind of personal care are underrated? The risotto is boiling, and I give it a quick stir, then glance into the living room. Millie is sitting on an overstuffed chair holding court. Jeanette is to her left on the rocker. Xiaona has taken the ottoman to Millie's right. Sandee has pulled over the piano bench. Marilyn has stolen a chair from the dining room, and Julie is perched on the edge of the couch. Millie's fingers are wrapped up in her mermaid's yellow yarn hair, which she is watching closely for signs of movement. But when Marilyn starts speaking, Millie grins. Someone else chimes in—another familiar voice—and Millie starts laughing, a sound that begins deep in her belly and ends in a tone like the wind chimes behind my back door.

I scheduled this dinner to welcome Sandee and Julie to Millie's team. It has been a year since I went on leave from the local university. I am spending half my time in Manhattan or on the road, and I wanted to give Millie's care providers a chance to get to know each other better and to thank them for their hard work. But instead of taking their glasses of wine onto the deck, the women have gathered around Millie and Xiaona, who has the evening shift. Millie rarely gets to see her care providers together in one place, and now they're encircling her, chatting happily. Someone tells a funny story about our dog, who is snoring on the sofa. Hrrrmmm, Millie purrs, then takes a breath. Then she starts giggling again. The women laugh with her. None of us knows for certain what Millie is thinking. But we have to believe she's glad everyone's here.

Millie is as close to these women as I am to anyone. Most people spend a large portion of their lives waking, dressing, eating, bathing, and toileting. But how many of us do these things in the constant company of attentive others? And not just with one attentive other, but an evolving series of attentive others, all intimately bound to us through these acts of care? This isn't a group home of the underfunded, impersonal sort described by the Finnish researchers, where each care provider is responsible for up to four clients. This also isn't the prom. There's no carpet, no cameras, no dance floor. But isn't this just as expansive a social world?

Which is to say, isn't this just as human a social world? In the appendix to *Narrowed Lives*, Benjamin L. Curtis and Simo Vehmas offer philosophical grounding for a truth that to my mind should go without saying: People like Millie are worthy of moral concern. Even if Millie spent her days lying motionless on a cot, her life would still count no less than that of anyone else. As Curtis and Vehmas see it, this is for a very precise reason: Millie possesses "the intrinsic property of possibly being a person."[23] To be a person is to possess "high-level intrinsic psychological properties." To possibly be a person is to be someone who could have possessed these properties, but does not. Millie was born of statistically typical people and could well have been a statistically typical person herself, if not for the silent genetic changes that set her on a different path.

This argument anchors Millie's moral status in the biological reality of inheritance and impairment. But the reality faced by Millie's loved ones is more complex. I've been with Millie for over twenty years. Although I can guess at what she's feeling, I may never know for sure. But in this, Millie is far from exceptional. We've all experienced those lulls that interrupt the flow of a conversation. I glance across the dinner table at my cousin. Is she thinking about what I told her or digesting her salad? Nobody can see someone's "high-level intrinsic psychological properties" in an X-ray or a scan. If cognitive mystery is the norm, not the exception, we are all consigned to the condition of "possibly being a person." I can never fully get inside the minds of Xiaona or Marilyn, or even my son, Ralph. We share homes, and we create ourselves through our relationships with others. But our social worlds always rest on a leap of faith.

"There is nothing outside of language." My training might have told me this, but my life has had something different to say. If you truly want to know what social worlds are made of, you have to pay heed to things that can't be written, pictured in a diagram, or spoken out loud. Millie, like all her fellow humans, is part of the "ongoing configuration and reconfiguration of the world." Whatever I have learned as an anthropologist only matters to the degree that it makes these matters plain.

The Rest of a Life

What strikes me most about the handout are the graphics. In the upper left-hand corner, next to the first paragraph, is a bicycle, pedaled by four riders. They are identical in size and shape, but with different hats and hairstyles, one with an enormous nose. "Transition Together" is emblazoned above this tandem-times-two. In the middle is a flow chart: "Individual Turns 18" marks the blue box that starts the process; the arrows point to two red boxes, with the alternatives "Receive a Diploma" and "Receive a Certificate of Completion and Continue to Post-Secondary Program." Diploma receivers choose between the green boxes "Pursue Further Education (College/University)" and "Attend a Day Program or Vocational Program (Funded by SARC/DOR)." Certificate receivers can "Attend Public School Post-Secondary Program and Complete at Age 22," before choosing between purple boxes: "Attend a Day Program or Vocational Program (Funded by SARC/DOR)" or "Explore"—not Pursue—"Further Education (College Classes)."

At the bottom of the page, to the right of a list of residential options, is a signpost with arrows pointing every which way. The destinations are

"Independence," "Autonomy," "Freedom," and "Self-Reliance." I flip the page over and find the same graphic on the other side, but with the arrows pointing to "Job," "Career," "Work," and "Opportunity." Peculiar. I think I understand what they mean by "pursuing" and "exploring" further education. It boils down to the difference between taking a psychology class at the local community college and showing up with your aide for adaptive aerobics. And I can understand the impulse to present the riders as identically embodied, even if many of the people they represent are more likely to transition in a wheelchair than on a bike. But aren't the words on each of those signposts synonyms? Do you really need to head in different directions to be "independent" or "free?" Isn't a "job" also an "opportunity" and possibly even a "career"?

The handout is labeled "Transition Toolbox: The Nuts and Bolts of Exiting the School System." "Transition," it tells us, "is the purposeful, organized, and outcome-oriented process designed to help a student 'at risk'"—why the scare quotes? at risk of what?—"move from school to employment and a quality adult life." Until recently, Millie was in the green box marked "Attend Public School Post-Secondary Program and Complete at Age 22." She rode the bus every morning to Soquel High, where she spent the day with her teacher Andrew and his sweet-tempered crew of aides and deeply atypical young adults. The "Transition Toolbox" is the map to Millie's future.

MY HEART WAS RACING when I trotted down the stairs from my home office to let in Tammy Hayes, our new SARC service coordinator. SARC, which stands for the San Andrea Regional Center, was one of several acronyms I had to master during our first befuddling months in California. I quickly learned what SARC could do for us—it covered the cost of therapeutic horseback riding for Millie. It took me longer to figure out what SARC was. Regional centers are community-based nonprofits funded by the California Department of Developmental Services. They are responsible for the health, welfare, and education of developmentally disabled children and adults. Tammy was here for our annual meeting, and we were going to talk about what would happen when Millie finished school. A service coordinator is both a guide and a gatekeeper. Tammy's job was to inform me of the services that SARC could offer and gather the information used to determine how much support Millie would receive.

I had kept myself busy until the last second before our appointment, rifling through papers looking for a letter I'd received earlier that month informing me that Millie's Medi-Cal had been cut. SARC is just one star in the constellation of bureaucracies that provides for Millie. The Department of Health is another, and now it was threatening to withdraw its funding. This was a crisis. We were doing fine now. But in the coming years, as I grow older and our expenses mount, Millie will need every bit of state support we can muster. I could quit my job and care for Millie myself, but it's not clear how we'd afford to eat. I pictured myself, bent and frail, helping Millie into her wheelchair. As this grim image filled my mind, I ignored the faint sound of Marilyn shuffling around in the kitchen, putting away the groceries she'd just bought for Millie. Then I heard a knock from far below me at the front door.

Millie's most recent Individual Program Plan from SARC observes that she lives with her mother "in a big and spacious family home." Our house is just that, with twenty-foot ceilings and a master bedroom large enough to hold my partner's New York apartment. It's not just big; it's ornate, with lattice ceilings and gleaming woodwork, a carved banister adorned with rosettes, and a washbasin shaped like a cherub. The widow who built it in 1874 initially wanted an Italianate mansion, tastefully symmetrical with large square rooms and big windows. Then, in a fit of architectural FOMO, she slapped on a turret and wedding cake cornices so it counted as Stick and Eastlake, too.

In the 1990s, the real estate magnate I bought it from added Vegas-worthy monstrosities, including "Caesar's Bathroom" and a carriage house my neighbors call the "Taj Ma-Garage." My house is on a leafy dead-end street of Victorians, beach cottages, typical twentieth-century homes, and low-end rentals a few blocks from downtown Santa Cruz. It has a gate, a hedge, a palm tree, and a circular driveway watched over by a second-floor balcony, where I could stand if a crowd gathered and I wanted to give a speech. Behind the Taj Ma-Garage stands the little outbuilding I use as a studio, where I've put my childhood twin beds and a desk for when I escape to write. Brian, a computer programmer who helps with the landscaping, lives with his partner in a cottage on the other side of the property. Behind it is a low-slung building with more rental units; it houses Candice, another care provider, with her daughter and grandson; our friend Diana, a retired children's book illustrator and former producer for Black Sabbath; and Susan, a middle-aged mortgage broker who complains about the utility costs, but is always friendly when she walks past the deck to get to her car.

My heart was racing because this was my first meeting with Tammy Hines, and I'm always embarrassed by the grandeur in which Millie lives, which makes me wonder whether we should be getting any help from social service agencies at all. On top of that, I couldn't find the relevant documents, the possession of which is one of the few things that gives me a claim to the status of "good mother." These days, other people bathe Millie, feed her, and wake her up for school. I pay the bills and take care of the paperwork needed to keep the operation afloat. I spend over half of my salary on Millie's care providers; at this rate, I'll never be able to retire. Millie requires 24/7 care. In a world where care providers made a decent living—the only world I want to live in—the total would come to over $300,000 per year. If you keep your care providers below the poverty line, as most government agencies do, the total is still over $100,000 per year. And that's without food, shelter, and clothing, let alone medical supplies and equipment, which the health care industry has made astronomically expensive. I make as much money as anyone in my field, but this is still more than I can afford. Never retire? Without state support, I'll never be able to die.

There is a word used by Tibetan Buddhists to describe the sensation I was feeling: "wind energy," which should have been peacefully resting in my abdomen but was racing around my brains and heart. I breathed into my belly as I opened the door and shook hands with Tammy, who was friendly but guarded. "Let's sit in here," I said, guiding her into the living room, past a couch covered with dog fur, and a chair my mom reupholstered in fabric covered with cats. Somehow, I ended up in Millie's rocker, the only truly comfortable seat in the house, while Tammy took the leatherette chair with the lumpy, peeling cushion. Marilyn joined us from the kitchen, greeted Tammy briskly, and then shot me a smile. "Let's take care of the boring stuff first." Tammy rummaged in her bag for our file.

It surprised me, this nervousness. I'm usually happy to meet emissaries from agencies like SARC: people whose job it is to ask me about Millie, pay attention to what I say, and take an interest in little details, like the fact she is getting better at watching TV. Why the dread? I felt a shameful pang of jealousy. A colleague's son, who is Millie's age, had just gotten into a doctoral program in physics. Millie's cousin was starting medical school. She was also going to get a PhD. Those parents were living the dream. I thought of the missing papers—where was that damn letter?—and how little time I spent with Millie. Would I need to tell Tammy about my job with the foundation in Manhattan and all my trips abroad? Tammy finished reviewing our file; now she was reaching for her clipboard. My stomach tightened into a knot.

Staring at the clipboard, Tammy ticked off a few short questions. "Birth date?" "Diagnosis?" "Still the same primary care physician?" "Does she get SSI?"

"No." I swallowed. SSI stands for Supplemental Security Income. The payments are small, but they are the ticket to other benefits. Most disabled adults get it. But not Millie. I'd tried.

Tammy looked up, eyebrows raised. "No?"

"No." I glanced toward the stairway and thought of my filing cabinet. "She gets survivor benefits from her dad."

"Mmm?"

"They continued after she turned eighteen. Because she's disabled."

"How much does she get?"

My mind went blank. Six months earlier, the number had been etched in my brain. I had been applying for In-Home Supportive Services, or IHSS, which I hoped would help pay for Millie's care. The system worked like a row of dominoes. Millie was supposed to get IHSS automatically once she had Medi-Cal. She was supposed to get Medi-Cal automatically once she had SSI. But most government programs are needs-based, and you're not allowed to reject whatever benefits you have coming to you. As it turned out, Millie had no choice but to accept a continuation of the survivor benefits she began receiving when Craig died, which made her ineligible for SSI, which meant she didn't get Medi-Cal automatically. Even worse, the monthly checks she received to make up for losing her dad put her above the income limit for Medi-Cal, which meant she didn't qualify for IHSS.

"Uh. I'll have to check."

The social security folder was the one I hadn't brought down. Marilyn would have to entertain Tammy. I abruptly rose and headed to the stairs. In the office, I opened and shut file drawers, growling. Do all anthropologists have trouble coming up with mutually exclusive categories? Yes, everything is connected, and labels are arbitrary. These are helpful dictums for the classroom but less useful when you're trying to manage your affairs. The notice with the new amount had vanished. All I could find was the notice from the year before. Clutching it in my fist, I stumbled back down to the living room.

"It used to be $2,013." I mumbled as I rifled through the IHSS file one more time. Wait. There was the right monthly rate, in plain sight, on the application I'd submitted after Medi-Cal miraculously came through. "$2,073."

Tammy jotted down the sum, unmoved by my struggle. My neck stiffened. She was supposed to be here to help us. I was getting pissed. It wasn't Millie's fault that her dad died.

I blurted out an anxious chain of words. "It was hard to get Medi-Cal, and we got them to make an exception last year, but I just got a letter from them telling me that Millie no longer qualifies, and I'm afraid I'll need to make the case again, and I'll have to do it every year." Ending abruptly, I glared at Tammy as if it were her fault.

Tammy glanced up at me blandly. "We work with them on SARC waivers for children, but we don't have anything to do with Medi-Cal for adults." This wasn't her problem. She turned back to the forms. I swallowed and stared out the window at the base of the palm tree. The patch of earth around it was overgrown with weeds. I hadn't believed the letter, but I should have called to check. Was it too late to appeal?

"Have you thought about where Millie is going to live?" Tammy put down the clipboard and pulled a handout from her bag.

"What?"

"Have you thought about where Millie is going to live?"

Startled, I glanced at Marilyn, then back at Tammy. "Here?"

I waited for Tammy to answer. She looked back at me. I took a breath. Then I launched into an explanation. I told her about Millie's wonderful care providers, about the rental units on the property where some of them already lived, and about Millie's ramp and tub and friends. About how I was thinking of inviting other disabled people and their care providers to move in so we could share expenses. About the circle of companions who would gather around Millie and how happy we all would be.

Tammy had placed the handout on the thrift-store side table. She had her pen and was making a little star next to one of the list of options. "SLS. Supported Living Services. That would be the most appropriate. She could go into a group home, but the closest ones are in San Jose, so that wouldn't be ideal."

Millie could go into a group home? In San Jose? On the other side of the coastal range? I knew about group homes. Or at least about the scandals. I dropped that thought fast, as if I'd accidentally picked up a snake. SLS. Could be better. Sounded familiar. One of the many crucial tidbits of information I kept learning and forgetting.

Tammy went on. "SLS would cover twenty-four-hour care, beyond what Millie is getting with IHSS. And you could keep the same care providers."

Bingo. That was what I had been looking for. Funding for a commune. I pictured waking up each morning in a household filled with smiling people. Brian could help me remove the remaining grass, and there would be a vegetable garden and more roses and picnics and Millie and her people drinking lemonade made from our own trees.

"That's great! This sounds exactly like what I've been thinking we should do!"

"But she couldn't live here."

My picnic dissolved. "What?"

"She couldn't live with her parents. If she lived here, you'd have to move out."

What? I looked away and tried to gather my thoughts. Our resident black squirrel, who had been scuttling up the palm tree, turned tail and raced toward the ground.

"What about her brother?" Ralph was caring and attentive, when it came to Millie. Flaky as hell, but someday he'd grow up.

"Is he a conservator?"

I nodded.

"Then no."

I let out a big breath. Tammy's tone softened.

"The point is that Millie should be independent. Parents who can afford it can pay for a place for their kids to live. But the kids need to have their own lives."

Their own lives? Millie's life was my life. Without her, nothing in my life would be the same. I met Tammy's eyes.

"For a lot of parents, it's really hard when their kids are adults. They are so used to caregiving; they don't want to let their kids grow up."

There went my fantasy of growing old with Millie, side by side in our wheelchairs. Would I really have to leave Millie when I needed her the most? I glanced out the window. A raven pecked at something on the driveway. The squirrel had disappeared.

I looked at Marilyn, who was inspecting something in her lap. I couldn't live without Millie. I didn't want to live without Millie. I sat for a moment, taking all this in. Then a lightbulb went off. Maybe there was a way around this. "Could I visit?"

"I don't see why not." Tammy smiled.

"What about the rental properties? Could I use one of those?"

"Officially, you and your kid are supposed to have separate addresses. But with the housing crisis, they're loosening this requirement. People are having their kids live in an accessory dwelling unit on their property, and they're letting it slip."

"So, I could use the cottage?" I thought of the neat little one bedroom with the gas fireplace, a few feet from the house. I could trade homes with Brian and his partner. Or, better, Susan the mortgage broker's small apartment, with its deck and broken hot tub and view of the boardwalk. She had told me several times that she was thinking about getting married and moving out.

"Yes, Millie could live in the cottage, and you could visit her."

"I'm talking about me."

"That, too. They just don't want parents hovering."

Marilyn, who had been listening intently, finally chimed in. "Hovering has never been Danilyn's strong suit." She caught my eye and winked.

This was absurd. Here I was, all worried about what Tammy would think of the fact I spend half my time in New York. It was like someone had waved a magic wand. Poof. I was a bad mom; now I was a good one. I was already living apart from my child.

The sound of the backdoor cut short that train of thought. "Hi! We're home!" Jeanette called out cheerfully as she rolled Millie into the bathroom. I paused to greet them, then turned back to the business at hand. Tammy helped me strategize. I told her about my idea of getting Millie a roommate—"That would be great. Lots of people do that"—and how to manage the paperwork—"There are agencies that can handle all of this."

"I'm trying to think about what happens when I'm gone."

"That's a good idea."

I looked up and Tammy followed my eyes. Jeanette and Millie were approaching, Jeanette holding her by her gait belt as Millie marched toward us.

"Hey, Millie! Come on in!"

Millie paused and listened, then chuckled in recognition at the sound of my voice.

I got up to give Millie the rocker and pulled over the ottoman next to it, as Jeanette positioned her on the cushion and used the gait belt to get her to sit up straight. Millie grimaced—she doesn't like being messed with—then settled in. I put my hand on Millie's leg, and she reached for it, smiling and rocking, then glanced up at Tammy before looking away. Millie's smile is contagious. I smiled at Tammy, and she smiled back at me.

"Lots of giggling today." Jeanette, who was standing next to Marilyn's chair, was smiling, too.

"I can help you with that letter from Medi-Cal. I can't do anything about their decision, but I can look her up to see whether she's actually been dropped."

THAT NIGHT, I SPENT some time thinking about the small apartment and my retirement. I could fix the hot tub and get some nice furniture and come up every evening to make dinner in Millie's house. The apartment would be my writing refuge and a peaceful place to sleep. I was using up way too much space in the main house; others could live there instead. Maybe other disabled people. For sure, some of Millie's care providers. It would be better this way. I used to mourn the fact that Millie would never live independently. For a few moments, I was terrified she would. People my age aren't supposed to spend this much wondering how long they have left on this planet. But I can't map out the rest of Millie's life without mapping out the rest of mine.

What would Craig make of what's become of us in his absence? Like me, he'd be worried about our future, with the Sierras burning, sea levels rising, and the likelihood of our species surviving shrinking by the day. But he'd also be pleased. He'd be happy we are back in California, in Santa Cruz, no less, the beach town where he and his best friend taught themselves to surf. He'd be glad I took my mother's advice and found a big house and lots of help. He'd be tickled that we ended up adopting a hunting dog, even if fetching bird carcasses is the last thing on Biak's mind. He'd see that both his children have good souls.

And while he'd shake his head in gentle wonder at the mess I've made of his filing system, he'd be happy with where Millie has landed. Would he think about all the things we might have done together for Millie if he had lived? I hope not. I like to think he'd be too busy noticing the sunshine streaming into Millie's bedroom and the way it glitters in her hair. Craig and I met in a co-op, where we cooked together in a kitchen full of people. Thanks to Millie, I cook in a kitchen full of people all the time. Life has come full circle, even with him gone.

Millie could have had more of me. She could have more of me now. What has it cost her to have a mother who loves her job, loves her hobbies, and loves her friends, and somehow spends time on them all? Is it wrong to answer, not that much? Millie seems happy when we're together, but she's also happy when we're not, and for that I'll forever be grateful. When we're apart, I miss her the same way I miss Ralph, with a longing mixed with relief at the fact that he seems to be making his way. I'm living a life that my forty-year-old self feared would be a nightmare. I think about her a lot. I wish I could tell her it would be okay.

This is what I would share with her if I could. It's a sunny, blustery day in July, a month before Millie's twenty-third birthday, and I'm watching Millie's face. We're on the patio at my new favorite hangout, Shrine Coffee, named after the Shrine of St. Joseph, Guardian of the Redeemer. We walked here along West Cliff past ice plants and couples walking dogs, the deep blue of Monterey Bay stretching out beside us, sea spray in the air. If Shrine Coffee has an evangelical mission, it wears it lightly. Waiting for the bathroom, I read the spine of the only book on the built-in bookshelves; it was an edition of the New Testament, a quiet presence in the expanse of polished concrete and reclaimed wood. I wrestled Millie out of a wet diaper and replaced it with a dry one. I'm creaky and out of practice; someone knocked, and I called out an apology. I was ready to be embarrassed, but the woman smiled at us when I wheeled Millie past her on our way to get our drinks.

It was one of those days—and I used to have more of them—when every smell, every sight, every whisper of breeze, registers in my consciousness with miraculous clarity. No longer the background noise to whatever plans I happen to be making, the flowers, the breakers, the sunshine, and the tourists expanded to fill the entire frame. I had Millie for the entire afternoon, something that rarely happens these days. Maybe that's why the colors seemed so much more vivid. Maybe that's why I recognized the strangers we passed on our way to the Shrine when I saw them again on our way home.

And now it's Millie who has my full attention. She's sitting very still, her fingers caressing the buckle on her stroller. Her lips are pursed. What is she thinking about? I ponder her expression. Then I hear them, too. A flock of ravens have gathered in the grove behind Millie's head, high above us in the crown of the tallest tree. Wind rattles the leaves, and their cries are plaintive: *caw caw . . . caw caw caw*. A moment passes, then another, as we listen together. For the first time in months, I'm completely relaxed. I feel more alive than I've felt in years.

As the birds scold and summon each other, Millie and I listen. Then I join them. *Caw*, I croak. Millie's face dissolves into hilarity; she knows that I just made a joke. Since moving to Santa Cruz, we've seen a geneticist once, an elegant German woman with short gray hair who inspected Millie with interest. "Pitt-Hopkins," she announced. The test came back negative, and life moved on. Friends ask me whether I've had Millie's entire genome sequenced. I could, and someday I might, but I haven't felt the need. I know what our lives will be like when Millie is older. If we're lucky, much like this. These days, that's more than enough for me.

Epilogue

In 2017, on a perfect June morning, I woke up in Hyde Park. I was back in my old neighborhood for the first time in years.

The workshop I was attending left me free until midday, and I set out in the direction of our old townhouse. I ended my walk at a coffee shop that took up the first floor of the building where Ralph had once taken ceramics lessons. It was right around the corner from the row of homes where we had lived.

I ordered a chai and gazed at the park across the street—our park—which bordered Lake Shore Drive. Disease had taken some of the elms and ash trees. But others still stood, rising high above the lawn, like so many leafy giants standing watch over the skyscrapers downtown. I took in the meandering walkways, the vast expanses of grass, the tennis court, and the spacious playground where I'd pushed Millie in the baby swing, while Craig chased Ralph, who shrieked with pleasure. It was like looking through a telescope at a distant star; those days felt so far away.

Sitting there, so close to the place where Craig had died, I thought of the monk parakeets. On the way to the coffee shop, it had been hard to find our townhouse in the series of identical homes. The new owners had installed a birdbath. Nothing was growing in the tiny front yard except some tasteful groundcover and a bush. The sunflowers my mother had planted were long gone. Something rustled high in a treetop, and I looked up, waiting for birds to explode from the foliage. But it was just the wind.

THE WORKSHOP WENT WELL, and at 6 a.m. the next morning, a Lyft arrived to take me to the airport so I could catch my flight home. The driver, a woman about my age named Sonia, rearranged some bags to make room for my suitcase in the trunk.

I settled into the back seat, and Sonia turned the car around and drove in the direction of the nearest entrance to Lake Shore Drive. I looked out the window as we passed a Whole Foods. "Hyde Park sure has changed."

Sonia glanced at me in the rearview mirror. "Yeah. You used to have to go the whole way downtown to find a Marshall's. Now there's one on 49th."

I gazed past the grass toward the blue strip of lake as the car picked up speed. Then I turned back to the front seat. "How long have you been driving?"

"Two years." Sonia sighed. "But before that I worked for twenty-five years in the Chicago Public Schools. Severe and profound."

I'd been caught in my own thoughts, only partly listening, but now I was all ears. "My daughter was in that program."

"Really? I was an aide at Blair. Then Christopher."

I leaned forward, excited. "Millie went to both those schools!"

Sonia studied me in the mirror, her eyes widening. "I remember Millie! Millie was in my class!"

My breath caught. "Really? That's amazing!" Over the years, a half-dozen women had waited for Millie on the bus and accompanied her to school every morning. Why hadn't I paid more attention? Which one had she been? Sonia smiled, catching my eye. "I remember all those kids. They were just like my own."

It was a quick ride to O'Hare—no traffic this early on a Saturday—and soon we were pulling up to the curb.

"Here's Millie today." I showed Sonia a picture on my phone of Millie and me standing together in the sun with the ocean stretching out behind us. I'm holding her in an embrace to keep her upright.

Sonia sighed. "They grow up so fast." She helped me with my suitcase, then gave me a big hug. "Say hi to her for me."

"I will."

I turned, and a lump came to my throat. Almost ten years had passed since we left Chicago. Few signs remained of my life in this city. But Millie was remembered, and she'd been loved. She had drawn others to her, and they warmed themselves in her presence. She'd found her flock. And she'd ruled her realm. It had never been just down to me.

ACKNOWLEDGMENTS

This book has been a long time coming. Over the years, I presented sections of it to audiences at Columbia University, Harvard University, the London School of Economics and Political Science, New York University, Princeton University, Rice University, Stony Brook University, the University of California at San Diego, the University of Chicago, the University of Colorado, the University of Virginia, and Western University, and at conferences hosted by the American Association of Anthropology, the Danish Anthropology MEGA-seminar, the Franke Institute, the Society for Applied Anthropology, and the Society for Linguistic Anthropology. I'm grateful to Josh Babcock, Chris Ball, Sandra Bamford, Ira Bashkow, Anya Bernstein, João Biehl, Pam Block, Summerson Carr, Lucien Castaing-Taylor, Amy Clark, Jennifer Cole, Biella Coleman, Eve Danziger, Shannon Dawdy, Lis Dobrin, Austin Duncan, Terra Edwards, Mathew Engelke, Michele Friedner, Sue Gal, Kate Goldfarb, Faye Ginsburg, Byron Good, MaryJo Good, Mara Green, Gökçe Gunel, Nick Harkness, Michael Herzfeld, Vikram Jaswal, Andrew Johnson, Arthur Kleinman, Doreen Lee, Mathew Liebmann, William Mazzarella, Carol McGranahan, Shayla Monroe, Erin Moore, Fred Myers, Constantine Nakassis, Alejandro Paz, Beth Povinelli, Laurence Ralph, Rayna Rapp, Kamala Russell, Bambi Schieffelin, the late Michael Silverstein, Tauna Szymanski, Sunaura Taylor, Chika Watanabe, and Rihan Yeh for their insights and hospitality.

A special shout-out to Julia Elyachar, my partner in proprioception, for her wisdom and references; Michael Lempert and Miyako Inoue, for bringing me into the conversation on technology, semiotics, and mediation; Julianne Obadia, for the conversation she started on intimacy and proximity; Rachel Adams and Don Kulick for their encouraging words; and Deb Thomas and Joseph Masco, whose expanded vision of sovereignty prompted my thinking on vulnerability, care, and power. Thanks to Helena Dietz, Khaled Furani, Brendan Hart, Dagmar Herzog, Webb Keane, Erin Rafferty, Joshua Reno, and Tyler Zoanni for being ongoing sources of conversation and inspiration. Eva Kittay responded to an email out of the blue and became a valued interlocutor. Aisha Beliso de Jesús, Chip Colwell, and Richard Grinker talked through the project with me and helped me strategize. Jim Siegel planted ideas in my brain that provoke me still.

As part of my day job, I was on hand for pathbreaking conversations at two extraordinary meetings: the Wenner-Gren Symposium, Disability Worlds in Tucson in 2018, and our first Wenner-Gren Seminar, A Workshop in Radically Humanist Praxis in Cape Town in 2022. Faye Ginsburg and Rayna Rapp, who supported this project (and me) when I moved to New York, had a strong influence on my thinking, and I learned much from conversations with S. Can Aciksoz, Renu Addlakha, Tom Boellstorff, Patrick J. Devlieger, Arseli Dokumaci, Michele Friedner, Richard Grinker, Cassandra Hartblay, the late Devva Kasnitz, Beatriz Miranda-Galaraza, Herbert Muyinda, Laurence Ralph, Rayna Rapp, Ayo Wahlberg, Susan Whyte, and Tyler Zoanni. In Cape Town, Kamari Clarke, Kelly Gillespie, and Deb Thomas showed me how to create a new kind of space for thought and action; I am only now beginning to fathom everything I learned at that meeting from Su'ad Abdul Khabeer, Donna Auston, Lucia Cantero, Ruchi Chaturvedi, Victoria Collis-Buthelezi, Jason De León, Justin Dunnavant, Ntone Edjabe, Divine Fuh, Karelle Hall, Ryan Jobson, Aja Lans, Nosipho Mngomezulu, Wayne Modest, Julie Nxadi, Suren Pillay, Kwame Otu, Lesego Rampolokeng, Ciraj Rassool, Savannah Shange, Audra Simpson, Tendayi Sithole, Marlon Swai, Ahmed Veriava, Rachel Watkins, and Leniqueca Welcome.

No one writes alone; that's as true for me as it is for other authors. In New York and later online, I shared chapters with Elsa Davidson, Maura Finkelstein, Elayne Oliphant, Annabelle Pitkin, and Andrea Voyer. As soon as we discovered we were working on similar topics, Patrick McKearney, Joshua Reno, and Tyler Zoanni joined forces with me to share and discuss drafts. Kelly Gillespie read an early version and made pivotal suggestions. At a critical juncture, Maura Finkelstein and Deb Thomas read the entire manuscript swiftly and generously. I had professional help from Jane Roseman and Rose Skelton; along with Nomi Stone, Rose Skelton runs Field Studio, which hosted the workshop where I wrote the prologue to this book.

At the University of Chicago Press, I benefited from conversations with Mary Al-Sayed and Dylan Montanari; at Fordham University Press, I deeply appreciate Thomas Lay's belief in this project, and the wonderful discussions I had with Clara Han and Andrew Braudel. At Princeton University Press, Fred

Appel commented helpfully on a chapter I thought was finished. (It wasn't.) Five anonymous readers evaluated the manuscript thoroughly and astutely. I benefited from their advice.

Ken Wissoker at Duke University Press deserves his own paragraph. I contacted him with a vague question concerning genre. I expected an equally vague answer. Instead, he read and critiqued the entire Frankensteinian draft. His comments on how to situate the book in the "blur" between academic and literary writing served as my guide throughout this process. This book is so much better than it would have been without his help.

If I have come even close to nailing the landing, I have these colleagues to thank. But without the support I received in Santa Cruz, this project never would have taken off. I owe a huge thanks to Laura Davis, my writing teacher, and my talented classmates, especially Jen Astone, Susan Burrowes, Leslie Carlin, Sheila Coonerty, Vanya Erickson, Melinda Iuster, Cathy Krizik, Barb Martin, Magali Morales, Katie Olson, Molly Segale, Phoenix Song, Eileene Tejada, and Renee Winter. My colleague Megan Moodie shared her street smarts; her beautiful prose has long been an inspiration. Karen Barad prompted my thinking early on. I received a National Science Foundation (NSF) Scholar's Award in 2016, which allowed me to take courses in language development and augmentative and alternative communication at San Jose State from Lyle Lustigman and Shannon McCord. I benefited from the education in developmental psychology I received from my mentor, Nameera Akhtar, along with Janette Dinishak, Vikram Jaswal, and Barbara Rogoff. Vikram Jaswal and Linda Burkhart read and commented on the chapter on PODD. Ralph Lombreglia, whose own work is so good it makes me never want to touch my computer again, scoured the manuscript for clichés and untangled some twisted patches of prose.

A word about dialogue. I recorded the interviews and speech therapy sessions described in "Proximity to Disability," "The Sovereignty of Vulnerability," and "Becoming an Operating System"; for the first chapter I had sound, and for the second and third I had video, which I transcribed, described, and edited for the purpose of these chapters. I based the rest of the scenes on notes, documents, and memory. While my portrayal is true to the impression these events left in my mind, I realize that others may recall these happenings differently. I offered individuals mentioned in the book an opportunity to catch these discrepancies; a few suggested corrections, which I gratefully made. I contacted Karen Baca, Marylin Baddawi, Hana Beddawi, Darcy Bellman, Cassidy Bellman, Karin Best, Ralph Best, J. P. Brown, Fenella Cannell, Adriana Coronado, Cameron Croghan, Julie Croghan, Leia Delabahan, Tim Duane, Gitta Dunn, Rachel Fulton, Dan Haifley, Julia Haifley, Rebecca Haifley,

Marion Jordan, Wendy King, Marilyn Landon, Lisa Larson, Eszter Lazlo, Amy Lebichuck, Diana Lehr, Jeanette Lopez, Kim Locke, Vicky Nunez, Karen Park, Katy Petersen, Max Poen, Scott Richerson, Adriana Rivera, Janine Roeth, Clare Rogowski, Emma Rogowski, Ron Rogowski, Geo Rutherford, Jim Rutherford, Natalie Rutherford, Sandra Rutherford, Suzannah Rutherford, Tom Rutherford, Veronica Rutherford, Aniek van Ham, Andrew Whitehead, Jack Ziegler, Marlis Ziegler, and Xiaona Zhang. I would have contacted the late Brigitte Best, Dick Best, Donald Rutherford, Marilyn Rutherford, and Bill Wyman if I could have. In the book, I used pseudonyms for the named characters who didn't want to be identified or whom I was unable to reach—that is, with two significant exceptions. Melitta Best did not read the manuscript, though she helped me write it. I think of Craig Best every day.

Readers interested in more technical versions of the book's argument will find them in the following venues:

> "How Structuralism Matters," *Hau* 6, no. 3 (2016): 61–77.
> "Proximity to Disability," *Anthropological Quarterly* 93, no. 1 (2020): 1453–81.
> "Becoming an Operating System: Disability, Difference, and the Ethics of Communication in the United States," *American Ethnologist* 48, no. 2 (2021): 139–52.
> "The Sovereignty of Vulnerability," in *Sovereignty Unhinged: An Illustrated Primer for the Study of Present Intensities, Disavowals, and Temporal Derangements*, edited by Deborah A. Thomas and Joseph Masco (Durham, NC: Duke University Press, 2023).

That's the work; then there's life. Here, I'm at a loss. I'm indebted to many more people than I can name. But there are three I must mention. While finishing *Beautiful Mystery*, I hit some milestones: My son became an adult, I remarried, and my mother passed away. You need to spend some time with Ralph Best ("R1") and my beloved husband and fellow poodle parent, Ralph Lombreglia ("R2"), if you're confused about the meaning of kindness, curiosity, and honor. When I was a toddler, Marilyn Rutherford hung all the pictures at my eye level. Need I say more? I dedicate this book to them.

NOTES

WORLDS WITHOUT WORDS

1 Joseph Shapiro, "As Hospitals Fear Being Overwhelmed by Covid-19, Do the Disabled Get the Same Access?," *All Things Considered*, December 14, 2020, https://www.npr.org/2020/12/14/945056176/as-hospitals-fear-being-overwhelmed-by-covid-19-do-the-disabled-get-the-same-acc.
2 Michele Friedner and Emily Cohen, "Inhabitable Worlds: Troubling Disability, Debility, and Ability Narratives," *Somatosphere*, April 20, 2015, *Inhabitable Worlds* series, http://somatosphere.net/2015/inhabitable-worlds-troubling-disability-debility-and-ability-narratives.html/, p. 1. Friedner and Cohen draw from the philosopher Martin Heidegger's notion of "worlding," which anthropologist Mei Zhan takes up in her description of worlds as "emergent socialities entangled in dynamic imaginaries of pasts, futures, and presents." See Zhan, *Other-Worldly*, loc. 251. Like Zhan, I am interested in exploring (and, to be honest, defending) the "plural ways of being human that are contained in the very different orientations of the world." See Zhan, *Other-Worldly*, loc. 561. I am also inspired by Ginsburg and Rapp, "Disability/Anthropology"; and Ginsburg and Rapp, *Disability Worlds*.
3 For students of semiotics, a sign is an object that stands for another object to a mind. My understanding of what language does, and what signs more generally do, is drawn from the American philosopher Charles Sanders Peirce. See Parmentier, *Signs in Society*.
4 Goode, *World Without Words*, loc. 710.
5 Goode, *World Without Words*, loc. 752.
6 Zola, foreword to *World Without Words*, loc. 44.
7 In addition to Reno's remarkable study, Friedner and Wolf-Meyer, "Becoming Malleable," provides a bibliography of recent work. Green, *Making Sense*, shares my interest in the emergence of conventions and how we need to understand this as a matter of ethics. See also Edwards, *Going Protactile*.
8 Keane, *Ethical Life*, 16, makes this point adroitly; so does Keane, *Animals, Robots, Gods*.

9   Haraway, *Companion Species Manifesto*; Harding, "Convicted by the Spirit"; Luhrmann, *When God Talks Back*; Keane, *Signs of Recognition*; and Bubandt, *Empty Seashell*, provide good examples of this.
10 Boyer, *Religion Explained*.
11 Rogoff et al., "Firsthand Learning"; Rochat and Callaghan, "What Drives Symbolic Development?," 27.
12 See Rogoff, "Cognition as a Collaborative Process"; Rogoff et al., "Interaction with Babies"; Bates and Elman, "Learning Rediscovered"; and Namy and Waxman, "Symbols Redefined," 274. Vygotsky, *Mind in Society*, inspired much of this work. Grove et al., "See What I Mean," extends the insight to interactions with disabled people. "It is extremely common to encounter claims that a person with a disability can communicate complex information in ways that are hard for outside observers to verify. Such beliefs result not only from an understandable commitment to realizing the potential of individuals, but from the nature of interactions with people who function at an early level of communicative development, and the developmental path of intentional states" (197). Jorgensen, "Least Dangerous Assumption," pioneered this approach.
13 Mel Baggs, "In My Language," *YouTube*, January 14, 2007, video, 8:37, https://www.youtube.com/watch?v=JnylMIhI2jc. See also Mukhopadhyay, "Five Poems"; Ochs and Solomon, "Autistic Sociality"; Autistic Self-Advocacy Network and Bascom, *Loud Hands*; Wolf-Meyer, *Unraveling*; and Botha, "Academic, Activist, or Advocate?"
14 Carlson, "Philosophers of Intellectual Disability"; Carlson, *Faces of Intellectual Disability*; S. Taylor, *Beasts of Burden*; and Kittay, *Learning from My Daughter*, also cover this fraught ground.
15 Hannah-Jones et al., *1619 Project*, 376. See also Coates, *Between the World and Me*.

WHAT TO EXPECT

1   Bérubé, "Life as We Know It"; see also Bérubé, *Life as We Know It*.
2   What to Expect First Year Month-by-Month, "6-Month-Old Baby," accessed January 15, 2015, http://www.whattoexpect.com/first-year/month-by-month/month-6.aspx.
3   Eisenberg et al., *What to Expect*, 245.

DIAGNOSIS

1   Davis, *Enforcing Normalcy*, 3–12; Davis, *Bending Over Backwards*, 92. See also Shakespeare, "Disability Studies"; and Shakespeare and Watson, "Defending the Social Model."
2   Davis, *Enforcing Normalcy*, 10.
3   See McKearney and Zoanni, "Introduction"; see also Friedner and Wolf-Meyer, "Becoming Malleable."

EARLY INTERVENTION

1. In 1975, Congress passed the Education for All Handicapped Children Act. Early intervention became part of it in 1986 when the Act was reauthorized (and renamed). See Center for Parent Information and Resources, "Early Intervention, Then and Now," updated March 2014, May 2023, https://www.parentcenterhub.org/ei-history/.

NO FUTURE

1. For a vivid and horrific portrait of this place, see Chao, *In the Shadow*.
2. Chao, *In the Shadow*, 178.
3. Vonnegut, *Cat's Cradle*, 91.

PROXIMITY TO DISABILITY

1. Obadia, "Introduction," 1343.
2. Landsman, *Reconstructing Motherhood*. Other accounts include Grinker, *Unstrange Minds*; Silverman, *Understanding Autism*; and Ginsburg and Rapp, *Disability Worlds*.
3. Gammeltoft, *Haunting Images*, describes this.
4. I'm drawing on Schneider, *American Kinship*; Weston, *Families We Choose*; and Povinelli, "Notes on Gridlock." For the deeper history behind this view of kinship, see Warner, *Letters of the Republic*; and Rutherford, "Proximity to Disability."
5. Douglas and Michaels, *Mommy Myth*; Orenstein, *Flux*; Ennis, *Intensive Mothering*; and Giles, *Mothering in the Age of Neoliberalism*, also describe this trend.
6. Buck, *Child Who Never Grew*. Pearson, *Ordinary Future*, 78, mentions Buck's article and its impact.
7. Buck, *Child Who Never Grew*, 21.
8. Buck, *Child Who Never Grew*, 27.
9. See Schweik, *Ugly Laws*; Burgdorf and Burgdorf, "History of Unequal Treatment"; Garland-Thomson, *Staring*; Carlson, *Faces of Intellectual Disability*; Goodey, *History of Intelligence*; and Nielsen, *Disability History*.
10. See Grinker, *Nobody's Normal*, 14–15; Semonin, "Monsters in the Marketplace"; and Berger, *Disarticulate*, 15–43.
11. Cook, "Of Men," 147.
12. Cook, "Of Men," 145.
13. Davis, *Enforcing Normalcy*, loc. 645, 744, makes this connection. See also Garland-Thomson, "Cultural Work"; Adams, *Sideshow U.S.A.*; and Davis, *Bending Over Backwards*, 92.
14. Simplican, *Capacity Contract*, 49, 56–57.
15. See Ginsburg and Rapp, *Disability Worlds*, 87; Carey et al., *Allies and Obstacles*, 38. See also Nielsen, *Beyond the Miracle Worker*.
16. As Johnson said to one photographer, "I don't want this unusual story diluted with a distracting visual narrative of the Amazing Crippled Attorney!" Johnson, *Too Late*, 231. See also Garland-Thomson, *Staring*, 91, 188.

17 Ginsburg and Rapp, *Disability Worlds*, 4, call this the "doubled telos of modernity."
18 Merceira, *Living Otherwise*, 139.
19 J. Taylor, "On Recognition."
20 Garfinkel, *Studies*, 47–48, in Keane, *Ethical Life*, 90.
21 See Mauss, *Gift*; Derrida, *Given Time*.
22 Images of this work are available online. See *Ron Mueck*, an exhibition at the Museum of Fine Arts, Houston, which began on February 26, 2017, and ended on August 13, 2017 (https://www.mfah.org/exhibitions/ronmueck).
23 Hart, "Autism Parents and Neurodiversity," makes this point; so does Ochs et al., "Communication"; and Ginsburg and Rapp, *Disability Worlds*.
24 See Ferry, review of *Static Encephalopathies*.
25 Kafer, *Feminist, Crip, Queer*, 47–68. See also Razack, "From Pity to Respect."
26 Carey, *On the Margins of Citizenship*, 183. Carey et al., "Sometimes Allies"; and Carey et al., *Allies and Obstacles*, also discuss this history.
27 Kafer, *Feminist, Crip, Queer*, 67.
28 Kafer, *Feminist, Crip, Queer*, 67.

THE SOVEREIGNTY OF VULNERABILITY

1 I'm drawing from Agamben, *Homo Sacer*; Hansen and Stepputat, "Sovereignty Revisited"; Cattelino, *High Stakes*; Derrida, *Beast and the Sovereign*; Rutherford, *Laughing at Leviathan*; and Rutherford, *Living in the Stone Age*. See also Foucault, "Governmentality."
2 Mani, *Contentious Traditions*, describes this history.
3 See Wadsworth et al., "Integrating Remote Sensing."
4 See Ginsburg and Rapp, *Disability Worlds*, 73–74.
5 Bayo Akomolafe, "Astray, Awkwardly: An Autistic Politics (Republished)," *Bayo Akomolafe*, August 16, 2022, https://www.bayoakomolafe.net/post/astray-awkwardly-an-autistic-politics-copy.
6 Foucault, *Society Must Be Defended*, 15–16; Michael Hardt, "War by Other Means," *Sidecar* (*New Left Review* blog), January 21, 2021, https://newleftreview.org/sidecar/posts/war-by-other-means.
7 Akomolafe, "Astray, Awkwardly."
8 See Furani, "Mastering Submission," 701. Furani proposes doing away with the concept of sovereignty; I'd rather repurpose it as "unhinged from the state," along the lines proposed by Thomas and Masco, *Sovereignty Unhinged*.
9 Simplican, *Capacity Contract*, 99. See also Davis, *Enabling Acts*.
10 Habermas, *Structural Transformation of the Public Sphere*.
11 See Berlant, *Queen of America*; Edelman, *No Future*.
12 Compare Cannell, *Power and Intimacy*.
13 Goodwin, "Competent Speaker."
14 Adler-Bolton and Vierkant, in *Health Communism*, discuss the relationship between capitalism and health. The idea that work should be part of the rehabilitation of disabled people has a long history.

15 "IDEA—the Individuals with Disabilities Education Act," http://www.parentcenterhub.org/repository/idea/.
16 Morrison, *Nobel Lecture*, in Ochs, "Experiencing Language," 149. See also Mead, "Self."
17 Heidegger, *Poetry, Language, Thought*, 207.
18 In a similar spirit, the speech therapist turns to Liam with a paper towel she's just used to wipe the table. "Okay, Sir Liam. Can you help me throw it away?"
19 I have in mind something like the "otherwise" Povinelli describes in *Economies of Abandonment*.
20 Arendt, *Human Condition*, 28–37.
21 Simplican, *Capacity Contract*, 119–20.
22 Kittay, *Love's Labor*; Kittay, "When Caring Is Just."
23 Nussbaum, *Frontiers of Justice*.
24 Pamela Block explores this insight in research undertaken with Gerald McKinley. "People have generally looked at the 'burden' of care for the non-disabled person, but care can be reciprocal, it is a relationship of care." Rob Rombouts, "Supporting Mutual Care Relations," *Western Social Science News and Updates*, July 25, 2022, https://www.ssc.uwo.ca/news/2022/Pamela_Block_mutual_care_relationships.html.
25 Piepzna-Samarasinha, *Care Work*.
26 Maura Finkelstein, "In Defense of Academic Freedom: Defamation, Intimidation, and Suspension," statement presented in a webinar organized by DC, Maryland, and Virginia Faculty for Academic Freedom, cosponsored by the MESA Task Force on Civil and Human Rights, Gaza in Context Collaborative Project, and Faculty for Justice in Palestine Network, March 21, 2024, https://www.jadaliyya.com/Details/45860. See also Jeremy Scahill, "'Man-Made Hell on Earth': A Canadian Doctor on His Medical Mission to Gaza," *Intercept*, May 23, 2024, https://theintercept.com/2024/03/23/intercepted-doctor-gaza-interview/.

BECOMING AN OPERATING SYSTEM

1 Cusk, *A Life's Work*, 91.
2 See Silverstein, "Language Structure and Linguistic Ideology"; Woolard and Schieffelin, "Language Ideology"; Irvine and Gal, "Language Ideology and Linguistic Differentiation"; Carr, *Scripting Addiction*; and Carr, *Working the Difference*. Saussure, in *Course in General Linguistics*, describe this (mistaken, in his view) understanding of language.
3 Derrida, "Signature, Event, Context," 307–8. Derrida also refers to the way people speak of communicating a "movement or tremor." But he does not privilege the nonsemiotic meaning of the word. You need the idea of communication as the transfer of meaning to conceive of these metaphorical usages.
4 See Agha, *Language and Social Relations*; Silverstein, "Shifters."
5 Goossens et al., in *Engineering the Preschool Environment*, describe this approach.
6 Swift, *Gulliver's Travels*, 170.
7 Linda Burkhart, personal communication, August 9, 2019. "Symbols can be spoken words, sign language, or pictographs in a robust AAC [augmentative and

alternative communication] system. Patterns and rules reflect both the spoken language of the AAC as well as the patterns of vocabulary organizations and also strategic conventions for using a limited set of symbols at different speeds, through different access methods."

8 I shared this chapter with Linda, and she sent me the following note: "One can not learn a language on just one day, we only barely started. I was focusing on connection—facial expressions, tone of voice, waiting and responding in a respectful turn taking dance with Millie, then beginning to overlay the language on top of that. Connection is the basis of language—the desire to connect and communicate with another person is what makes language something to be interested in learning. . . . Communication and desire for connection are inborn drives that are built into every individual and were around long before any languages existed. In my mind, languages evolved because of that human need. Languages serve to add details and expand upon that desire to connect with others, not replace it. I think that's what you're arguing." Linda Burkhart, personal communication, August 9, 2019. See also Erna Alant, "Being with Another: Basis for AAC Intervention?," *Erna Alant Consultancy*, August 5, 2019, https://ernaalantconsultancy.com/2019/08/05/being-with-the-basis-for-aac-intervention/.

9 See Kliewer et al., "Who May Be Literate?"

10 Jaswal et al., "Eye-Tracking." See also Heyworth et al., "Perspective." Jaswal and Akhtar, in "Being Versus Appearing Socially Uninterested," include commentaries from prominent psychologists, several of whom take issue with their well-documented findings challenging the presumption that people with autism lack social motivation. These critics call into question insights that Jaswal and Akhtar draw from autistic people, to the extent these informants relied on the "discredited techniques" of facilitated communication and the rapid prompting method. See Vyse et al., "Whose Words Are These?"; and Rutherford, "Benefits of Modesty."

11 Compare Bialecki, "No Caller ID for the Soul."

12 Gal, "Politics of Translation"; Inoue, "Speech Without a Speaking Body"; and Silverstein, "Translation, Transduction, Transformation," make this point. See also Benjamin, "Task of the Translator."

13 McKearney, "Limits of Knowing Other Minds." See also Kulick, "Problem of Speaking for Others *Redux*."

14 "Erin Sheldon: Literacy in Angelman Syndrome Workshop (Saturday Afternoon Panel #1)," *YouTube*, December 7, 2014, https://www.youtube.com/watch?v=IRSErkJUZiM.

15 See Harry, *Melanie*.

16 Harry, *Melanie*, 2, 15.

17 Harry, *Melanie*, 132.

PROPRIOCEPTIVE SOCIALITY

1 See Akhtar, "Is Joint Attention Necessary?"; and Akhtar and Gernsbacher, "Joint Attention and Early Vocabulary."

2 See Keane, *Ethical Life*, 51, 137; and Keane, *Signs of Recognition*.
3 Sherrington, *Integrative Action of the Nervous System*. See also Elyachar, "Anthropology of Proprioception."
4 This is Irving Goffman's term from "Alienation from Interaction." Sidnell builds on it in insisting on the importance of "dyadic, mutual involvement and attunement," in "Architecture of Intersubjectivity," 365–66.
5 I draw my version of this story from Cole, *Pride and a Daily Marathon*, 10, passim.
6 See Heidegger, *Being and Time*; and Heidegger, *Question Concerning Technology*.
7 Edwards, "Bridging the Gap"; Edwards, "Sign-Creation"; Edwards, "Re-Channeling Language."
8 See Puig de la Bellacasa, *Matters of Care*. See also Hart, "Autism Parents and Neurodiversity," on "somatic modes of attention."
9 I'm drawing this description from Brentari and Edwards, "Feeling Phonology"; and Edwards and Brentari, "Grammatical Incorporation of Demonstratives."
10 We could replace the word *framing* with *articulation*. Friedner and Helmreich, "Sound Studies Meets Deaf Studies," 80.
11 Cole, *Pride and a Daily Marathon*, 26.
12 Cole, *Pride and a Daily Marathon*, 26.
13 Mauss, "Techniques of the Body," 70.
14 Russell, "Facing Another," 316.
15 Reddy, *How Infants Know Minds*, 56.
16 Reddy, *How Infants Know Minds*, 100.
17 Cole, *Pride and a Daily Marathon*, 163.
18 Cole, *Pride and a Daily Marathon*, 166.
19 Cole, *Pride and a Daily Marathon*, 166.
20 Quoted in Puig de la Bellacasa, *Matters of Care*, loc. 1729. But as Puig de la Bellacasa goes on to argue, "The generative character of touch is not given, it emerges from contact with a world, a process through which a body learns, evolves, and becomes." Puig de la Bellacasa, *Matters of Care*, loc. 1968.
21 Our journey entails the shared "passing into pleasure" that Annelieke Driesson describes in "Pleasure and Dementia." Walking with Millie involves "active-passive surrender" on Millie's part and attunement to an "appreciating subject" on mine.
22 Vikram Jaswal pointed out to me that this warning exaggerates the risk: "Rarely have neighbors, friends, peers ever doubted the nonspeaking folks I know who communicate with assistance. It's only when we get to institutions where there is some expert knowledge about the way people are supposed to be that these issues of belief arise." Vikram Jaswal, personal communication, July 17, 2022.
23 Compare "Carolyn Lazard's Crip Time," *MoMa Magazine*, April 7, 2021, https://www.moma.org/magazine/articles/529.
24 Savarese's works "Swoon," "Tongue," and "Blanch-Ink-Jet Maneuver" beautifully describe this.
25 Weheliye, *Habeas Viscus*.
26 Agamben, *Homo Sacer*.
27 Julia Elyachar makes this point. See "Anthropology of Proprioception."

28 Speaking of her experience as a dancer, Deborah Thomas writes, "We *knew* and became conscious by doing something with our bodies—together, and in this way became human." *Political Life in the Wake of the Plantation*, 207. To meet the demands of the work of repair—in this case, the repair required to come to terms with the racist foundations of modernity—Thomas proposes grounding a politics in the "embodied self." Quoting Thomas Csordas, Thomas foregrounds the unknowability of the other—"the ongoing indeterminacy and flux of adult cultural life"—while maintaining the possibility of connection. Csordas, "Embodiment as a Paradigm," 40, quoted in Thomas, *Political Life in the Wake of the Plantation*, 219.
29 See Napolitano, "On the Touch-Event," 86, 87.
30 See Ochs and Solomon, "Autistic Sociality"; Rapp and Ginsburg, "Enabling Disability"; Rapp and Ginsburg, "Reverberations"; Rafferty et al., "Lonely Joy"; Friedner and Helmreich, "Sound Studies Meets Deaf Studies"; Merceira, *Living Other*wise*; and McKearney and Zoanni, "Cognitive Disability."
31 Durkheim, *Elementary Forms of the Religious Life*, 163.
32 Ginsburg and Rapp, *Disability Worlds*, 120–53.

CROSS COUNTRY

1 Macdonald, *Vesper Flights*, 43.
2 Macdonald, *Vesper Flights*, 44.

WHAT SOCIAL WORLDS ARE MADE OF

1 Arnold, *Testimony of Steve Biko*, loc. 924.
2 Césaire, *Discourse on Colonialism*, 73, in Scott, "Re-Enchantment of Humanism," 121. See also Wynter, "Unsettling the Coloniality of Being," 260; Weheliye, *Habeas Viscus*; Thomas, "Time and the Otherwise"; and Thomas, *Political Life in the Wake of the Plantation*, 1–66. Some of the most potent theorizations of the limits of Western understandings of the human have come from scholars who have paid heed to the intersections between racism and ableism. See Ralph, *Renegade Dreams*; Connor et al., "Dis/ability Critical Race Studies (DisCrit)"; and Piepzna-Samarasinha, *Care Work*.
3 See Herzog, *Unlearning Eugenics*; and Herzog, *Question of Unworthy Life*. In the decades leading up to World War II, German psychiatrists, religious leaders, and politicians measured the worth of a life by gauging a person's ability to engage in productive labor. Millie would have belonged to the category of "useless eaters."
4 Ralph, "Becoming Aggrieved."
5 See Latour, "On Interobjectivity."
6 Geertz, *Interpretation of Cultures*, 55.
7 Jim preferred Jacques Derrida's writings on the relationship between language and social life. See Siegel, *Naming the Witch*; and Derrida, "Structure, Sign, and Play."
8 As I learned by reading Carsten and Hugh-Jones, "Introduction"; Cannell, *Power and Intimacy*; McKinnon, "Domestic Exceptions"; and McKinnon, "Houses and Hierarchy." See also Lévi-Strauss, "Clan, Lineage, House."

9   See Gell, "Strathernograms," 65.
10 Edwards, "Language Emergence," 142, describes this.
11 See Russell, "Facing Another."
12 Friedner, *Sensory Futures*, 3.
13 Barad, *Meeting the Universe Halfway*, loc. 4492.
14 Sahlins, *What Kinship Is*, xi.
15 Lévi-Strauss, *Elementary Structures of Kinship*, 84–85.
16 Solomon, *Far from the Tree*, 74.
17 Lévi-Strauss, *Elementary Structures of Kinship*, 59. See also Miyazaki, *Method of Hope*.
18 Vehmas and Mietola, *Narrowed Lives*, 14.
19 Vehmas and Mietola, *Narrowed Lives*, 26.
20 Vehmas and Mietola, *Narrowed Lives*, 5.
21 Tim Tebow Foundation, "Watch the Official 2021 Night to Shine Worldwide Highlight Video," accessed July 25, 2021, https://www.timtebowfoundation.org/ministries/night-to-shine; Branch and Pilon, "Tim Tebow."
22 Same-sex couples don't fit the script either, but this also doesn't seem to matter. Sexuality of any sort is considered out of bounds for people like Millie, at least in the United States. See Kulick and Rydström, *Loneliness and Its Opposite*.
23 Curtis and Vehmas, "Appendix," 209. Curtis and Vehmas borrow this phrase from Kagan, "What's Wrong with Speciesism?"

BIBLIOGRAPHY

Adams, Rachel. *Sideshow U.S.A.: Freaks and the American Cultural Imagination*. Chicago: University of Chicago Press, 2001.
Adler-Bolton, Beatrice, and Artie Vierkant. *Health Communism: A Surplus Manifesto*. New York: Verso, 2022.
Agamben, Giorgio. *Homo Sacer: Sovereign Power and Bare Life*. Translated by Daniel Heller-Roazen. Stanford, CA: Stanford University Press, 1998.
Agha, Asif. *Language and Social Relations*. Cambridge: Cambridge University Press, 2007.
Akhtar, Nameera. "Is Joint Attention Necessary for Early Word Learning?" In *The Development of Social Cognition and Communication*, edited by C. Tamis-LeMonda and B. D. Homer. Mahwah, NJ: Erlbaum, 2005.
Akhtar, Nameera, and M. A. Gernsbacher. "Joint Attention and Early Vocabulary: A Critical Look." *Language and Linguistics Compass* 1 (2007): 195–207.
Arendt, Hannah. *The Human Condition*. Second ed. With a foreword by Danielle Allen. Chicago: University of Chicago Press, [1958] 1998.
Arnold, Millard W., ed. *The Testimony of Steve Biko*. Johannesburg: Picador Africa, [1978] 2017.
Autistic Self-Advocacy Network and Julia Bascom. *Loud Hands: Autistic People, Speaking*. Washington, DC: Autistic Press, 2012.
Barad, Karen. *Meeting the Universe Halfway: Quantum Physics and the Entanglement of Matter and Meaning*. Durham, NC: Duke University Press, 2007.
Bates, Elizabeth, and Jerry Elman. "Learning Rediscovered." *Science* 274, no. 5294 (1996): 1849–50.
Benjamin, Walter. "The Task of the Translator." In *Illuminations: Essays and Reflections*, edited by Hannah Arendt; translated by Harry Zohn. New York: Harcourt, Brace, and World, [1923] 1968.
Berger, James. *The Disarticulate: Language, Disability, and the Narratives of Modernity*. New York: New York University Press, 2014.
Berlant, Lauren. *The Queen of America Goes to Washington City*. Durham, NC: Duke University Press, 1997.

Bérubé, Michael. *Life as We Know It: A Father, a Family, and an Exceptional Child*. New York: Knopf Doubleday, 1996.

Bérubé, Michael. "Life as We Know It: A Father, a Son, and a Genetic Destiny." *Harper's Magazine*, December 1994.

Bialecki, Jon. "No Caller ID for the Soul: Demonization, Charisma, and the Unstable Subject of Protestant Language Ideology." *Anthropological Quarterly* 84, no. 3 (Summer 2011): 679–703.

Botha, Monique. "Academic, Activist, or Advocate? Angry, Entangled, and Emerging: A Critical Reflection on Autistic Knowledge Production." *Frontiers of Psychology* 12, section *Developmental Psychology* (September 28, 2021): 4–12. doi:10.3389/fpsyg.2021.727542.

Boyer, Pascal. *Religion Explained*. New York: Basic Books, 2021.

Branch, John, and Mary Pilon. "Tim Tebow, a Careful Evangelical." *New York Times*, March 27, 2012.

Brentari, Diane, and Terra Edwards. "Feeling Phonology: The Conventionalization of Phonology in Protactile Communities in the United States." *Language* 96, no. 4 (2020): 819–40.

Bubandt, Nils. *The Empty Seashell: Witchcraft and Doubt on an Indonesian Island*. Ithaca, NY: Cornell University Press, 2014.

Buck, Pearl S. *The Child Who Never Grew*. Bethesda, MD: Woodbine House, [1950] 1992.

Burgdorf, Marcia Pearce, and Robert Burgdorf Jr. "A History of Unequal Treatment: The Qualifications of Handicapped Persons as a 'Suspect Class' Under the Equal Protection Clause." *Santa Clara Law Review* 15, no. 4 (1975): 855–88.

Cannell, Fenella. *Power and Intimacy in the Christian Philippines*. Cambridge: Cambridge University Press, 1999.

Carey, Allison C. *On the Margins of Citizenship: Intellectual Disability and Civil Rights in Twentieth-Century America*. Philadelphia: Temple University Press, 2009.

Carey, Allison C., Pamela Block, and Richard K. Scotch. *Allies and Obstacles: Parents of Children with Disabilities and Disability Rights*. Philadelphia: Temple University Press, 2020.

Carey, Allison C., Pamela Block, and Richard K. Scotch. "Sometimes Allies: Parent-Led Disability Organizations and Social Movements." *Disability Studies Quarterly* 39, no. 1 (2019). doi: 10.1806/dsq.v39i1.6281.

Carlson, Licia. *The Faces of Intellectual Disability: Philosophical Reflections*. Bloomington: Indiana University Press, 2009.

Carlson, Licia. "Philosophers of Intellectual Disability: A Taxonomy." In *Cognitive Disability and Its Challenge to Moral Philosophy*, edited by Eva Feder Kittay and Licia Carlson, 315–30. Maldon, MA: Wiley Blackwell, 2010.

Carr, E. Summerson. *Scripting Addiction: Politics of Therapeutic Talk and American Sobriety*. Princeton, NJ: Princeton University Press, 2011.

Carr, E. Summerson. *Working the Difference: Science, Spirit, and the Spread of Motivational Interviewing*. Chicago: University of Chicago Press, 2023.

Carsten, Janet, and Stephen Hugh-Jones. "Introduction." In *About the House: Lévi-Strauss and Beyond*, edited by Janet Carsten and Stephen Hugh-Jones, 1–46. Cambridge: Cambridge University Press, 1995.

Cattelino, Jessica R. *High Stakes: Florida Seminole Gaming and Sovereignty*. Durham, NC: Duke University Press, 2008.

Césaire, Aimé. *Discourse on Colonialism*. Translated by Joan Pinkham. New York: Monthly Review Press, 2021.

Chao, Sophie. *In the Shadow of the Palms: More-Than-Human Becomings in West Papua*. Durham, NC: Duke University Press, 2022.

Coates, Ta-Nehisi. *Between the World and Me*. New York: Spiegel and Grau, 2015.

Cole, Jonathan. *Pride and a Daily Marathon*. Cambridge, MA: MIT Press, [1991] 1995.

Connor, David J., Beth A. Ferri, and Subbing A. Annamma. "Dis/ability Critical Race Studies (DisCrit): Theorizing at the Intersections of Race and Dis/ability." In *DisCrit: Disability Studies and Critical Race Theory in Education*, edited by David J. Connor, Beth A. Ferry, and Subbing A. Annamma, 9–32. New York: Teachers College Press, 2015.

Cook, James W. "Of Men, Missing Links, and Nondescripts: The Strange Career of P. T. Barnum's 'What Is It?' Exhibition." In *Freakery: Cultural Spectacles of the Extraordinary Body*, edited by Rosemarie Garland-Thomson, 139–57. New York: New York University Press, 1996.

Csordas, Thomas. "Embodiment as a Paradigm for Anthropology." *Ethos* 18, no. 1 (1990): 5–47.

Curtis, Benjamin L., and Simo Vehmas. "Appendix: On Moral Status." In *Narrowed Lives: Meaning, Moral Value, and Profound Intellectual Disability*, by Simo Vehmas and Reetta Mietola, 185–212. Stockholm: University of Stockholm Press, 2021.

Cusk, Rachel. *A Life's Work: On Becoming a Mother*. London: Picador, 2001.

Davis, Lennard J. *Bending Over Backwards: Disability, Dismodernism, and Other Difficult Positions*. New York: New York University Press, 2002.

Davis, Lennard J. *Enabling Acts: The Hidden Story of How the Americans with Disability Act Gave the Largest U.S. Minority Its Rights*. Boston: Beacon, 2016.

Davis, Lennard J. *Enforcing Normalcy: Disability, Deafness, and the Body*. New York: Verso, 1995.

Derrida, Jacques. *The Beast and the Sovereign*. Vol. 1. Translated by Geoffrey Bennington. Chicago: University of Chicago Press, 2009.

Derrida, Jacques. *Given Time: I. Counterfeit Money*. Translated by Peggy Kamuf. Chicago: University of Chicago Press, 1992.

Derrida, Jacques. "Signature, Event, Context." In *Margins of Philosophy*, translated by Alan Bass, 307–30. Chicago: University of Chicago Press, [1972] 1985.

Derrida, Jacques. "Structure, Sign, and Play in the Discourse of the Human Sciences." In *Writing and Difference*, translated by Alan Bass, 278–94. Chicago: University of Chicago Press, [1967] 1980.

Douglas, Susan J., and Meredith W. Michaels. *The Mommy Myth: The Idealization of Motherhood and How It Has Undermined All Women*. New York: Free Press, 2004.

Driesson, Annelieke. "Pleasure and Dementia: On Becoming an Appreciating Subject." *Cambridge Journal of Anthropology* 36, no. 1 (2018): 23–39.

Durkheim, Émile. *Elementary Forms of the Religious Life*. Translated by Carol Cosman. Oxford: Oxford University Press, [1912] 2001.

Edelman, Lee. *No Future: Queer Theory and the Death Drive*. Durham, NC: Duke University Press, 2004.

Edwards, Terra. "Bridging the Gap Between DeafBlind Minds: Interactional and Social Foundations of Intention Attribution in the Seattle DeafBlind Community." *Frontiers of Psychology* 6, no. 1497 (2015). doi:10.3389/fpsyg.2015.01497.

Edwards, Terra. *Going Protactile: Life at the Limits of Language*. Oxford: Oxford University Press, 2024.

Edwards, Terra. "Language Emergence in the Seattle DeafBlind Community." PhD diss., University of California, Berkeley, 2014.

Edwards, Terra. "Re-Channeling Language: The Mutual Restructuring of Language and Infrastructure Among DeafBlind People at Gallaudet University." *Journal of Linguistic Anthropology* 28, no. 3 (2018): 273–92.

Edwards, Terra. "Sign-Creation in the Seattle DeafBlind Community: A Triumphant Story About the Regeneration of Obviousness." *Gesture* 16, no. 2 (2017): 307–32. doi: 10.1075/gest.16.206dw.

Edwards, Terra, and Diane Brentari. "The Grammatical Incorporation of Demonstratives in an Emerging Tactile Language." *Frontiers in Psychology* 11, no. 579992 (2021). doi: 10.3389/fpsyg.2020.579992.

Eisenberg, Arlene, Heidi E. Murkoff, and Sandee E. Hathaway. *What to Expect the First Year*. New York: Workman Press, [1989] 1996.

Elyachar, Julia. "Anthropology of Proprioception: Endurance and Collectivity on Unstable Grounds in Postrevolutionary Cairo." *American Anthropologist* 124, no. 5 (2022): 525–35.

Ennis, Linda Rose. *Intensive Mothering: The Cultural Contradictions of Modern Motherhood*. Bradford, Ontario: Demeter Press, 2014.

Ferry, Peggy C. Review of *Static Encephalopathies of Infancy and Childhood*. *American Journal of Disabled Children* 147, no. 6 (1993): 696.

Foucault, Michel. "Governmentality." In *The Essential Foucault: Selections from Essential Works of Foucault, 1954–1984*, edited by James Faubion and translated by Robert Hurley, part 3: 201–22. New York: New Press, 2000.

Foucault, Michel. *Society Must Be Defended: Lectures at the Collège de France 1975–1976*, edited by Arnold J. Davidson; translated by David Macy. London: Picador, 2003.

Foucault, Michel. *Technologies of the Self: A Seminar with Michel Foucault*, edited by Luther H. Martin and Huck Gutman, 16–50. Amherst: University of Massachusetts Press, 1988.

Friedner, Michele. *Sensory Futures: Deafness and Cochlear Implant Infrastructures in India*. Minneapolis: University of Minnesota Press, 2022.

Friedner, Michele, and Stefan Helmreich. "Sound Studies Meets Deaf Studies." *The Senses and Society* 7, no. 1 (2012): 72–86.

Friedner, Michele, and Matthew Wolf-Meyer. "Becoming Malleable: How Orienting to Disability, Communication, and the Senses Further Commits Anthropology to Its Moral Project." Forum: *What Good Is Anthropology? Celebrating 50 Years of American Ethnologist*. *American Ethnologist* 51 (2024): 78–83. doi: 10.1111/amet.13239.

Furani, Khaled. "Mastering Submission: Palestinian Poets Measuring Sounds of Freedom." *American Anthropologist* 120, no. 4 (2018): 697–710.

Gal, Susan. "Politics of Translation." *Annual Reviews in Anthropology* 44 (2015): 225–40.

Gammeltoft, Tine M. *Haunting Images: A Cultural Account of Selective Reproduction in Vietnam*. Berkeley: University of California Press, 2014.

Garfinkel, Harold. *Studies in Ethnomethodology*. New York: Wiley, 1967.

Garland-Thomson, Rosemarie. "The Cultural Work of American Freak Shows, 1835–1940." In *Extraordinary Bodies: Figuring Physical Disability in American Culture and*

Literature, by Rosemarie Garland-Thomson, 55–80. New York: Columbia University Press, 1997.

Garland-Thomson, Rosemarie. *Staring: How We Look*. Oxford: Oxford University Press, 2009.

Geertz, Clifford. *The Interpretation of Cultures*. New York: Basic Books, 1973.

Gell, Alfred. "Strathernograms, or The Semiotics of Mixed Metaphors." In *The Art of Anthropology: Essays and Diagrams*, by Alfred Gell, edited by Eric Hirsch, 29–75. London: Athlone Press, 1999.

Giles, Melinda Vandenbeld, ed. *Mothering in the Age of Neoliberalism*. Bradford, Ontario: Demeter Press, 2014.

Ginsburg, Faye, and Rayna Rapp. "Disability/Anthropology: Rethinking the Parameters of the Human." Introduction to Wenner-Gren Symposium Supplement 21. *Current Anthropology* 61, no. S21 (2020): S4–S15.

Ginsburg, Faye, and Rayna Rapp. *Disability Worlds*. Durham, NC: Duke University Press, 2024.

Ginsburg, Faye, and Rayna Rapp, eds. *Disability Worlds*. Wenner-Gren Symposium Supplement 21. *Current Anthropology* 61, no. S21 (2020): S1–S140.

Goffman, Erving. "Alienation from Interaction." *Human Relations* 10, no. 1 (1957): 47–60.

Goode, David. *A World Without Words: The Social Construction of Children Born Deaf and Blind*. With a Foreword by Irving Kenneth Zola. Philadelphia: Temple University Press, 2010.

Goodey, Christopher F. *A History of Intelligence and "Intellectual Disability": The Shaping of Psychology in Early Modern Europe*. Farnham, UK: Ashgate, 2011.

Goodwin, Charles. "A Competent Speaker Who Can't Speak: The Social Life of Aphasia." *Journal of Linguistic Anthropology* 14, no. 2 (2004): 151–70.

Goossens, Carol, Sharon Sapp Crain, and Pamela Elder. *Engineering the Preschool Environment for Interactive, Symbolic Communication: An Emphasis on the Developmental Period 18 Months to Five Years*. Birmingham, AL: Southeast Augmentative Communication Conference Publication, 1992.

Green, E. Mara. *Making Sense: Language, Ethics, and Understanding in Deaf Nepal*. Berkeley: University of California Press, 2024.

Grinker, Richard Roy. *Nobody's Normal: How Culture Created the Stigma of Mental Illness*. New York: W. W. Norton, 2021.

Grinker, Richard Roy. *Unstrange Minds: Remapping the World of Autism*. New York: Basic Books, 2008.

Grove, Nicola, Karen Bunning, Jill Porter, and Cecilia Olsson. "See What I Mean: Interpreting the Meaning of Communication by People with Severe and Profound Intellectual Disabilities." *Journal of Applied Research in Intellectual Disabilities* 12, no. 3 (1999): 190–203.

Habermas, Jürgen. *The Structural Transformation of the Public Sphere: An Inquiry into the Categories of Bourgeois Society*. Translated by Thomas Burger. Cambridge, MA: MIT Press, 1991.

Hannah-Jones, Nikole, Caitlin Roper, Ilena Silverman, and Jake Silverstein. *The 1619 Project: A New Origin Story*. New York: New York Times Company, 2021.

Hansen, Thomas Blom, and Finn Stepputat. "Sovereignty Revisited." *Annual Review of Anthropology* 35 (2006): 295–315.

Haraway, Donna J. *The Companion Species Manifesto: Dogs, People, and Significant Otherness*, edited by Matthew Begelke. Chicago: Prickly Paradigm, 2003.

Harding, Susan F. "Convicted by the Spirit: The Rhetoric of Fundamental Baptist Conversion." *American Ethnologist* 14, no. 1 (1987): 167–81.

Harry, Beth. *Melanie, Bird with a Broken Wing: A Mother's Story*. Baltimore, MD: Brookes, 2010.

Hart, Brendan. "Autism Parents and Neurodiversity: Radical Translation, Joint Embodiment, and the Prosthetic Environment." *BioSocieties* 9, no. 3 (September 2014): 284–303.

Heidegger, Martin. *Being and Time*. Translated by John Macquarrie and Edward Robinson. New York: Harper and Row, [1927] 1962.

Heidegger, Martin. *Poetry, Language, Thought*. Translated by Alfred Hofstadter. New York: Harper and Row, 1971.

Heidegger, Martin. *The Question Concerning Technology and Other Essays*. Translated with an introduction by William Levitt. New York: Harper and Row, 1977.

Herzog, Dagmar. *The Question of Unworthy Life: Eugenics and Germany's Twentieth Century*. Princeton, NJ: Princeton University Press, 2024.

Herzog, Dagmar. *Unlearning Eugenics: Sexuality, Reproduction, and Disability in Post-Nazi Europe*. Madison: University of Wisconsin Press, 2018.

Heyworth, Melanie, Timothy Chan, and Went Lawson. "Perspective: Presuming Autistic Communication Competence and Reframing Facilitated Communication." *Frontiers of Psychology* 13, no. 864991 (2022). doi: 10.3389/fpsyg.2022.864991.

Inoue, Miyako. "Speech Without a Speaking Body: 'Japanese Women's Language' in Translation." *Language and Communication* 23, no. 3–4 (July–October 2003): 315–30.

Irvine, Judith T., and Susan Gal. "Language Ideology and Linguistic Differentiation." In *Regimes of Language: Ideologies, Polities, and Identities*, edited by Paul V. Kroskrity, 35–83. Santa Fe, NM: School of American Research Press, 2000.

Jaswal, Vikram K., and Nameera Akhtar. "Being Versus Appearing Socially Uninterested: Challenging Assumptions About Social Motivation in Autism." *Behavioral and Brain Sciences* 42 (2019): 1–73.

Jaswal, Vikram K., Allison Wayne, and Hudson Golino. "Eye-Tracking Reveals Agency in Assisted Autistic Communication." *Scientific Reports* 10, no. 7882 (2020). doi: 10.1038/s41598-020-64553-9.

Johnson, Harriet McBryde. *Too Late to Die Young: Nearly True Tales from a Life*. New York: Picador, 2005.

Jorgensen, Cheryl. "The Least Dangerous Assumption: A Challenge to Create a New Paradigm." *Disability Solutions* 6, no. 3 (2005): 1–15.

Kafer, Alison. *Feminist, Crip, Queer*. Bloomington: Indiana University Press, 2013.

Kagan, Shelly. "What's Wrong with Speciesism?" Society for Applied Philosophy Annual Lecture 2015. *Journal of Applied Philosophy* 33 (2016): 1–21. doi: 10.1111/japp.12164.

Keane, Webb. *Animals, Robots, Gods: Adventures in the Moral Imagination*. New York: Penguin, 2024.

Keane, Webb. *Ethical Life: Its Natural and Social Histories*. Princeton, NJ: Princeton University Press, 2015.

Keane, Webb. *Signs of Recognition: Powers and Hazards of Representation in an Indonesian Society*. Berkeley: University of California Press, 1997.

Kittay, Eva Feder. "At the Margins of Moral Personhood." *Ethics* 116, no. 1 (2005): 100–131.
Kittay, Eva Feder. *Learning from My Daughter: The Value and Care of Disabled Minds*. Oxford: Oxford University Press, 2019.
Kittay, Eva Feder. *Love's Labor: Essays on Women, Equality, and Dependency*. New York: Routledge, 1999.
Kittay, Eva Feder. "When Caring Is Just and Justice Is Caring: Justice and Mental Retardation." *Public Culture* 13, no. 3 (2001): 20–31.
Kliewer, Christopher, Douglas Biklen, and Christi Kasa-Hendrickson. "Who May Be Literate? Disability and Resistance to the Cultural Denial of Competence." *American Educational Research Journal* 43, no. 2 (Summer 2006): 163–92.
Kulick, Don. "The Problem of Speaking for Others *Redux*: Insistence of Disclosure and the Ethics of Engagement." *Knowledge Cultures* 3, no. 6 (2015): 14–33.
Kulick, Don, and Jens Rydström. *Loneliness and Its Opposite: Sex, Disability, and the Ethics of Engagement*. Durham, NC: Duke University Press, 2015.
Lacan, Jacques. "The Mirror Stage." In *Écrits*, by Jacques Lacan, 75–81. Translated by Bruce Fink. New York: W. W. Norton, 2006.
Landsman, Gail Heidi. *Reconstructing Motherhood and Disability in the Age of "Perfect" Babies*. New York: Routledge, 2009.
Latour, Bruno. "On Interobjectivity." *Mind, Culture, and Activity* 3, no. 4 (1996): 228–45.
Lévi-Strauss, Claude. "Clan, Lineage, House." In *Anthropology and Myth: Lectures 1951–1982*, by Claude Lévi-Strauss, translated by Roy G. Willis, 153–94. London: Basil Blackwell, 1984.
Lévi-Strauss, Claude. *The Elementary Structures of Kinship*. Edited by Rodney Needham. Translated by James Harle Bell, John Richard von Sturmer, and Rodney Needham. Boston: Beacon, [1949] 1969.
Luhrmann, T. M. *When God Talks Back: Understanding the American Evangelical Relationship with God*. New York: Vintage, 2012.
Macdonald, Helen. *Vesper Flights*. New York: Grove Atlantic, 2020.
Mani, Lata. *Contentious Traditions: The Debate on Sati in Colonial India*. Berkeley: University of California Press, 1998.
Mauss, Marcel. *The Gift: Forms and Functions of Exchange in Archaic Societies*. Translated by Ian Cunnison. New York: W. W. Norton, [1925] 1967.
Mauss, Marcel. "Techniques of the Body." [1935] *Economy and Society* 2 (1973): 70–88.
McKearney, Patrick. "The Limits of Knowing Other Minds: Intellectual Disability and the Challenge of Opacity." *Social Analysis* 65, no. 1 (2021): 1–22.
McKearney, Patrick, and Tyler Zoanni, eds. "Cognitive Disability." Special issue, *Cambridge Journal of Anthropology* 36, no. 1 (2018): 1–119.
McKearney, Patrick, and Tyler Zoanni. "Introduction: For an Anthropology of Cognitive Disability." *Cambridge Journal of Anthropology* 36, no. 1 (2018): 1–22.
McKinnon, Susan. "Domestic Exceptions: Evans-Pritchard and the Creation of Nuer Patrilineality and Equality." *Cultural Anthropology* 15, no. 1 (2000): 35–83.
McKinnon, Susan. "Houses and Hierarchy: The View from a South Moluccan Society." In *About the House: Lévi-Strauss and Beyond*, edited by Janet Carsten and Stephen Hugh-Jones, 170–88. Cambridge: Cambridge University Press, 2005.
Mead, George Herbert. "Self." In *The Social Psychology of George Herbert Mead*, edited by Anselm Strauss, 199–246. Chicago: University of Chicago Press, [1934] 1965.

Merceira, Duncan P. *Living Otherwise: Students with Profound and Multiple Learning Disabilities as Agents in Educational Contexts*. Rotterdam: Sense, 2013.

Miyazaki, Hirokazu. *The Method of Hope: Anthropology, Philosophy, and Fijian Knowledge*. Stanford, CA: Stanford University Press, 2004.

Morrison, Toni. *The Nobel Lecture in Literature*. New York: Alfred A. Knopf, 1994.

Mukhopadhyay, Tito Rajarshi. "Five Poems: Tito Rajarshi Mukhopadhyay." *Disability Studies* 30, no. 1 (2010). https://dsq-sds.org/index.php/dsq/article/view/1192/1256.

Murphy, Robert F. *The Body Silent: The Different World of the Disabled*. New York: W. W. Norton, 2001.

Namy, Laura L., and Sandra R. Waxman. "Symbols Redefined." In *Symbol Use and Symbolic Representation*, edited by Laura L. Namy, 269–78. New York: Taylor and Francis, 2005.

Napolitano, Valentina. "On the Touch-Event: Theopolitical Encounters." *Social Analysis* 64, no. 4 (2020): 88–91.

Nielsen, Kim E. *Beyond the Miracle Worker: The Remarkable Life of Annie Sullivan Macy and Her Extraordinary Friendship with Helen Keller*. Boston: Beacon, 2009.

Nielsen, Kim E. *A Disability History of the United States*. Boston: Beacon, 2012.

Nussbaum, Martha C. *Frontiers of Justice: Disability, Nationality, Species Membership*. Cambridge, MA: Harvard University Press, 2006.

Obadia, Julienne. "Introduction: Overwhelmed by Proximity." *Anthropological Quarterly* 93, no. 1 (2020): 1329–53.

Ochs, Elinor. "Experiencing Language." *Anthropological Theory* 12, no. 2 (2012): 142–60.

Ochs, Elinor, and Olga Solomon. "Autistic Sociality." *Ethos* 38, no. 1 (2010): 69–92.

Ochs, Elinor, Olga Solomon, and Laura Sterponi. "Communication." *Discourse Studies* 7 (2005): 546–83.

Orenstein, Peggy. *Flux: Women on Sex, Work, Kids, Love, and Life in a Half Changed World*. New York: Anchor, 2020.

Parmentier, Richard J. *Signs in Society: Further Studies in Semiotic Anthropology*. Indianapolis: University of Indiana Press, 1994.

Pearson, Thomas W. *An Ordinary Future: Margaret Mead, the Problem of Disability, and a Child Born Different*. Berkeley: University of California Press, 2023.

Piepzna-Samarasinha, Leah Lakshmi. *Care Work: Dreaming Disability Justice*. Vancouver: Arsenal Pulp, 2018.

Povinelli, Elizabeth. *Economies of Abandonment*. Durham, NC: Duke University Press, 2011.

Povinelli, Elizabeth. "Notes on Gridlock: Genealogy, Intimacy, Sexuality." *Public Culture* 14, no. 2 (2002): 215–38.

Puig de la Bellacasa, Maria. *Matters of Care: Speculative Ethics in More Than Human Worlds*. Minneapolis: University of Minnesota Press, 2017.

Rafferty, Erin, Kevin Vollrath, Emily Harris, and Laura Foote. "Lonely Joy: How Families with Nonverbal Children with Disabilities Communicate, Collaborate, and Resist in a World That Values Words." *Journal of Pastoral Theology* 29, no. 2 (2019): 101–15.

Ralph, Laurence. "Becoming Aggrieved: An Alternative Framework of Care in Black Chicago." *RSF: The Russell Sage Foundation Journal of the Social Sciences* 1, no. 2 (2015): 31–41.

Ralph, Laurence. *Renegade Dreams: Living Through Injury in Gangland Chicago*. Chicago: University of Chicago Press, 2014.

Rapp, Rayna, and Faye Ginsburg. "Enabling Disability: Rewriting Kinship, Reimagining Citizenship." *Public Culture* 13, no. 3 (2001): 533-56.

Rapp, Rayna, and Faye Ginsburg. "Reverberations: Disability and the New Kinship Imaginary." *Anthropological Quarterly* 84, no. 2 (2011): 379-410.

Razack, Sherene. "From Pity to Respect." In *Looking White People in the Eye: Gender, Race, and Culture in Courtrooms and Classrooms*, 130-56. Toronto: University of Toronto Press, 1998.

Reddy, Vasudevi. *How Infants Know Minds*. Cambridge, MA: Harvard University Press, 2008.

Reno, Joshua. *Home Signs: Life Beyond and Beside Language*. Chicago: University of Chicago Press, 2024.

Rochat, Philippe, and Tara Callaghan. "What Drives Symbolic Development? The Case of Pictorial Comprehension and Production." In *Symbol Use and Symbolic Representation*, edited by Laura L. Namy, 25-46. New York: Taylor and Francis, 2005.

Rogoff, Barbara. "Cognition as a Collaborative Process." In *Cognition, Perception, and Language*, vol. 2 of *The Handbook of Child Psychology*, edited by D. Kuhn and R. S. Siegler, 679-744. New York: Wiley, 1998.

Rogoff, Barbara, Catherine Malkin, and Kathleen Gilbride. "Interaction with Babies as Guidance in Development." In *Children's Learning in the "Zone of Proximal Development,"* edited by Barbara Rogoff and J. V. Wertsch. San Francisco: Jossey-Bass, 1984.

Rogoff, Barbara, R. Paradise, R. M. Arauz, et al. "Firsthand Learning Through Intent Participation." *Annual Reviews in Psychology* 54 (2003): 175-203.

Russell, Kamala. "Facing Another: The Attenuation of Contact as Space in Dhofar, Oman." *Signs and Society* 8, no. 2 (2020): 290-318.

Rutherford, Danilyn. "The Benefits of Modesty." *Behavioral and Brain Sciences* 42 (2019): 45-46. https://doi.org/10.1017/S0140525X18002443.

Rutherford, Danilyn. *Laughing at Leviathan: Sovereignty and Audience in West Papua*. Chicago: University of Chicago Press, 2012.

Rutherford, Danilyn. *Living in the Stone Age: Reflections on the Origins of a Colonial Fantasy*. Chicago: University of Chicago Press, 2018.

Rutherford, Danilyn. "Proximity to Disability." *Anthropological Quarterly* 93, no. 1 (2020): 1453-81.

Sahlins, Marshall. *What Kinship Is—and Is Not*. Chicago: University of Chicago Press, 2014.

Saussure, Ferdinand de. *Course in General Linguistics*. Edited by Charles Bally and Albert Sechehaye, with the collaboration of Alfred Riedlinger. Translated by Roy Harris. Peru, IL: Open Court Classics, [1916] 1986.

Savarese, D.J. "Blanch-Ink-Jet Maneuver." In *A Doorknob for the Eye*. Unrestricted Editions, 2017. http://www.djsavarese.com/3d-flip-book/doorknobfortheeye/.

Savarese, D.J. "Swoon" and "Tongue." *Seneca Review* 47, no. 1 (2017): 5-7.

Savarese, Ralph James. *Reasonable People: A Memoir of Autism and Adoption*. New York: Other Press, 2021.

Schneider, David M. *American Kinship: A Cultural Account*. Chicago: University of Chicago Press, 1968.

Schweik, Susan M. *The Ugly Laws: Disability in Public*. New York: New York University Press, 2010.

Scott, David. "The Re-Enchantment of Humanism: An Interview with Sylvia Wynter." *Small Axe* 8 (September 2000): 119-207.

Semonin, Paul. "Monsters in the Marketplace: The Exhibition of Human Oddities in Early Modern England." In *Freakery: Cultural Spectacles of the Extraordinary Body*, edited by Rosemarie Garland-Thomson, 69–81. New York: New York University Press, 1996.

Shakespeare, Tom. "Disability Studies Today and Tomorrow." *Sociology of Health and Illness* 27, no. 1 (2005): 138–48.

Shakespeare, Tom, and Nick Watson. "Defending the Social Model." *Disability and Society* 12, no. 2 (1997): 293–300.

Sherrington, Charles Scott. *The Integrative Action of the Nervous System*. Silliman Memorial Lectures. New Haven, CT: Yale University Press, 1908.

Sidnell, Jack. "The Architecture of Intersubjectivity, Revisited." In *The Cambridge Handbook of Linguistic Anthropology*, edited by N. J. Enfield, Paul Kockelman, and Jack Sidnell, 364–99. Cambridge: Cambridge University Press, 2014.

Siegel, James. *Naming the Witch*. Stanford, CA: Stanford University Press, 2005.

Silverman, Chloe. *Understanding Autism: Parents, Doctors, and the History of a Disorder*. Princeton, NJ: Princeton University Press, 2012.

Silverstein, Michael. "Language Structure and Linguistic Ideology." In *The Elements: A Parasession on Linguistic Units and Levels*, edited by Paul Clyne, William Hanks, and Carol Hofbrauer, 193–247. Chicago: Chicago Linguistics Society, 1979.

Silverstein, Michael. "Shifters, Linguistic Categories, and Cultural Description." In *Meaning in Anthropology*, edited by Keith Basso and Henry A. Selly, 11–55. Albuquerque: University of New Mexico Press, 1976.

Silverstein, Michael. "Translation, Transduction, Transformation." In *Translating Culture: Perspectives in Translation and Anthropology*, edited by Paula J. Rubel, 75–106. Oxford: Berg, 2003.

Simplican, Stacy Clifford. *The Capacity Contract: Intellectual Disability and the Question of Citizenship*. Minneapolis: University of Minnesota Press, 2015.

Solomon, Andrew. *Far from the Tree: Parents, Children, and the Search for Identity*. New York: Scribner, 2012.

Swift, Jonathan. *Gulliver's Travels*. New York: E. P. Dutton, [1726] 1906.

Taylor, Janelle S. "On Recognition, Caring, and Dementia." *Medical Anthropology Quarterly* 22, no. 4 (2008): 313–35.

Taylor, Sunaura. *Beasts of Burden: Animal and Disability Liberation*. New York: New Press, 2018.

Thomas, Deborah A. *Political Life in the Wake of the Plantation: Sovereignty, Witnessing, Repair*. Durham, NC: Duke University Press, 2019.

Thomas, Deborah A. "Time and the Otherwise: Plantations, Garrisons, and Being Human in the Caribbean." *Anthropological Theory* 16, no. 2–3 (2016): 177–220.

Thomas, Deborah A., and Joseph Masco, eds. *Sovereignty Unhinged: An Illustrated Primer for the Study of Present Intensities, Disavowals, and Temporal Derangements*. Durham, NC: Duke University Press, 2023.

Vehmas, Simo, and Reetta Mietola, eds. *Narrowed Lives: Meaning, Moral Value, and Profound Intellectual Disability*. Stockholm: Stockholm University Press, 2021.

Vonnegut, Kurt. *Cat's Cradle: A Novel*. New York: Dell, [1963] 1998.

Vygotsky, Lev. *Mind in Society: The Development of Higher Psychological Processes*, edited by Michael Cole, Vera John-Steiner, Sylvia Scribner, and Ellen Souberman. Cambridge, MA: Harvard University Press, 1978.

Vyse, Stuart, Bronwyn Hemsley, Russell Lang, et al. "Whose Words Are These? Statements Derived from Facilitated Communication and Rapid Prompting Method Undermine the Credibility of Jaswal and Akhtar's Social Motivation Hypothesis." *Behavioral and Brain Sciences* 42 (2019): 48–49. doi:10.1017/S0140525X18002236.

Wadsworth, William T. D., Kisha Supernant, Ave Dersch, and the Chipewyan Prairie First Nation. "Integrating Remote Sensing and Indigenous Archaeology to Locate Unmarked Graves: A Case Study from Northern Alberta, Canada." *Advances in Archaeological Practice* 9, no. 3 (2021): 202–14.

Warner, Michael. *The Letters of the Republic: Publication and the Public Sphere in Eighteenth-Century America*. Cambridge, MA: Harvard University Press, 1990.

Warner, Michael. *The Trouble with Normal*. Cambridge, MA: Harvard University Press, 1999.

Weber, Max. *The Protestant Ethic and the Spirit of Capitalism*. Translated by Talcott Parsons. New York: Penguin Classics, [1905] 2002.

Weheliye, Alexander G. *Habeas Viscus: Racializing Assemblages, Biopolitics, and Black Feminist Theories of the Human*. Durham, NC: Duke University Press, 2014.

Weston, Kath. *Families We Choose: Lesbians, Gays, Kinship*. New York: Columbia University Press, 2005.

Wolf-Meyer, Matthew J. *Unraveling: Remaking Personhood in a Neurodiverse Age*. Minneapolis: University of Minnesota Press, 2020.

Woolard, Kathryn A., and Bambi B. Schieffelin. "Language Ideology." *Annual Review of Anthropology* 23 (October 1994): 55–82.

Wynter, Sylvia. "Unsettling the Coloniality of Being/Power/Truth/Freedom: Toward the Human, After Man, Its Over-Representation—an Argument." CR: *The New Centennial Review* 3, no. 3 (Fall 2003): 257–337.

Zhan, Mei. *Other-Worldly: Making Chinese Medicine Through Transnational Frames*. Durham, NC: Duke University Press, 2009.

Zola, Irving Kenneth. Foreword to *A World Without Words: The Social Construction of Children Born Deaf and Blind*, by David Goode. Philadelphia: Temple University Press, 2010.

INDEX

Note: Page numbers in italics indicate figures.

ableism, 141, 206n2. *See also* racism
Agamben, Giorgio, 146
Akomolafe, Bayo, 94
American Anthropological Association, 48
American Sign Language, 96, 121, 136
Americans with Disability Act (ADA), 42, 95
Amsterdam, Netherlands, 41, 42
Ann Arbor, Michigan, 50, 58
anthropology, 7, 8, 14, 15, 22, 26, 48, 55. *See also* kinship; language; Mauss, Marcel; Rutherford, Danilyn
Arendt, Hannah, 104
Ashley X, 88, 89
autism, 6–7, 37–38, 94, 97, 128, 145, 157, 173. *See also* communication

Baggs, Mel, 7
Ball, Mike, 96–98
Barad, Karen, 171
Barnum, P. T., 76
Bérubé, Michael, 15–16
Best, Craig: ashes of, 57; and biking, 57; and cancer, 25, 28, 33; as a certified public accountant, 14; and chemotherapy, 50; and children, 14, 15, 18, 26, 43–44, 45, 49, 52, 56, 57, 60, 62, 189, 191; classmates of, 50; college life of, 14; death of, vii, viii, 43, 47, 48, 50, 51, 52, 53, 55–60, 62, 63, 67, 73, 153, 168, 185, 191; and Dovita, 49; and education, 99, 107; family of, 62, 91, 188–89; father of, 50, 57, 62, 65; finances of, 51; and fishing, 56; heart condition of, viii, 48, 50; and *Henny Penny*, 45; and hunting, 48, 57; and Karin (sister), 26, 42; and loss, 57; and marriage, 14, 15, 56; memorial services for, 51, 52, 56, 172; memories of, 52, 62; and Millie's birth, 16, 17; and Millie's condition, 28, 31–32, 33, 34, 35, 36, 38, 39, 40, 42, 56, 62, 65; and Millie's eyesight, 22–24, 28; mother of, 65, 159; and nature, 15, 57; parents of, 14, 62, 65, 172; and Ralph, 29, 33; sisters of, 50, 57, 62, 172; and special education, 42; and video camera, 43–44, 45; and visit with Dr. Kelly, 26, 27–28
Best, Melitta Alta Rutherford (Millie): and accepting help, 133–34; and Adri, 157, 160; as an adult, viii, 3, 8, 141–44; and alternating estropia, 23, 25; and Amy, 164; ancestors of, 164, 169; and Andrea, 143; artwork of, 110; as a baby, vii–viii, 13, 16, 17–19, 21, 22–25, 26, 27, 33–37, 38, 40, 41–42, 44–45, 62, 191; bathing of, 141–42, 143; birthdate of, 169, 184; birthplace of, 8, 17; biting of, 81, 101, 102, 119, 122–23, 160, 176; body of, 78, 79, 81, 141, 142, 143, 144, 164; and Cameron, 160; cards for, 163, 164; and care providers, 17, 41, 59, 65, 79, 81, 84, 93, 103, 104, 119, 123, 124, 125, 143, 144, 148, 151–52, 155–61, 164, 167–69, 170, 175, 177–78, 183–84, 186; as a child, 62, 64–65, 104, 107–11, 133, 135, 144, 153; and Christopher Elementary School, 64–65, 192; and cognitive

Best, Melitta Alta Rutherford (Millie) (*continued*)
disability, 5, 24, 62, 131, 143, 161, 178, 192; cousins of, 58, 167, 184; development of, 41, 143; diagnoses of, 7, 17, 23-24, 25, 31, 39-41, 45, 53, 66, 110, 125, 184; and Dovita, 38, 44, 50; and drinking a smoothie, 102; and early intervention, 32, 41, 53; and eating, 9, 36-37, 38, 41-42, 61, 96, 119, 123, 125, 134, 142, 159, 206n3; and emotions, 3, 19, 34, 38, 62, 74, 78, 93, 101, 102, 109-10, 119, 133, 142, 144, 160, 164, 178; and empowerment, 89; father of, 13, 16, 17, 18, 19, 22, 24, 25, 33, 35, 37, 38, 39, 40, 43, 44, 51, 52, 56, 61, 62, 67, 79, 110, 168, 171, 173, 174, 184; gait belt of, 142, 144, 188; and glasses, 63; and "global developmental delay," 37, 41, 42; and Grace, 157; graduation of, 147; grandmother of, vii, 9, 29, 32, 42, 45; grandparents of, 51, 57; and Greta, 119, 123; and head circumference, 17, 26, 29; homes of, 166-69, 175, 183, 186, 188; and Individualized Education Program (IEP), 61, 67, 133, 134, 145; and infant development specialist, 38-39; and Iryna, 144; and Jeanette, 2, 159, 176, 177, 188; and jobs, 99, 135, 148; and Julie, 3, 148, 159, 164, 177; and kindness of strangers, 50; and language, 39, 42, 52, 60, 61, 62, 108, 115; and laughter, 93, 102, 103, 142, 160, 169, 170, 174, 177, 188; leg braces of, 63; lessons from, 3, 8, 9, 52, 55, 88, 111, 148; and love, 103, 110, 169; and Mardi Gras beads, 60, 109, 110; and Marilyn, 157, 169, 176, 177; and Max, 163-64, 165; and medical history, 16; and memory, 52, 56; and moral personhood, 7, 178; mother of, viii, 3, 4, 7, 8, 9, 14, 15, 16-19, 22-29, 31, 32, 33, 34, 37-44, 49-53, 55-57, 60-67, 72, 73, 74, 76-77, 78, 80, 83, 84, 86, 88, 93, 95, 96, 98-103, 107, 110-13, 116, 119, 123, 124, 127, 128, 131, 133-35, 138, 139, 141, 144-46, 148, 154, 160, 161, 166, 168, 169, 171, 176-78, 183-87; and movement, 34, 37, 40, 44-45, 61, 62, 122-23, 133-34, 136, 138, 142-44; and MRI, 28, 31, 131; and music, 9, 36, 73, 74, 75, 78, 144, 159, 164; and normality, 21, 41; and orthotics, 4; and parental help, 136, 144-45; and personhood, 164, 168, 170, 175, 178, 179; and physical therapy, 144, 145, 147; pictures of, 13, 17-18, 62, 63, 64, 110, 111, 122, 177, 192; and PODD books, 120-24; and politics, 95, 98; privilege of, 175; prom experience of, 176-77, 178; and relationships, 169-70; and riding horses, 147, 182; and Sandee, 177; and school, 32-33, 52, 56, 60-65, 67, 98, 99, 102, 103, 107-10, 133-34, 135, 144, 145, 182, 192; and "Severe/Profound Cognitive Impairment," 62; and skills, 41, 66, 110, 143; and sleeping, 51, 102, 103; and social life, 9, 67, 169, 171, 173, 174, 175-78, 186; and speaking, viii, 3, 36, 37, 38, 40, 42, 99, 102, 108-9, 112, 117, 142, 160, 165, 169; and speech therapy, 98, 100-101, 102, 105, 108-9, 147-48; and spinal tap, 45; and standing, 144-45; and Steve, 169; and teachers, 6, 9, 43, 61, 67, 98, 107, 108, 109, 135, 182; as a teenager, 79-80, 81, 123-25, 143; and therapy, 33-37, 39, 40, 41, 42, 43, 60, 61, 62, 67, 99, 101, 105, 107, 108, 109-10, 133-35, 143, 147-48, 182; and time with in-laws, 56, 62; and touch, 143, 144, 166; and Vanessa, 148; and Vermont, 155; vision of, 18, 22-24, 25, 28, 37, 63, 78, 98, 110, *120*, *121*, 142; and visit with Dr. Kelly, 26-28, 39; and vulnerability, 94, 100; and walking, viii, 3, 38, 40, 41, 142-44, 169, 188, 205n21; and wheelchairs, viii, 4, 43, 64, 67, 74, 81, 93, 96, 103, 105, 125, 142, 152, 156, 176, 183, 187; and Xiaona, 98, 119, 121, 123, 124, 125, 134, 144, 169, 176, 177, 178; and Yosselin, 169. *See also* Blair School

Best, Ralph: as an adult, 45; and Amy, 151-53, 156; and AP world history, 157; as a baby, 79; and band concert, 64; and ceramics lessons, 191; as a child, viii, 14, 57-60, 62, 63, 64, 91-92, 93, 134, 144; cousins of, 50, 58, 62; and crawling, 43-44; and Dr. Monroe, 22; and dysgraphia, 60; and dyslexia, 60; and emotions, 19; and engraved placard, 168; father of, 47, 48, 49, 51, 52, 57, 67; and father's death, 49-50, 51, 58; and graduate student, 58; grandparents of, 43-44, 57; and Halloween costume, 110; and kindness of strangers, 50; and language, 19, 59-60; and Lewis and Clark, 155; and Millie, 187; mother of, vii, 14-15, 17, 18, 19, 47, 48-49, 56, 57, 58-60, 66, 67, 91-93, 178, 189; and pack trip, 56-57; pictures of, 110; and Rachel, 47, 49; and reading, 60; and sailing, 58; and school, 29, 49, 56, 59, 60, 64, 91; and skiing, 57; and support

222 INDEX

group, viii; and surfing, 62; and talking, 19; and walking, 18; and zombies, 47-48. *See also* Best, Craig; education
Biko, Steve, 164
Black Sabbath, 183
Blair School, 42, 43, 49, 52, 60-62, 63, 64, 133, 192
Boardmaker, 119
Body Silent, The (Murphy), 8
Boyer, Pascal, 6
Buck, Carol Lossing, 74, 75, 77, 78
Buck, Pearl, 74, 75, 78
Burkhart, Linda, 113, 116-17, 118-22. *See also under* communication; Rutherford, Danilyn
Bush, George, 155
Butler, Judith, 140, 144

California: Bakersfield, 151; Berkley, 66; community-based nonprofits, 182; Department of Education, 99; Department of Health, 182-83; East Bay, 118; and Latinx women, 96; and Legislation Day, 96; Los Angeles, 58; and Medi-Cal, 182, 185, 188; Monterey Bay, 189; Palo Alto delegation, 96, 97-98; and road trips, 155; Sacramento, 99; San Andrea Regional Center (SARC), 182, 183, 184, 185; San Francisco, 158; San Jose, 176, 186; Santa Cruz, 2, 4, 43, 66, 67, 80, 84, 87, 93, 96, 99, 102, 103, 110, 125, 141, 147, 151, 154, 157, 158, 164, 173, 183, 189-90; Santa Cruz delegation, 96, 97, 98; social services system, 103, 182-86; Special Education Local Plan Area (SELPA), 99; Supported Living Services (SLS), 186; Ventura, 9, 13, 17, 62, 63
capitalism, 33, 104, 202n14
Cat's Cradle (Vonnegut), 66
Césaire, Aimé, 164
Chao, Sophie, 55, 56
Chesney, Kenny, 2
Chicago, Illinois: African Americans in, 63; American Anthropological Association meeting, 48; Chicago Public Schools, 42, 60, 192; Child Protective Services, 92, 93; Craig's firm, 15; Hyde Park, 42, 43, 63, 191, 192; Lake Shore Drive, 191, 192; medical treatment in, 104; and Millie, 193; and social worlds, 165; and Sonia, 192; South Side of, 8, 63, 92;

therapists in, 42, 57; time spent in, viii, 66, 67, 139, 191-92, 193; townhouse in, 44, 191-92
China, 74, 79, 151
climate change, 188-89
cognitive mystery, 5-7, 9, 88-89, 95, 98, 101, 165, 178
Cohen, Emily, 3, 199n2
Cole, Jonathan, 137, 138, 139
communication: assistive, 5, 87, 112, 113, 116, 127-28, 205n22; and assistive technologies, 109; augmentative, 87, 112, 127, 203-4n7; and autistic people, 204n10; and awareness, 5, 139; and bodies, 139; and body language, 80, 115, 126; and books, 115, 119-20, 122, 123, 129; and Caleb, 117, 118; and care, 136; and Cassidy, 117, 118, 123, 124, 127; and children, 116-17, 125-26; and Closing the Gap, 112-18; development of, 200n12; and disabled children, 112-27, 130; and disabled people, 3, 6, 77, 119-20, 136-37, 200n12; and facial expressions, 5, 204n8; and finger-spelling, 77; and foam board, 119; and games, 2, 5; and gestures, 3, 4, 5, 80, 138-39, 145; and help from parents, 118, 145; and icons, 116, 119-20, 121, 122, 125-26, 129; and intentionality, 6; and Linda Burkhart, 123, 126, 128; and love, 77, 83; and Millie, viii, 61-62, 77, 108-9, 111, 113-14, 116, 118, 119, 120, 121, 147, 160, 174; and movement, 118, 122-23; and personhood, 124, 127; and PODD (Pragmatically Organized Dynamic Display), 130, 145; and PODD books, 120-24, 120, 125; and PODD partners, 115, 116, 119, 120; and sight, 137; and sign use, viii, 3, 5, 77, 83, 125, 128, 133; and sounds, 3, 5, 7, 9, 123, 124, 135; and speaking, 77, 89, 98, 109, 110-13, 115, 122-24, 126, 127, 128, 135, 137; and symbols, 113, 114-15, *114*, 119, 125, 203-4n7; and technology, 109, 113, 115-18, 121, 122-23, 129; and therapists, 38, 108-10; and touch, 84, 118, 127, 128, 135, 136-37, 141, 205n20; as transfer of meaning, 203n3; and understanding others, 3, 4-6, 9, 85-86, 89, 110, 117, 118, 129, 130, 135, 148, 160; and vegetative states, 5; and vocalizations, 130, 160, 174; and words, 77, 80, 84, 85, 87, 110, 119, 120, 122, 127, 129, 130, 203-4n7. *See also* cognitive mystery; language
COVID-19 pandemic, 1, 2, 9, 43, 147
Cusk, Rachel, 108

Davis, Lennard J., 21
DeafBlind people, 136–37, 141, 171
democracies, 76, 95
dependency, 104–5, 148, 169, 170
Derrida, Jacques, 112, 203n3, 206n7
Didion, Joan, 57
difference, 171, 172–73, 174, 175
disability: and accepting help, 139, 141; access trail for disabled, 156; and Agent Orange, 73; and Alzheimer's disease, 80; and Ana, 124–27; and Angelman syndrome, 125, 127; and ataxia, 40; and awareness, 4, 9, 43, 65; and Bianca, 4–5; and blind children, 77; and care providers, 1, 2–3, 6, 59, 81, 85, 87, 88, 93, 103, 104, 105, 115, 128–30, 145; and cerebral palsy, 37, 88; cognitive disabilities, 4–5, 9, 24, 37–39, 62, 71–72, 76, 80, 82–84, 88, 104, 125, 130–31, 146–48, 175, 176, 177; cortical visual impairment, *120*, *121*; and deaf people, 77, 173; and death, 131; and dementia, 9, 65, 159; and depression, 97, 98; disability activists, 95, 146; disability justice, 88, 89; disabled children, 15–16, 33–36, 39, 42, 52, 53, 56, 59, 62, 64, 65, 71–84, 85, 88, 93–98, 99, 100, 108–9, 112–27, 128, 131, 177; disabled people, viii, 1–9, 15–16, 72, 75–78, 79, 88–89, 104, 115, 128, 128–30, 134–44, 145, 161, 164–65, 169, 173, 175–79, 186, 202n14; and Down's mosaicism, 28; and Down syndrome, 15–16, 71, 72, 73, 173, 176, 177; and dysgraphia, 62; and dyslexia, 62; and emotions, 126; and eyesight, 140; and families, 80–86; and genetics, 37, 39–40, 65–66, 78, 125, 178, 190; and Guillain-Barré syndrome, 137–38; and Helen Keller, 127; and hypomyelination, 82; Individuals with Disabilities Education Act (IDEA), 32, 42, 99; and Jane, 80, 81–88, 89; and laughter, 67, 74, 78, 81, 82, 83, 84, 85, 93; and Liam, 100; and life-saving measures, 1–3; and love, 79–80, 81, 83, 84, 88, 93, 94, 108; and Luisa, 124–27, 128, 129; and Melanie, 131; and movement, 139–40; multiple disabilities, 4, 88, 99, 131–32, 164–65, 176; and neurological difference, 141, 173; and normality, 21, 74–75, 76, 78, 79, 87–88, 95, 140, 141, 145, 147, 165, 177; and parents altering children, 88; and parents demanding access, 87–88; and parents' help, 115, 145; and personhood, 7, 74–76, 77, 78, 84, 85–87, 88, 108, 124, 129; and Pitt-Hopkins, 190; and politics, 95, 104, 145–46; and Rett syndrome, 40, 41, 66, 123; and scoliosis, 85; and social worlds, 166, 176; and solitude, 139; and speaking, viii, 1, 76, 77, 85, 99, 122–23, 127, 145; and speaking equipment, 113, 123; and special education, 4, 96–98, 127, 128; and special needs children, 82, 103; and speech therapy, 82, 97, 100–101, 127; and technology, 115–16, 131, 136; and touch, 136–38, 145; and Training School, 75, 77–78; and walking, 131; and wheelchairs, 71, 72, 80, 81, 84, 85, 87, 100, 112, 113, 141. *See also* Americans with Disability Act (ADA); autism; Best, Melitta Alta Rutherford (Millie); cognitive mystery; communication; DeafBlind people; education
disability studies, 21
Dortmund, Germany, 164
Dovita, 17, 26, 27, 31, 32, 34, 35, 36. *See also under* Best, Craig; Best, Melitta Alta Rutherford (Millie)
Dunn Early Childhood Center, 42
Durkheim, Émile, 147
Dynavox, Tobii, 113

education: and Blair School, 192; and boarding schools, 93; and careers/jobs, 182; and Chicago Public Schools, 42, 60; and community advisory councils, 99; and community colleges, 182; and disabled children, 43, 64–65, 99, 100, 111, 128, 201n1; and disabled people, 6, 32, 147; and early intervention, 201n1; and English teaching, 14; and fear, 164–65; and foam board, 107, 108, 110; and Individualized Education Programs (IEPs), 42, 61, 67, 133; and Individuals with Disabilities Education Act (IDEA), 32, 60, 99; and kindergartens, 135, 148; levels of, 181; and Liam, 98; and love, 164–65; and PECS (Picture Exchange Communication System), 108; and personal goals, 181–82; and PODD (Pragmatically Organized Dynamic Display), 115, 117; and preschool, 107–8; and private treatment centers and schools, 99; and protests, 63; and Ralph's schools, 14, 26, 29, 41, 59, 64, 66, 91, 110; and San Lorenzo Valley High School, 98; and school systems, 5, 97, 98–99, 128,

134–35, 182; and sovereignty, 99; and special education, 4, 6, 42, 96–98, 99, 108, 127, 128, 164–65; and technology, 5, 87, 100, 135, 148; and "Transition Toolbox," 182; and truant children, 99; and wheelchairs, 63, 182; and Zoom school, 9
Edwards, Terra, 136, 141
eugenics, 76, 88
European refugees, 161

Far from the Tree (Solomon), 173
Finkelstein, Maura, 105
French and Indian War, 7
Friedner, Michele, 3, 171, 199n2

Galton, Sir Francis, 21
Garfinkel, Harold, 80
Gaza hospitals, 105
Geertz, Clifford, 166
Global South, 103
Goode, David, 4, 5
Goodwin, Charles, 99
Grove, Dr., 37, 38, 39
Gulliver's Travels (Swift), 116

Habermas, Jürgen, 98
hand-over-hand assistance, 133–35
Harry, Beth, 130, 131
Hawking, Stephen, 109, 115
Heidegger, Martin, 101, 199n2
Hines, Tammy, 183–88
Hobbes, Thomas, 59
Home Signs (Reno), 5
Hopper, Carol, 32, 33, 34, 35
humanism, 164–66
Hume, David, 59

Individuals with Disabilities Education Act (IDEA), 32, 42, 99
Indonesia, 14, 41, 166, 167

Jamaica, 131
Johnson, Harriet McBryde, 78
Johnson, William Henry, 76

Kafer, Alison, 88, 89
Keller, Helen, 77, 127
Kelly, Dr., 26, 27–28, 31, 38, 39

kinship, 73, 168, 171, 172, 173–74, 201n2
Kittay, Eva Feder, 7, 104

Lab School, 41, 59, 63–64, 66
Lacan, Jacques, 39
La Honda, California, 57
Landsman, Gail, 73
language: "aided language stimulation," 115; American Sign Language, 96, 121, 136; and animals, 6; Arabic, 125; and babies, 6, 36, 39, 115; body language, 80, 101, 126; and Cassidy, 120; and Charles Sanders Peirce, 199n3; and children, 108, 117, 128–29; and community, 3, 117, 128–29; and connection, 204n8; and conversations, 101, 102; and creation of worlds, 3, 175; and culture, 166; Danish, 117; development of, 39, 129; and disabled children, 111, 129–30, 175; and disabled people, 7; and doctors, 45; English, 115, 117, 166; and existence, 179; expressive, 37; and freedom, 146; German, 117; and gestures, 101; and help from parents, 111, 115; and humans, 104, 165, 166; and icons, 117; and Indonesian, 166; and labeled objects, 111; and language pathologists, 33, 35, 127; and Liam, 101, 102; and Millie, 37, 42, 52, 60, 61, 62, 64, 101, 115; and motherhood, 169; Norwegian, 117; and PODD (Pragmatically Organized Dynamic Display), 112, 113–18, 119, 128, 129; and Ralph, 59–60; and reading, 108; and relationships, 169, 170–71; and semiotics, 199n3; sign language, 96, 101, 121, 136, 203–4n7; and sign use, 199n3; and social life, 206n7; and sounds, 101; and sovereignty, 101; Spanish, 64, 125; and speaking, 101, 115, 116, 117, 120, 127; and speech therapy, 36, 62, 82, 98, 100, 108–10; and structuralists, 167, 174; Swedish, 117; and symbols, 108–9, 110, 117; and technology, 111; and theory class, 59; and utterances, 113, 115, 116, 117, 128, 138; verbal, 117; and vocalizations, 5; and words, 100, 101, 108, 109, 116, 129, 167, 170; and writing, 127–28. *See also* communication
Lebanon, 125
Lévi-Strauss, Claude, 174
Lithuania, 31
Locke, John, 59, 95
London, England, 14, 15, 17, 79

Macdonald, Helen, 160, 161
Marilyn, 81–84, 143, 148, 155, 156. *See also under* Best, Melitta Alta Rutherford (Millie); Rutherford, Danilyn
Marind people, 55
Master and Commander (film), 48
Mauss, Marcel, 139
McKearney, Patrick, 128, 129
McSweeney, Sarah, 1–3, 8, 9
Mead, George Herbert, 138
Mendota Institute, 71, 72
Merceira, Duncan, 78
Mexico, 104
Miracle Worker, The (film), 77
"Mirror Stage, The" (Lacan), 39
monk parakeets, vii, viii, 139, 191
Monroe, Dr., 22, 23, 24, 28
Morrison, Toni, 101
Mueck, Ron, 86
Murphy, Robert F., 8
Music Together, 73, 74, 78
mutual care, 203n24

Nairobi, Kenya, 50
Narrowed Lives: Meaning, Moral Value, and Profound Intellectual Disability, 175, 176, 178
National Public Radio, 1, 2, 8
New York, New York, 3, 4, 103, 122, 167, 170, 177, 187
Nobody's Normal (Grinker), 21
Nussbaum, Martha, 104

Obadia, Julienne, 73
O'Brian, Patrick, 56
Ochs, Elinor, 101
Oregon, 1

Pediatric Neurology, 27
pediatric neuro-osteopath, 82–83
Porter, Gayle, 113, 115
Pragmatically Organized Dynamic Display (PODD), 112, 113–18, *114*, 119, 120–26, 127. *See also* communication; language
Pride and a Daily Marathon (Waterman), 140, 141
Princeton, New Jersey, 14, 16, 22, 24, 175
proprioception, 135–41, 142, 143, 146–47, 206n28
Protestant Ethic and the Spirit of Capitalism, The (Weber), 33

Quetelet, Adolphe, 21

racism, 75, 76, 104, 146, 206n2, 206n28
Ralph, Laurence, 165
Ray, Rachel, 100
Reddy, Vasudevi, 139
religion: and Catholic principal, 42, 52, 53; and Christians, 6, 95, 166; and church, 7, 166, 176; discussion of, 60; and God, 6, 75, 95, 177; and gods, 6, 80, 165; and the Koran, 167; leaders of, 206n3; and love, 177; and ministers, 7; and Mormons, 172; and New Testament, 189; and the Pope, 146; and predestination, 33; and Presbyterian church, 166; and spirits, 6; and Tibetan Buddhists, 184
Roberts, Julia, 4
Russell, Kamala, 139
Rutherford, Danilyn: and Adriana, 158; and American Marriage Ministries, 157; ancestors of, 7, 75, 169; and Annie, 158; as an anthropologist, 7, 8, 15, 18, 22, 116, 136, 167, 168, 169–70, 179, 185; Biak friends of, 167–68; boyfriend of, 66, 67, 155; California home of, 183; and Cassidy, 112–13; college life of, 166, 167, 172; and connection to daughter, 76–79, 116, 118, 128, 135, 139, 166, 169, 170, 171, 175, 184, 187, 188, 190; and cost of care, 184; and Craig, viii, 64; and creation of social worlds, 175–76; and disabled people, 188; and education, 3, 7, 14, 18, 22, 55, 56, 63–64, 72, 73, 155, 166, 167, 171–72; and elementary school, 112; and emotions, 102; and English teaching, 166; family of, 7, 50, 58, 62; father of, 134, 135, 159, 169; and field work, 152, 167; and freedom, 103; and grace, 55; graduate training of, 172; and identity, 171; and In-Home Supportive Services, 185; and Izzy, 158; and journey of life, 15; and Katy, 158; and kindness of strangers, 50; and language, 64; and Leia, 158; and Linda Burkhart, 119, 124, 127, 145; and loss, 66, 118, 154; in Manhattan, 103, 177, 184; and Marilyn, 158, 173, 178, 183, 185–87; and Marind people, 55; marriage of, 14, 45, 49, 51, 56, 67; and memory, 168–69, 193; and Millie's therapy, 36–37, 109–10; as a mom, 104, 168, 178, 182, 188, 189–90, 193; mother of, vii, 42, 45, 72, 78, 138, 154, 159, 166,

226 INDEX

169, 189, 192; and move to Santa Cruz, 110; and New York, 3, 122; and normality, 172, 174; parents of, 7, 9, 25, 42, 45, 58, 72, 134, 169; partner of, 159, 183; and PhD, 15, 167; and PODD (Pragmatically Organized Dynamic Display), 112, 113-18; and pregnancy, 14, 15, 16, 171; and raising children, 103; and relationships, 170-71; and rental units, 183, 186, 187; and retirement, 184, 188; road trips of, 151-57, 173-74, 177; and rowing, 152; and school council, 63; and Scott, 158; and silent retreat, 111; sister of, 131; and social services help, 183; and social theory, 41; and social worlds, 178-79; and teaching, viii, 41, 59; as a teenager, 71-72; and therapy, 57, 66; and touch, 170; and trips abroad, 184; and understanding others, 9, 61, 62, 144; and Vermont, 144, 145, 151, 155, 157, 158, 173; and volunteer work, 71; and watercolor lessons, 56; as a writer, 14-17, 59, 67; and Xiaona, 158, 168. *See also* Best, Craig; Best, Melitta Alta Rutherford (Millie); Best, Ralph

Savarese, D.J., 111, 127-28
Savarese, Emily, 111
Savarese, Ralph James, 111, 127
Seattle, Washington, 51, 58, 136
self-help groups, 77
sexuality, 168, 173, 207n22
Sheldon, Erin, 129
Sherrington, Charles Scott, 135
Siegel, Jim, 167, 175, 206n7
Simon, Paul, 82
Simplican, Stacy Clifford, 95, 104
slavery, 7, 127, 145-46
social life, 9, 139, 140-41, 146-47, 164, 167-68, 171, 172. *See also* Best, Melitta Alta Rutherford (Millie)
Solomon, Andrew, 173
Soquel High, 182
South Africa, 164
sovereignty, 92, 93, 94, 95, 98, 105; concept of, 202n8; and language, 101, 102; and school setting, 99
Special Education Liaison Administrators' conference, 96-98
Special Olympics, 78
Special Parenting (magazine), 31

spirituality, 6, 55, 94, 130, 184, 189
St. Augustine, 59
Sullivan, Annie, 77, 127
Swift, Taylor, 79

Taylor, Janelle, 80
Tebow, Tim, 177
Tokyo, Japan, 5
Toronto, Canada, 130
Trinidad, 131
Trouble with Normal, The (Warner), 171-72
touch: and care, 137; and communication, 127, 128, 136-37; and DeafBlind people, 136-37, 141; and disability, 136-38, 145; and illness, 141; and language, 136-37; and Millie, 84, 135, 137, 143, 144, 166; and parents, 118; and proprioception, 137, 141; and relationships, 136-37; and transfer of meaning, 137, 203n3
Twin Talk, 109, 110, 113

Ukraine, 144
United States: and Afghan villages, 37; and African Americans, 63, 76, 93, 165; and assumptions about words, 110; and Black and Brown families, 93; Boston, 77; California, 2, 4, 8, 13, 14, 26, 57, 58, 62, 63, 84, 87, 96, 99, 166; Colorado, 57, 156; Congress of, 99, 201n1; and disabled people, 161, 167, 207n22; Florida, 157; government agencies, 166-67; Idaho, 155; Illinois, 166; and immigration system, 104; Indiana, 57; Iowa town, 156; and Latinx immigrants, 63; and love of children, 73-74; and Medicare coverage, 147; and memory, 80; Montana, 14, 15, 51, 155, 158; and Native American land, 7, 168; and Native Americans, 93, 156, 168; Nebraska, 156; Nevada, 156; New Jersey, 169; New York, 3, 4, 75; Pipestone National Monument, 156; political system of, 95; and relationships, 170; and September 11, 37; Sierras, 56, 66, 151, 188; and slavery, 7, 127; and unusual minds, 21-22, 164; Vermont, 66, 67, 99, 110, 144, 145, 151, 155, 166, 173; Vineland, New Jersey, 75, 77; Washington, DC, 18, 19, 22, 41. *See also* Ann Arbor, Michigan; Chicago, Illinois; New York, New York; Oregon; Princeton, New Jersey

University of California (Santa Cruz), 66–67, 155, 171
University of Chicago, 15, 63, 67

Vermont Law School, 66
Vico, Giambattista, 59
Vietnam, 73

Waterman, Ian, 136, 137–41, 142, 143, 144, 146
Weber, Max, 33
Weheliye, Alexander, 145, 146
West Papua, 42–43, 55, 167–68

What Kinship Is—and Is Not (Sahlins), 172
What to Expect the First Year, 18, 21
Wheatley, Phillis, 127
Williams, Lucinda, 156
Wisconsin, vii, 15, 26, 29, 42, 134
Wood, Dr., 39, 40, 41
World War II, 206n3
World Without Words, A (Goode), 4, 5

Yeltsin, Boris, 170

Zhan, Mei, 199n2